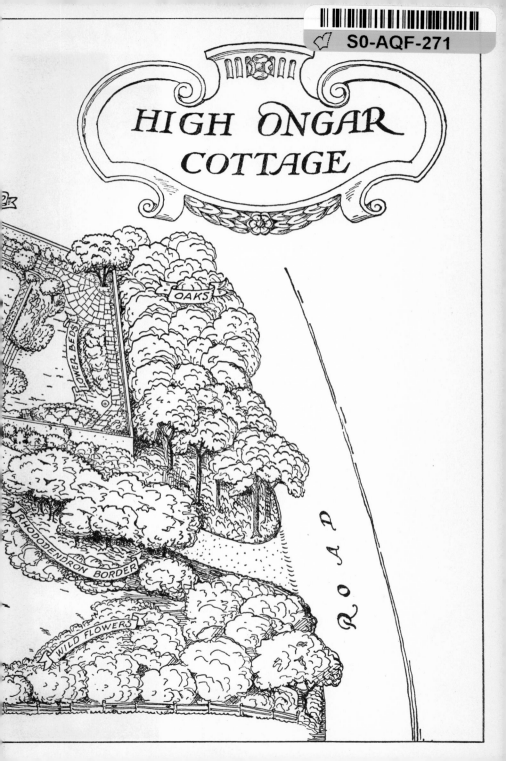

# The Growing Year

# THE
# GROWING YEAR

## MONTH BY MONTH IN A HOME GARDEN

CLIFTON LISLE

FARRAR, STRAUS AND YOUNG

NEW YORK

To my Father and my Mother
Robert Patton Lisle
Fanny Hollingsworth Lyman Lisle

Who taught me the wondrous beauty of the world about
us, the ordered plan, the glory of the growing year, God's
handiwork in wind and sky and tree and flower

# Contents

Note

The Growing Year

I. JANUARY:
    The Month of Promise . . . . . . 5
    JANUARY CHECK LIST . . . . . 16

II. FEBRUARY:
    The Month of Trees . . . . . 18
    FEBRUARY CHECK LIST . . . . . 37

III. MARCH:
    The Now-or-Never Month . . . . 39
    MARCH CHECK LIST . . . . . 56

IV. APRIL:
    The Month of Fulfillment . . . . 59
    APRIL CHECK LIST . . . . . 77

V. MAY:
    The Merry Month . . . . . . 79
    MAY CHECK LIST . . . . . . 99

VI. JUNE:
    The Happy Month . . . . . 102
    JUNE CHECK LIST . . . . . 124

VII. JULY:
    The Month of Change . . . . 126
    JULY CHECK LIST . . . . . 149

VIII. AUGUST:
    The Month of Thanksgiving . . . . 152
    AUGUST CHECK LIST . . . . . 173

IX. SEPTEMBER:
The Month of Returning Gold . . . 176
SEPTEMBER CHECK LIST . . . . 198

X. OCTOBER:
The Month of the Leaf . . . . . 201
OCTOBER CHECK LIST . . . . . 224

XI. NOVEMBER:
The Month of Blessings . . . . . 226
NOVEMBER CHECK LIST . . . . 245

XII. DECEMBER:
The Month of Cheer . . . . . 248
DECEMBER CHECK LIST . . . . . 263

# *Note*

In the making of the humblest garden we may be sure that many hands have been at work as well as many kindly hearts. It would not be possible to acknowledge properly the help and the encouragement received through the years. The story of the garden has likewise been heartened by friendly counsel and sound advice.

I am most grateful to my wife for her aid in editing manuscript and proofs. Mrs. S. Laurence Bodine of Greenbank Farm has been a friend indeed when it came to whipping the book into final shape. Mr. Raymond Thomas, Mr. William Gantz, Mr. Peter Ferrilli, Mr. Vick of Wildgardens fame, Miss Anne McGarry, each of them gave to the garden time and skill and love of green things growing. I am indebted to them one and all. I am also grateful to Mr. E. Sculley Bradley, editor of the *General Magazine and Historical Chronicle* of the University of Pennsylvania, who has graciously given permission to use in this book certain parts of the manuscript first published serially in the *General Magazine*.

C. L.

# The Growing Year

"Nay, if you come to that, Sir, have not the wisest men in all ages, not excepting Solomon himself, have they not had their Hobby-Horses?" says Tristram Shandy in Laurence Sterne's most delectable of books. "For my hobby-horse is a sporting little filly-folly which carries you out of the present hour—a maggot, a butterfly, a picture, a fiddle-stick, or an any thing which a man makes shift to get astride, to canter it away from the cares and solicitudes of life. . . . 'Tis as useful a beast as in the whole creation—nor do I see how the world could do without it."

Note that Tristram refers to the maggot. He could have spared us that. For the maggot, though perhaps no relation of the slug or the sowbug, the chafer, the cutworm or the beetle, the aphid, the leaf-hopper, the mite, the snail, or even of the earwig, the borer, or the thrips, yet the maggot reminds us of the connection between such loathsome destroyers and the hobby-horse we find most alluring to ride, perhaps to be raced away with—down to the garden's end. Round-the-year work with flowers—that has run away with us more than once, which is, of course, the cream of the fun.

## THE FRIENDLY MONTHS

March to October gardening is easy, even competing with Pennsylvania blizzards, March winds, July droughts, the Lammas floods and the mildews, the blackspot and blight, the wilt, the rot and the rust, the hungry hordes of bug and beetle, worm and midge, that cut and sting and bore, blister and chew and suck and bite through all the lovely growing year.

November is easy. Hardy rearguards hang on. But by mid-October much has been sacrificed for the new bulbs. They have to be fitted in somewhere; so up come the marigolds, the late mums, and zinnias

1

still brave in Indian Summer glory. November leaves, too, must be dealt with. Why not bank down the beds while we're at it—leaves around the laurels and rhododendron, good cow manure, salt hay, what you will, on beds and borders?

All too often, long before Thanksgiving the garden is fast in a sleep that can hold through dark December and the gaining light and deepening cold of January and the coldest bite of all—February's ice and sleet and thaw and freeze, most killing of weathers. Three months dormant—there's the rub. There's the Hobby-Horse that had better not be mounted at all unless one is game for the gallop. December, January, February—no gardeners to help; all bloom to be out-of-doors. That is the Hobby-Horse never forgot.

## THE CHALLENGE

To start with the rules of this gardening game: all that grows outdoors should count—flower or shrub or leaf or tree. No cover or shielding of glass should count, but leaves, a handful or so here and there, are fair. So is advantage taken of garden wall or terrace angle, the sun trap below the library window, the bank by the drive where cherry laurels have made safe covert for Christmas roses nestled in their lee. All these are fair. The prize: something in flower out-of-doors from New Year's around to Christmas.

## THE PLAN

It is obviously impossible to catch between the pages of a book the ordered miracle of growth, the wonder and the beauty of the growing year whose pageantry enchants us. Such splendours come from God.

We hope, however, that we may share with others, at least in some small measure, the joy that a garden brings to us, the gifts of heartsease and happiness and beauty rich past telling. We hope that others may find of use some of the things we have been doing in our

2

own small garden in return for what our garden has done for us. Perhaps even the list of chores, our workaday schedules, tucked in between the demands of earning a living elsewhere, may serve as encouragement to those who, like us, love gardening but cannot give to it the time they would like.

Flowers, trees, shrubs, each in its appointed season, weave for us a pattern of delight. Each fragrant branch, each tiny flower, has earned its place. In due time, if we be patient, we reap their sure reward.

It is our plan to follow here, month by month, the sweet unfolding of a year.

CHAPTER I

# JANUARY
## *The Month of Promise*

The first year that something bloomed in January and so gave us a chance at listing blossoms throughout the year, our tally was small, quite pitiful in fact: blue periwinkle and the Christmas roses. Winter berries and the holly trees were bright above the snow, but at first they were not reckoned in our flower score. They were not things in bloom and they had not come in January. Yet they did add colour and they did eke out the green brought indoors for Christmas. So in the end greens were counted fair quarry, if we could use them.

A start had been made, at least, with actual midwinter blossoms. It was worth a try. The next year we did better. On New Year's Day, again the faithful blue periwinkle, *Vinca minor*, was reasonably starred with bloom, especially where it had been sheltered by the cottage walls and lay on either side of the door, exposed to the winter sun. Oddly enough, across the drive on a bank facing north-west, a most exposed bank at that, the periwinkle had also blossomed a bit by the first week of January. Here, however, the blossoms were not so exposed. They were in bloom all right, only an odd one here and there, bright as the bluest sky above, though low-lying, tucked deeper in the protecting leaves.

## PERIWINKLE CARE

The periwinkle, both on the bank and in the sheltered sun trap flanking the door, has been given, year by year, a bale of peat-moss each spring, scattered loosely over it and allowed to soak down with

5

the April rains. The past two years the peat has been reinforced by an additional dressing of peat-moss and cow manure well rotted together. The cost of this, even in these price-soaring days, is still reasonable and has proved money well spent, for the periwinkle has rooted deeply in the soil below the peat, and moisture is retained through the driest summer. As a result, the plants are unusually thick and vigorous, well over a foot in height, forming a dense mass of ground-cover, as fresh and green at zero as they are in spring.

It was in this deep growth that the blossoms hid in January—enough of them right on from New Year's Day to keep a few indoors where their lovely, sky-washed blue outdid the African violets, *Saintpaulia ionantha,* sulking under a crotchety spell in the window where they were supposed to add a touch of colour to the statue of the Madonna and Child that stood there.

## MADONNA

Our statue has a story back of it, for it was made in Baden, Germany, at Karlsruhe on the edge of the Schwarzwald, where we were stationed for almost a year at the end of the recent war, resting on our arms, as it were, and scarcely knowing what to expect but hoping that some enduring peace might come. Small statues like this one stand in niches on every farmhouse end. We often saw them there. Our statue, however, was a new one. When it was cast, the mold was broken, so that this particular Madonna might be the only one of its design. When the clay had been baked and coloured and baked and glazed again, the people of Baden brought it to us as a gift, asking that in spite of regulations forbidding the acceptance of such things by the military, this statue, at least, might be received in the spirit in which it was offered—a spirit of understanding and good will and of prayer that, as the occupation of their land by those who had conquered had not led to the bitterness and the hatred they feared, so this statue of the Blessed Mother and Child might serve as a reminder that they, the people of Baden, had tried in their turn to share in the task of restoring peace.

Naturally, military regulations forbidding gifts seemed ill-designed for such a request, so the statue was accepted in the spirit in which it was given. We packed it in sawdust—the full three feet of it—and in the straw covers made for wine bottles—*stroh-hülse für flasche*. We crated it in a box to fit. And somehow or other, months later, it arrived unbroken and unscarred in Pennsylvania, to stand, as it does today, against the mullion that divides a broad window ledge stretching as wide as our cottage hall. Our Madonna is flanked there summer and winter by ferns and flowers, ivy and nephthytis, and philodendron hanging from baskets on the walls.

When January seems a far cry from any living thing outdoors, the sweet blue of the myrtle brings colour and life to the statue and heartens the memory of work done in Baden. It is indeed a harbinger of spring when all seems chilled in winter death.

## THE CHRISTMAS ROSE

Christmas roses made a particularly gallant show our first year of keeping a twelfth-month record of bloom, for some of them opened just in time for Christmas and offered bloom right through till spring—a few at a time, depending on the sun.

How they do it, often deep in snow, no one can tell. But the cherry laurel gives them shelter and they are well flanked by euonymus vines. Each year we feed them in the spring with a handful of bone-meal and powdered cow manure, worked well into the soil. A spoonful or so of commercial rose feed has also proved stimulating to growth, though they are as far from being roses as any plant could be, save in name.

The main things with them seem to be winter sun, summer shade, plentiful moisture, and a good cool stone tucked in somewhere about their roots on planting. These, and to be left alone. They do not like a move. In severe winters they need, too, a mulch of leaves about them from early December on. They should never be buried in leaves, but blanketed well up and loosely. Then, year by year, under the leaves and working bravely through them come the lovely snow-white blossoms with their golden stamens clustered in the centre. There are several varieties—the familiar *Helleborus niger,* always hardy with us and dependable. Then the larger, newer strain of *Helleborus niger altifolius,* a magnificent five-petaled flower three inches across.

If the Christmas rose is not moved, and if it has been given a good start, it will gradually spread, affording us a chance to cut these glorious blossoms all winter. Two or three of them make a real showing indoors, and often their stems grow surprisingly long, making them easy to use.

No frost seems able to kill these hardy blooms. In bitter weather, the buds are frozen as stiff as the leaves. Yet frost or no, sooner or later a warmer day comes—perhaps it is truer to say a day less cold —when winter sun reaches through the mulching of leaves and then the buds spread wide in what is, and must be, a major miracle of the growing year. No other flower in the herbal shows such magic. No other needs so little care yet gives so bravely to us of its beauty in the days when beauty is rare. Our very first Christmas rose came to us years ago as a gift from Glen Isle. It is living yet.

## THE HEARTSEASE

Also, on New Year's Day two other faithful, though forgotten, favourites give us of their bloom—a Johnny jump-up here and there and a scattering of autumn crocus. The Johnny-jump-ups, *Viola tricolor hortensis,* or *Viola bosniaca,* blossomed where they had sheltered deep in a mass of frost-killed sweet alyssum—the dwarf, white Little Gem, *Lobularia maritima.* No one knew they were there until their blue and gold and white peeped just above the covering that had tempted them to open. More blossoms, of course, were just under the blanket of dry alyssum stems. They looked as fresh and as rich in colour as any that would come, like daffodils, before the swallow dares and take the winds of March with beauty.

The older name for Johnny-jump-up still clings in places—it is the "heartsease" of the Elizabethans. Shakespeare knew it well, as he did all flowers, especially the wild ones, and so did John Bunyan when he wrote of the lad who lived a merrier life and wore more of that herb called heartsease in his bosom than he that was clad in silk and velvet.

The heartsease is one of our most persistent flowers. It must have been brought to this country by the earliest settlers, for always it has been a favourite here as well as in England. Actually a pansy, it has a way of clinging year after year to some out-of-the-way corner of the garden. To see it blooming on New Year's Day was a joy.

## THE AUTUMN CROCUS

The autumn-flowering crocus also gave us some January bloom; this was not the familiar snow crocus or the spring crocus which had almost two months to wait before it would appear above ground. The autumn crocus has an interesting history, being one of the oldest of our cultivated plants. The so-called saffron crocus, *Crocus sativus,* for instance, has been a drug-producing plant as well as a source of dye for as long as we have any record of such things. Far back in the days of the Roman Empire and even in the times of the Phoenicians this crocus was grown commercially and formed a staple of maritime trade.

The corms of these lovely blossoms, lavender in colour, had been planted in late August. Most of them, of course, had blossomed as expected, before much frost or shortly after it. A few, however, must have lain fallow a while longer, clumped along the base of our garden wall, where they suddenly challenged on New Year's Day.

## THE DAPHNE

On 21 January, the *Daphne mezereum* blossomed—a notable treat. The tiny flowers of this earliest of the daphnes are a pinkish purple, all the lovelier for their winter setting. These plants are not easy to grow in this country, but they are worth any amount of trouble if started right. They cannot stand drought or heat at all.

They must be planted where their roots stay cool and moist; always the soil must be deeply dug, yet well drained. A China fleece vine, *Polygonum Auberti,* grows near one of ours and seems to give the needed shade and coolness to its roots.

The *Daphne mezereum* lacks the fragrance of the *Daphne cneorum,* our so-called garland flower, which comes into bloom much later, yet the colour of the *mezereum* in January, small as its blossoms are, makes one feel that the worst of winter has passed and that we are rounding Tattenham Corner.

## THE WINTER GREENS

Apart from these blossoms, January has its greens, as useful after Twelfth Night as at Christmas for backing where other flowers are used. Holly berries, scarlet and sleek, and the orange-red sprays of the *Pyracantha coccinea*—the firethorn—are indispensable. The American holly, *Ilex opaca,* is, of course, more hardy than English holly, *Ilex aquifolium,* but the latter, if you can grow it, has the real Christmas Carol touch to its crisp and shiny leaves. Japanese holly, *Ilex crenata,* Chinese holly, *Ilex cornuta,* probably the loveliest of them all in the green of its foliage and the almost unbelievable sheen of its leaves, can always spare a spray or so to bring indoors.

Birds like the firethorn berries for dinner as much as we do for our decorations. They often have stripped our bushes by the end of fall, but always some berries are left. Luckily the firethorn is a lusty grower and will stand a lot of cutting, so when the berries are available, it does no harm to snip them back generously. *Pyracantha coccinea Lalandi,* pleached on a sunny wall, is especially lovely. There is pruning and to spare to keep it properly trimmed there.

The yew, *Taxus cuspidata,* which is the Japanese kind, especially the dwarf Japanese yew, *Taxus cuspidata nana,* and *Taxus Hicksi,* often allowed to grow upright until it becomes a tree, are easily pruned to give us winter greens. Spruce and hemlock and the retinosporas cannot be pruned so freely, for the scars remain, yet now and then an old branch may be spared and no harm done. Usually the so-called arborvitae, *Thuja occidentalis* and *Chamaecyparis pisifera aurea,* are clipped to desired size from time to time during the summer and hence do not lend themselves to cutting in winter. Many other shrubs do.

It is amazing what the growth about the smallest cottage, if it has been wisely planned and planted, can give in midwinter. The andromeda, *Pieris japonica,* for example, often yields us a branch or two, especially if cut where the shrub needed pruning anyway. *Leucothoe Catesbaei* grows luxuriantly in acid soil and under partial shade. Pruning never harms it, for what may be cut in January will be made good freshly enough by spring. Sprays of leucothoe, glossy-leaved and full of life, are a must in January. Laurel leaves, the *Kalmia latifolia,* can be lovely indoors but pruning is hard on these shrubs. The lower-growing cherry laurel, *Prunus laurocerasus schipkaensis,* seems to stand any amount of cutting back. It is a delightful shrub for background green, far more rewarding than mountain laurel as its leaves sweep close to the ground.

Ivy, the small-leaved English ivy, *Hedera helix,* from the high walls that shelter our lower garden, is always an asset in winter, for it offers the loveliest green indoors while busily making roots in winter for transplanting elsewhere later on.

## THE GROUND COVERS

Another green most useful in winter, if cut and used indoors, is the *Euonymus radicans coloratus,* the winter creeper. It, too, carries a cheery green all year, especially if one looks for the vines that have been covered a bit by the outer vines. The exposed leaves of the euonymus change their colour in the fall, not brightly, but bronzing deeply. The leaves, however, remain on all year.

*Pachysandra terminalis*—Japanese spurge—is still another of the ground covers that stands the bitterest weather apparently unharmed. In severe frosts it seems to wilt a bit, taking on a brittle look, but that is only temporary. While not particularly delicate in appearance, like periwinkle which is always delightful, the pachysandra

11

none the less has its place in the list of January greens.

Our cottage is small and the land about it even more limited, not so much as an acre all told. Of the shrubs and evergreens mentioned we have not too many of each, but the assortment is varied and grows through the years. There are, at the moment, some ninety varieties of shrubs and vines and all are useful.

## CLIMATE AND WINTER BLOSSOMS

Climate obviously is the limiting factor for winter bloom in the United States, as it must be everywhere where there is severe cold. In England, where the weather seems cold and the raw east wind sets a misery stirring in our bones, it usually is not very cold, so far as actual degrees of frost are concerned. Hence the richness of what can be done there in midwinter, not only in the milder confines of Cornwall and Devon, but in the north and east where it really is cold, regardless of what the thermometer says. Yet from a study of what can be grown in an English winter, we have experimented a bit here and been encouraged to see what some of their winter plants will do for us, especially when a mild winter helps them.

Winter aconite, of course, and winter jasmine, both grow well with us, though so far February is the earliest month they have come into blossom. *Sternbergia lutea,* the fall daffodil; *Berberis japonica;* wintersweet, *Chimonanthus fragrans,* we have not tried it yet, but it blooms with the Christmas rose in Britain; snowdrops, *Galanthus Elwesi; Forsythia intermedia; Corylopsis spicata,* the winter hazel; cyclamen; the saxifrages; the *Daphne mezereum,* with which we have had luck; various crocuses, especially *Crocus imperati;* winter heliotrope, *Petasites fragrans; Iris stylosa*—all these are definitely spring flowers, if they are tried. It seems hopeless to expect life from most of them in January, at least in our part of the world. Yet our *Daphne mezereum,* as said, has actually blossomed and blossomed well as early as the 21st of January.

It is, however, by realizing our climatic limitations, by taking a dare and by using generously the many and variously tinted greens that we do have at hand—it is by such measures, of course, that January can be tempted to unbend.

## A TOUCH OF SUMMER

No account of midwinter gardening would be complete without some reference to dried flowers and their use. Though they may have been grown in our own gardens in summer and given of their beauty so lavishly then, or though they may have been gathered as wild flowers by the dusty roadsides of August, if they are dried properly their loveliness seems even dearer in January than when they were actually growing. The secret, of course, lies in deciding in time what we want about us four or five months after we have selected and picked them and dried them properly.

All blooms must be picked at the right moment and they must be dried slowly in a dark place, free from any suggestion of damp; yet there must be fresh air, too. It is necessary to hang those drying and dried flowers in bunches upside down. They must be so hung immediately after they have been picked. To insure the rich colours natural to flowers, they should be picked just as you feel they are coming to their best or—better still—a little before it. Strawflowers, with us, seem to do some of their maturing while drying. A full-blown flower, obviously at its best on the stem, is likely to fade in drying—or become too brittle and lose its petals when touched.

## AUTUMN LEAVES

In gathering supplies for winter use indoors, do not overlook vividly coloured autumn leaves. They have to be pressed, of course, as well as dried. Ferns, too, are priceless yet easy to find, growing wild as they do so abundantly in our woodlands. They can easily be dried and pressed flat between pieces of paper. Best of all, they will keep their colour.

Choice of leaves is almost limitless. With us, the important thing is to gather them when colour is highest, but before the sap has drained from them. Otherwise, they become brittle. Dogwoods—pink and white; maples—the sugar maple, the yellow maple, and especially the scarlet-leaved red maple; the lovely golden-tinted sweet birch; the beeches; the hickories; and the oak—all of these except the beeches and some of the maples are at our door.

It is not so easy to prepare leaves for drying. To start with, they must be kept in a pool of water to prevent wilting before drying begins. When the actual work has started, each cluster of leaves (individual leaves, of course, are useless) must be smoothed perfectly flat. In gathering leaves for winter decoration, only those branches that seem flat to start with are worth cutting. As each cluster is laid flat, each leaf on that branch must be kept from overlapping any other leaf. Paper is laid on next and then another cluster of leaves. No two leaves must be allowed to touch. Finally a board is put on top of the layers being dried and the board weighted well to make sure that every leaf is held down. It takes usually a fortnight and more to press and dry leaves thoroughly. Then they can be handled without breaking.

Detested though it be by gardeners when allowed to run riot, bittersweet, Celastrus scandens, must not be spurned altogether. In addition to dried flowers and leaves which, though really an autumnal chore are put to use in January, the berries of the bittersweet can be most lovely when brought indoors.

I think my earliest recollection of Christmas in the country goes back to mountain laurel wreaths and white pine sprays—we seemed to have had little holly near by then—brightened by bittersweet and firethorn berries, with here and there a pine cone tied on with red ribbon and here and there a twist of the greenbrier from Holland Wood or Spring Bank corner, glossy leaves still on.

## A JANUARY POESY

It would be impossible, obviously, to list the wild flowers, the leaves and the berries that we may have picked for winter cheer. Wise gardeners gather most bloom in late summer and fall, enjoying the fruit of their labour now in January. Pine cones—not gilt or silvered, please—red cedar, the firs, dried everlasting, boneset, the most useful strawflower, wild yarrow, joe-pie, cattails—the list is endless. We have never used corn tassels—Indian corn—but much can be done with them as with sprays of dried wheat, if they are used carefully with other dried flowers and leaves and ferns. The trouble with corn is that it is too coarse, too mindful of a Harvest Home and the church windows at Thanksgiving. This is not true of dried wheat sprays, especially if used sparingly. Goldenrods and silverrods as well will dry admirably. Their varieties are legion and they grow everywhere. So does the broomsedge, most lovely with its tawny-russet yellow and its hint of autumnal sun aslant it on the hillside, redeeming the sadness of some abandoned farmstead where plough turns slowly to the wild again.

## PROMISE AND SURPRISES

Yes, even here where spring comes much later than in lands where the new year starts with the gaining light, January can surprise us. It is a month to prepare for well ahead and that is a challenge. It is a month that can bitterly disappoint—or thrill one as high June never can. Of course, we always look for more than we can possibly expect to receive, our climate being what it is; yet that, too, has an added savour about it that appeals to the sporting sense. If we knew that it was easy to grow things out-of-doors in midwinter, if we lived where nature did that for us so that we always got what we wanted, where would the fun be?

> "For getting whatever you want to get,
> Is like drinking tea from a fishing net."

Above all, January is the month of promise. The glory of the growing year lies before us. The sun itself tells us that. By Twelfth Night everyone knows that the change has come. It makes no difference how deep the snow may lie, how chill the wind may bite—light has come again. And light means growth. If, at our cottage door, we

15

are lucky enough to see the myrtle blooming; if through leaves, perhaps through snow itself, we catch the beauty of a Christmas rose or find our heartsease on the bank, though it be but a blossom, January's promise has come true.

## JANUARY CHECK LIST

January obviously is not a pressure month in gardening, but it can—and should—be a time for planning, checking, preparing, and ordering. The sequence is important.

Some care now in planning beds and borders, charting areas for annuals or the re-siting of perennials will save considerably in what we decide to order and the quantity needed of each.

A check of equipment is always a January chore, while there is time. Replacements or new gear can then be ordered when seed lists are sent in.

Have a look at the cold-frame if it has not been used during the winter, for it may need a bit of cement where the frame joins the foundation or the glass may need some putty.

Stored dahlias should be seen to at this time. Dusting them with a little sulphur helps to keep them sound. Make sure they are not cut off from a free circulation of air. Too often they are packed away in baskets with newspapers pressed down on top and then left to their fate in cellar or garret. This is a mistake. Dahlias and other stored bulbs and corms will stand reasonably cold fresh air far better than slow suffocation.

Start now to get seed-flats ready. This takes a good deal more preparation than a few lumps of frozen January clod thrown in a box. Sand, peat-moss, and well-thawed, well-sifted topsoil must be used.

Flats of the earliest (only the earliest) spring flowers, such as hardy poppies, forget-me-nots, heartsease, and pansies, may be started surprisingly soon in January. The key to success, however, is well-prepared soil in the flats, at least half-and-half peat-moss and soil. Not much sand is needed.

16

Pruning, at least a start at it, on mild days is definitely a January task. Begin it now if the weather is kind, but be careful not to cut back any of those early-flowering spring shrubs which have already been pruned in late spring or early summer after their flowering. January is seldom too early to prune fruit trees, and it is a good time to spray them while they are dormant.

Shrubs such as lilacs which are susceptible to oyster-shell scale and the like can be sprayed now, especially when days are mild. Miscible oil or lime-sulphur sprays are the things to use. Do not overlook the evergreens. They are aided by dormant sprays as much as fruit trees and shrubs.

When pruning, save such cuttings from trees and shrubs as will blossom if kept in water indoors. Keep them in a cool, shady place until the buds are ready to open. Never put them directly in the sun when they are first brought in. Forsythia, pussy willow, bush honeysuckle, flowering quince, as well as apple and peach are rewarding.

January is always brightened if we bring in a clipping or so of our greens, even when New Year's has passed. A spray of juniper or of retinospora or a branch of yew will help enormously as the days begin to lengthen. Often they will be as fresh as ever when spring comes round. Hollies will not last.

January also is the time to start our first indoor cuttings, especially mid-January and onwards. Cuttings may be made from house plants, if such dependables as begonias, fuchsias, and geraniums have responded to the encouragement of a sunny window. January is a good month to start indoors more hyacinths, lily-of-the-valley pips, and paper narcissus.

As January passes, keep an eye for more Christmas roses under their shelter of leaves. Be sure that the cover is loose. If it has matted down, now is the time to stir it up a bit.

Have a look for odd Johnny-jump-ups or perhaps a stray autumn crocus. They have a way of appearing even this early under leaves or deep in a myrtle bank. In January it pays to look for such treasure.

17

# CHAPTER II

# FEBRUARY

## *The Month of Trees*

<hr>

February Fill-Dyke is, I suppose, our most deceptive month. Light gains tremendously. Copse and covert, oak and ash, hickory, poplar, and the maple spinneys have deepened at the top till all our woodlands hang dark-shadowed and enriched against the sky. Swamps are quickening to a ruddier hue where the alder sap is rising. Every rill in the meadows has marked its course with a widening band of green as water cress and the bordering grasses come to life. It is spring for fair—hounds full cry on winter's traces—lisp of leaves—ah, no, not yet—ripple of rain, ah, yes! Aplenty! And some of our cruelest snow storms, our most prolonged and bitter ice spells, come in February. How can we think of gardens and of blossoms?

It is so different from England, where February does spell rain, chill, and bone-biting, or even passing snow. Yet the stir of spring is there in spite of it. Life in the hedgerow, the sure flow of green on slope and meadow! But here, most will agree that February is our bleakest month—surely our most discouraging.

Light shows with pitiless and particular candour how worn and torn, how grey and brown a lawn can be. Rhododendron leaves hang dejectedly in the grip of frost that can be more dangerous than anything January brought us. Laurel foliage, touched by the gaining sun and not liking it, shows all too often a sickly yellow. Even our faithful pachysandra loses heart of grace, now if ever, and presents a flattened look. Beds and borders are hopeless, of course, unless still mercifully blanketed, as they should be. Even the frozen ground thaws miserably at noon to trap unwary footsteps into scars, leaving hideous wounds that mar what green there is.

## PRUNING

This is the surface of February. And yet the year has turned and we know it in our hearts. Eyes, too, will tell us, if we but look beneath the wounds of winter. With spring in sight, there is work to do that has not been completed in December or January. Spring work now regardless of the chill. Shrubs and fruit trees must be pruned—some of them. Many a gardening tyro has pruned valiantly in winter, destroying with shears and pruning knife the last possibility of bloom next May by cutting off the summer growth of cane or branch upon which the blossoms of many a shrub must depend. We had an ardent lad once who pruned our Seckel pear so that it did not bear again for years. Why prune the pear at all? Nearly all flowering shrubs must, of course, be pruned as they finish blooming in the spring, for most shrubs blossom on this year's wood.

## SPRAYING

Needed winter pruning, however, should be finished in February if possible, before sap stirs too freely. This is especially so for fruit trees. Scale spray should be remembered, for March is an even busier month, with more spraying and all the mounting chores of spring. The first dormant spray should go on now in February. It is well to keep in mind that in these days of widespread pests and blights we are wise to spray not only our fruit trees for scale, but also the pines and spruces, witch hazels, lilacs, and the like, which are also subject to disease.

## THE HACKBERRY

We have a really magnificent hackberry tree, *Celtis occidentalis,* here, that must have stood on the bank by the door before our cottage was thought of. When one has a natural feature on even the smallest place that keynotes the rest, it is worth taking it into the over-all plan of building and planting and it also pays to tend it carefully. Here, this glorious old tree, some eleven feet in circumference at its base, one of the largest hackberries in Pennsylvania and said to be close to three hundred years old, obviously dominates house and garden, summer and winter. The great spread of its branches when they are bare of leaves, articulated against the winter skies, is as lovely and as graceful as is the welcome canopy of its foliage in the dog days.

Until recently witches-broom infested it. Every leaf in summer was scarred and blistered where aphids had been at them. We began, luckily in time, to give this tree a dormant spray of miscible oil when the other trees and shrubs were sprayed in February. Later, just as it comes into full leaf, we spray again, this time with a solution of DDT powder. As a result, the fine old tree has taken on new life. In February or March, we feed it now and then and that, too, has shown results. The dormant spray, of course, is useful against witches-broom as well as against scale.

February is the month we pay heed to our hackberry. Squirrels may like to (and once did) have their homes deep in the great hollows where branches have fallen from the trunk. These cavities, properly cleaned and filled, as they are now, mean a longer life for the tree itself. Other branches—for the tree has a spread and a height equalled by few oaks—have been wired with six or seven mutually supporting cables of heavy wire. That work, difficult and dangerous as it is, was handled by a man from our neighbourhood, a friend who loves trees and heals them with understanding. He even treats our shrinking purses with the same friendly consideration he shows our trees.

## TREE AND SHRUB PLANTING

Tree or shrub planting should be considered now or as soon as frost is out of the ground and the mud has dried a bit. Trees can be moved later than this, but the nearer they come into leaf the greater the chance of trouble when drought or warm winds parch them. We have found that it pays to handle most planting or transplanting of shrubbery as well as of trees early enough to get the work done in February or by early March.

In fact, February is essentially the tree month. In it we try to do our planting as well as our pruning and dormant spraying and—sad to admit—our thinning out. Some necessary cutting down, unfortunately, is the natural complement of growing up. Most new places are skimpy or bare of trees. Such places cry for anything green and all too often "anything" goes in. Then, too, few of us can visualize the surprising growth a tree will make, especially in its spread. Planning ahead and spacing both the trees and shrubs for the future are essential. February is the month for both.

An old place, of course, presents one problem; a new place another. On old ground, unluckily, we too often are trying to remedy past mistakes. With a new place, we should try to avoid them. One rule seems safe to follow on every sort of place. Put in trees at least twice as far apart as you are sure you will need them. Then add two or three yards more between them for luck. You may be sure that you will never have put them in quite far enough apart when they have grown. Make your closer planting with quick-growing shrubs that do not cost so much and that can serve the immediate purpose. Later, if necessary, these can be moved easily, pruned back, or thinned out. A tree once in likes to stay there.

## THE FOREST THAT WAS

Here, our hackberry, as has been said, dominates the cottage and all the ground about it. Everything else, large or small, has been planned with that in mind and subordinated to it.

Many of the older trees—the oaks, two tulip trees, a plane tree, a swamp maple or so, a hickory, the hackberries (we have two)—are evidently a remnant of what must have been an extensive forest, portions of which are still found to the south of us, spreading here and there for miles, far over past the parish of St. David's and up to the Newtown hills. Before a tree or a shrub was planted here, there stood about the cottage or near it several hackberries, *Celtis occidentalis;* tulip trees, *Liriodendron tulipfera;* red maples, *Acer rubrum;* white oaks, *Quercus alba;* hickory, *Hicoria;* wild dogwoods, *Cornus paniculata;* sour gum, *Nyssa sylvatica;* buttonwoods, *Platanus occidentalis;* sweet birch, *Betula lenta;* wild cherries, and two blighted chestnuts, *Castanea dentata,* one already dead, a majestic reminder of the forest that has gone.

We were fortunate, indeed, in these trees for some of them were woodland-grown with generations behind them. The hackberry probably goes back to the days when our road was the Indian trail that ran from the Schuylkill to the Conestoga, where Lancaster now stands, and thence on to the Susquehanna. Only a year or so ago, we found a perfectly knapped arrowhead within a few yards of the old tree.

The blighted chestnuts came down first of all. The wild cherries followed soon after, in spite of the lovely cherry blow each spring. We did this to lessen trouble with tent caterpillars. And then the new planting began. With or without mishaps, it has gone on ever since.

## FEEDING TREES

In feeding trees we have found that manure (cow manure preferably) and some bone-meal, well spaded in, does a better job than straight commercial fertilizer, useful as much of the latter is. The reason seems to be that organic matter attracts worms and without worms in quantity there can be precious little growing. They do our subsurface ploughing for us and harrowing as well, scot free.

## EARLY FERTILIZING

Apart from pruning, spraying, and planting trees and shrubs, other chores are waiting for us in February. Bone-meal and pulverized cow manure are sometimes spread on the fern bank at this time, and also on the beds and borders if winter cover has been removed. In milder years it is possible to do this. Great harm is done, however, if winter cover be lifted too soon—not so much by the cold as by the freeze and thaw of this treacherous in-between season. Yet now and then our beds and borders are given their first feeding this early, allowing time for the fertilizer to sink in.

## LIME

Our lawn is treated with ground limestone more often in February than in March, for it must be well limed before any real growing starts. This liming is a must, especially as we have so many flowering trees and shrubs that shade can be a problem and acid soil a costly liability unless we control it.

Again some care is needed in liming, for amateur gardeners such as we can easily be too generous with lime and spread it too near rhododendrons, laurels, azaleas, hollies, leucothoe, andromeda, and all the host of broad-leaved evergreen shrubs that are forest-bred by nature and must have acid soil and reasonable shade. We are likely to overlook as well the part that earthworms play in this. Our laurels may be in acid soil all right and our adjoining grass or borders as sweet as lime can make them—litmus tests to prove it—but that does not mean matters will stay so. Worms are great soil breakers. They literally eat and digest our acres, as well as break the clods for us. But also they are great rovers. Before you know it the lime on your lawn may go its way, a-progress through a worm, to your rhododendron clumps.

Actually lawns and beds must be limed each year, but carefully, and broad-leaved evergreen shrubs must be kept well supplied with humus. Rotted leaf mould is the best. An occasional sprinkling of aluminum sulphate, once, say, in the spring, near them, but never touching them, will remedy any lack of soil acidity.

## CHORES OF FEBRUARY

Dates sometimes bring to our consciousness more clearly the year's

23

majestic give and take, the ordered cycle of the world in which we live: the promise that seed time and harvest, and cold and heat, and summer and winter, and day and night shall not cease.

3 February—trimmed back virgin's-bower, *Clematis paniculata,* on the garden's northwest wall. Pruned some wisteria, *sinensis,* on its trellis —allowed it last fall to tangle a bit with ivy on the southeast corner. Ten degrees; ice on the ground, but no snow. Christmas roses, a few at a time, and periwinkle are blooming bravely. Snowdrops, *Galanthus nivalis,* along the drive, now open.

7 February—pruned apple trees—winesap and smokehouse. Gave all trees their first dormant spray of miscible oil.

9 February—more snowdrops, *Galanthus Elwesi,* now showing.

15 February—put 50 pounds of bone-meal and cow manure on lower beds and borders where salt hay had been removed. Roses, of course, still covered.

16 February—limed the lawns.

17 February—pruned our pin-oak, *Quercus palustris.*

22 February—more snowdrops in bloom. Fed the dogwoods, *Cornus florida,* in the sunken gardens and outside the wall.

25 February—winter aconite in bloom, brighter than gold.

26 February—50 pounds of bone-meal and cow manure on upper borders. No frost now in the ground—at least not on top. Now blooming: periwinkle, English daisies, Johnny-jump-ups, snowdrops, and still the Christmas roses.

The bloom, naturally, has not gained much over January in variety, but there is more of it. Plenty of blue myrtle can now be found in the bank and by the door.

## ENGLISH DAISIES

English daisies, *Bellis perennis,* can be dependable as a rock or can fade away at a touch of heat or drought. A few, however, tucked in at the base of our wall, and one or two others cramped and wedged between the cracks in a flagged walk (how they got there no one knows, or how they manage to survive there) and still other clumps in the east border—these have thrived for years. The English daisy is a perennial, but often gardeners seed in midsummer for next year's bloom. We have not done so.

## NO PAMPERING NEEDED

Originally, these English daisies were the large-flowered sort, hothouse forced, to be sold everywhere by roadside florists in spring. They bore scant resemblance to the lovely tiny flowers that star the English grass through most of the year. Yet, happily, they must be the same, for ours, neglected as they are, some of them cabin'd, cribb'd, confined by the flagstones of the path, have lost enormously in the size of their bloom. Lost, indeed, their look of cultivation, grown closer to the ground, but—thank God—seem healthy as ever and hardier than their betters. They are, in fact, the true English daisies now, the kind we know and love so well. To see them, low-growing there, cool, neat-headed, their colour and their beauty enhanced by natural size, is to catch a glimpse of England's grass once more and the unforgettable colour of England's green. We owe a lot to our English daisies. Daisies are a shallow-rooted plant, hence lack of moisture or excessive heat will destroy them.

## HEARTSEASE

Heartsease, the Johnny-jump-up, will bloom in February, just as it does now and then in January, provided the site for it is well sheltered and the weather has been reasonably mild. Ours have been growing for years in the corner of the terrace border and snuggled in at the base of the tool-house where they bloom amazingly early.

Heartsease, like most violas, is an annual or biennial for it lives through the years by reseeding itself. Or, of course, like the English daisies, it can be sown as seed in midsummer for next year's flowers. It stands a good deal of shade and like all spring-blooming flowers must have sufficient moisture to survive. Johnny-jump-up plants should be covered in winter. Salt hay makes a good cover, but it tends to mat somewhat when wet and so prevents much growth until spring.

There is something appealing about heartsease—so much jollity and so much of the irrepressible, such daintiness of coloring, such impishness of face, such unexpected springing up here and there where least expected—that it is small wonder the flower has won men's hearts through the ages as few others have.

Though usually regarded as a spring flower, it will bloom most of the year, provided it is damp-rooted, partly shaded, and constantly clipped. Once gone to seed, it does, of course, grow leggy, as all violas do, showing little or no more bloom as hot weather comes on. No other flower in all the wealth of summer lushness will give a cooler look to a room shaded from the August heat than a bowl of heartsease. It is February, however, we are concerned with now —not August. How quickly these Hobby-Horses bolt with us—six months on in a sentence!

## SNOWDROPS

The snowdrop, above all others, is the known harbinger of spring. Everybody looks for them in their accustomed places, just as year by year good people in London used to look for them in February, by the Serpentine in Hyde Park, near the Rabbit Warren there. Or as they looked for blue squills by the Grosvenor Gate or the golden carpet of crocuses by the Achilles. Even under the bombs they looked for them—we all did—and found them where they had always been.

It seems odd that snowdrops, though so fragile in appearance and coming so early, yet stay so long in bloom. Week after week, we see them here, as fresh and as cool as ever.

Sometimes snowdrops are confused with the lovely snowflakes that come somewhat later in spring. We have never had our snowflakes, *Leucojum vernum,* bloom before March, although that variety seems to be the earliest. There is another snowflake, very large, that blooms

26

as late as May, but so far we have not tried it. Now, however, in February, our snowdrops are the thing and how they do redeem the gloom of winter's damage! We have planted them as late as November, but it is far better to have them in the ground by September or October, if possible.

It is astonishing how even a few new bulbs each year will add up, before you know it, to lovely masses. Then, too, with the natural increase there is need for separating the clumps and replanting them from time to time. Our goal each year is to put in one hundred new snowdrops whenever we can fit them to our gardening budget.

## PLANTING SNOWDROPS

Snowdrops are extremely hardy. Nothing can replace them in the chill winds and lingering snow and ice of February and March. Snowdrops, naturally, like shade and some moisture the rest of the year. We have had many of them growing for years in our myrtle, where their delicate blossoms of purest white touched with green at the petal tips, pull at one's heartstrings. More of ours grow in a sheltered border below our library window, facing south. This is a prime sun trap all winter and it is here that the snowdrops show first, sharing the border with azaleas and daffodils that come two months later. Often, however, the snowdrops showing in February and the snowflakes in March will still be blooming in April with our earlier daffodils.

In planting snowdrops, do not be chary of leaf mould, for they thrive and increase in rich soil. If possible, they should be given a slope facing south—they do not mind a dry slope really—and earlier blossoms will be your reward.

## WINTER IS WINTER STILL

A word of caution is needed for all winter blossoms. Too often people have pictures in their minds of massed daffies in the breeze or of perennial borders in their summer glory or beds fall-painted

with dahlia and aster and the witchery of chrysanthemum and marigold. They look at the desolate grass and bare trees about the cottage
and ask: Where are the periwinkle and heartsease and the daisies
we boast of? Where are the Christmas roses? Yes, we see a few
snowdrops. But the rest? The answer may be disappointing, but it is
true. All are here, but they must of necessity show a few at a time
and usually well hidden at that. After all, winter is winter.

Part of the challenge is to give these venturesome pioneers a
chance to blossom at all, hidden if they like. Then, week by week,
through winter's darkest days, to be able to pick a few and bring
them indoors. A small bowl fresh with myrtle or euonymus leaves
and among them three or four Christmas roses, or a Johnny-jump-
up or so, or it may be an English daisy, picked in February snow,
will bring more magic to a room than masses of hothouse plants.
The same is true of snowdrops, but most of these wilt quickly so
we leave them to hearten us out of doors.

## BLOSSOMS AHEAD OF TIME

Though March is the more usual month for them, *Forsythia
spectabilis,* sometimes called by the lovelier name of golden bells;
the fragrant winter honeysuckle, *Lonicera fragrantissima,* and the
winter jasmine, *Jasminum nudiflorum,* all can be brought to the
freshest, most brightly coloured beauty imaginable, if their branches
are cut, even as early as February, dead twigs trimmed off, and the
sprays themselves placed in water. Jars filled with *Lonicera* have
filled our library with delectable scent year after year. As early as
the honeysuckle, we bring in the forsythia cuttings and they soon
fill our windows with gold, as does the jasmine. Pussy willow, *Salix
discolor,* must not be overlooked, for its catkins of the softest furlike
grey soon open and give character and height to any flower arrangement.

## SPRING GOLD

There are, of course, other shrubs that bloom indoors in water.

Most of them are yellow in blossom, spring's primary colour. The glint of their gold seems to have caught last year's brightest sun (as indeed it has) and saved it for us when we most long, in spite of gaining light, for the warm, sweet touch of spring. Why wait two months for all these lovely gifts of colour and scent when five minutes' clipping will bring them to us in abundance and make gardens for us on window ledge and table?

## A WINTER WINDOW

It is not our purpose here to discuss indoor plants at all, for that is a Hobby-Horse of quite another colour, yet it would not be a true picture to speak of winter greens and winter flowering sprays without at least a reference to what has been growing all this while in our winter window, giving toward the hackberry on the bank. Potted plants play their part there, of course.

Faithful geraniums; begonias, apparently ever blooming in their wealth of pink or red blossoms; fuchsias; shrimp plants; the African violet; a pot or two of miniature roses—tiny four-inch things taken in from their place in a low-growing border; oxalis; impatiens; pebble-grown narcissus—these and many more fill our winter window with warmth and colour and with sweetness. From time to time we move some of them to other rooms until they show that they need the sun again, then back they go to the larger window where a deep ledge awaits them with what winter sun there is. A few of these potted plants, backed up with flowering branches of forsythia or jasmine or honeysuckle produce an effect of far greater bloom indoors than there really is. All of them serve as reminders of spring and summer to come.

It is well to remember that the light and warmth which grow our plants indoors also encourage life in the pests that feast upon such plants. It takes a deal of doing to care for indoor flowers. They must be watered and aired and washed and sprayed as faithfully as any bed or border outdoors later on. Too many are smothered to death in steam heat and deadened air. Some plants are killed by unnoticed drafts, but very few by cold.

## LOOKING FORWARD

February is a planning month as well as a planting, pruning, spraying, liming, clean-up one. Bulbs can not tempt us now—at least not the buying of them for they have been in the ground since fall. All we can do on that score is poke into the salt hay or whatever covers them to see how far they are behind our venturesome snowdrops. Usually we find their bleached and yellow spears thrusting from the ground. There is thrill in that. But apart from bulbs, there is, perhaps, a bit of new planting or transplanting to be done. If there is, February is the time for it.

## VISTAS

A plan has been followed for years here and proved effective as well as saving on the budget. It is based on colour and vista. That sounds overpowering, but all it really means is that we have put, say, a silver bell tree, *Halesia tetraptera,* where it can be seen in the spring from our library window seat, but where it cannot be seen at all from what we call our upper garden. There is, though, a dogwood in the upper garden that ends a little view or vista across grass when seen from our wildflower path that winds through ferns and rhododendron and laurel toward the old road below. Close to the cottage itself a winesap apple tree stands at the end of a flagstoned path that passes between Norway spruce boughs, *Picea excelsa,* on one side and a tall cypress, actually *Chamaecyparis pisifera,* and arborvitae on the other; these evergreens form an arch to frame the apple tree. In blossom, it is lovely past telling.

Turning the corner of the cottage in spring, it is a delight to catch the splendour of the winesap bloom so framed at the end of that particular vista. In fall, its fruit is equally lovely—and most saving on the budget. Standing by the apple tree and facing the other way along the same path, past a low green gate in the garden wall, we have a large spreading *Viburnum tomentosum,* a glory of colour in spring and bright with berries in the fall. In summer it shades a stone-flagged corner of the garden where chairs and benches are always ready for a meal out-of-doors.

A witch hazel, *Hamamelis virginiana,* was planted years ago under and to one side of the hackberry because its November-December blossoming just fills the view from our winter window.

At the end of another path there is a laburnum *anagyroides,* the golden-chain tree—a thing of beauty every spring—and close to it a tree rose whose golden blossoms come a little later. No one could call this, or any of these, a vista; the distances are too ridiculously short for such a name, but in each case the tree or shrub at its end serves the purpose of a *point d' appui,* and, as a matter of fact, gives a pleasing illusion of depth and distance where they do not exist. Each view (again a misnomer—there are no "views" about our cottage) has been planned in either direction: the viburnum and the winesap apple, the golden-chain tree and, at the other end of that path, the lych gate and its climbing roses, leading out of the walled garden to the drive. The upper garden dogwood is faced down a stretch of lawn by fruit trees, narrowing to meet the start of the wildflower path—our newest venture.

In a word, we have tried to suggest what distances we could, in a very small space, by accenting certain views from windows indoors and from terrace or corner or path outdoors, and we have made use of a tree or shrub to add the needed colour at each short vista's end.

## THE UNEXPECTED

Early on, we learned that one tree or bush in flower, if properly flanked by more sober green, is worth a dozen crowded together or spread too profusely in view. We learned—again the hard way—that the loveliest bloom should not be in open view at all, but caught, unexpectedly wherever possible, around the cottage or through the lych gate eaves, or where the laurel serves us as a screen.

And we have learned not to repeat our surprises. There are flowering trees and shrubs aplenty to serve any number of views.

It pays to think of such things in February. One well-chosen, well-sited shrub, put in now, will delight you in May when its colour has come. Here we have relied all along on evergreens to flank our little *allées,* leaving it to the blossom of the tree itself or of the shrub to complete the picture. Rhododendron and laurel carry most of that burden, helped out by low-growing inkberries and yews, backed here and there by hemlocks and pines.

## TREES BY PLAN

Of trees planted according to this plan we have now about the cottage Norway spruce; white pine, *Pinus strobus;* hemlock, *Tsuja canadensis;* cypress; pin-oak, *Quercus palustris;* some seven or eight dogwoods, *Cornus florida,* both pink and white; a flowering crab, *Malus sieboldi;* silver-bell; golden-chain tree; arborvitae and cypress; several temple-trees, *Cryptomeria japonica Lobbi;* some double-file viburnums, so large that they are really more trees than shrubs; witch hazel; as well as cherries, apples and pears. All of these have been planted through the years as we could afford them, and are, of course, in addition to the older trees originally here and already listed.

Most of the new trees were put in during February or early March. All of them have lived. It has paid to follow a plan.

## POOR CHOICE

All too often, both with trees and shrubs, nurserymen will put in too many of what they have in full supply at the moment and what is easy to grow. As a result we find a plethora of privet hedges, always begging to be clipped, yet a privet hedge where you really need it can be lovely. We see masses of forsythia, most beautiful in spring, but why so much of it? We count bridal-wreath, spirea, and still more bridal-wreath. Not so many years back foundations planting consisted in mass upon mass of hydrangeas. Now the fashion seems to lean toward mass upon mass of azaleas and all of them magenta in colour.

All this massing of well-known shrubs, lovely in themselves, defeats its purpose. For one thing, too many of them bloom at the same time. A fortnight or so of spring colour and all is over. Then, too, these masses of bloom, in full view, are likely to cloy a bit. How wise the gardeners were, in Scotland particularly, when they placed their gardens—as most of them did in the old days—a little distance from the house, feeling that flowers, like a lovely view, were precious things to be sought and savoured, not stared at all day long.

## TIME OF BLOOM

In any February planting of flowering tree or shrub, thought must be given to time of bloom. A good nurseryman will gladly guide us in this and also post us as to proper time for planting. By putting in a few of each sort, perhaps only one of each at the start, and by selecting them now for the earliest bloom to the latest, beginners are surprised to find that an eight months' spread is not at all difficult. Not all shrubs can be planted as early as February. Roses for example, must wait until April is with us.

## MARCH

March gives *Forsythia spectabilis,* the showy border kind, or *ovata* or *suspensa* or *intermedia,* each of which is dependable according to the size and the shape of shrub desired. *Ovata* is usually the earliest to bloom. Also in March is winter jasmine, *Jasminum nudiflorum.*

## APRIL

For April we want flowering almonds, *Prunus triloba* or *Prunus gladulosa;* wintergreen barberry, *Berberis julianae;* andromeda; cherry blow —ours are ox-hearts; pear blossom, Seckels for us; the lovely shadbush, Amelanchier, in our wildflower corner; the azaleas including *nudiflora* or pinxterbloom, *kaempferi* or torch azalea, *mollis,* the Chinese azalea, *calendulacea* or flame azalea, *ledifolium album;* the pure white sort, lovely as them all; the flowering crab; the dogwoods; and the apple blossoms that seal each spring with beauty.

## MAY

May, of course, has different gifts and is most lavish of them. The lilacs, *Syringa vulgaris,* and all the lovely French forms that now are available anywhere; *Wisteria sinensis;* the silver-bell tree, *Halesia tetraptera;* holly grape, *Mahonia aquifolium;* winterberry, *Ilex verticillata;* the other hollies: American—*Ilex opaca,* English—*Ilex aquifolium,* the little leaf Japanese sort—*Ilex crenata* and *Ilex convexa,* there are many varieties, but tiny bloom will show and brilliant berries later on if male and female plants have been set out close by one another. People sometimes forget this. *Viburnum tomentosum* is at its peak in May, with bridal-wreath, *Spirea prunifolia.* Vanhoute is the commonest variety. It is found ad nauseam everywhere, but other sorts are quite nice, provided they are limited to one or two. Also in May are *Clematis montana rubens* and *montana undulata;* rock cotoneaster, *horizontalis.* Its flowers are tiny, but there all right. Its green, too, is charming; trumpet honeysuckle, *Lonicera sempervirens;* pink weigela, *florida rosea;* the golden-chain tree, *Laburnum anagyroides;* wild dogwood, *Cornus paniculata;* bush honeysuckle, *Diervilla lonicera;* beauty-bush, *Kolkwitzia amabilis;* all sorts and colours of climbing roses; mountain laurel, *Kalmia latifolia; Leucothoe Catesbaei; deutzia gracilis* or *scabra;* cherry laurel, *Prunus laurocerasus schipkaensis;* firethorn, *Pyracantha coccinea* and *coccinea Lalandi;* the golden rose, *Rosa Hugonis;* and cherries ripe for the picking.

## JUNE

June brings the mock orange or Philadelphus—there are endless types of them; the sweet bay, *Magnolia glauca;* inkberries, *Ilex glabra;* privet, *Ligustrum ovalifolium* (unclipped it can be quite useful as a high screen and bloom profusely); rose-bay, *Rhododendrom maximum;* butterfly bush, *Buddleia Davidi;* and naturally in June, all the roses.

## JULY

July gives us rose of Sharon, *shrub-althea* or *hibiscus syriacus;* trumpet-creeper, *Campsis radicans;* and *Abelia grandiflora,* which often blooms earlier in June.

## AUGUST

August shows still the rose of Sharon and the abelias; virgin's-bower; more trumpet honeysuckle; plenty of trumpet-creeper; all the floribunda roses—and masses of them there are; the tree roses; the bush hydrangeas (among them the usual *paniculata,* but the hills-of-snow, *Hydrangea arborescens grandiflora,* are still better); still some late blooming rhododendron; plus apples and pears galore to look at and eat.

## SEPTEMBER

September is rich, naturally, with colour, at least the start of it—leaf and berry. Abelia still blossoms and so do the floribunda roses; tree roses and the so-called monthly roses, our oldest stand-by. Dogwoods—pink and white and the wild ones, too, are gay with bronzing leaf and scarlet berries. The viburnums are rich with fruit. The drupes of the tupelo, the sour gum tree, add their colour—a deep, glossy blue. Colour shows, too, on the vines—the Virginia creeper, *Ampelopsis quinquefolia,* and the rest.

## OCTOBER

October is richer still in colour—the swamp maples come into their own now, the gum tree, and the gold of the sweet birch. Virgin's-bower still covers the north wall. Euonymus is bronzing.

## NOVEMBER

In November or even December the witch hazel blossoms—the last shrub of all to show its flower.

## NINE MONTHS OF BLOOM

It should be borne in mind that these flowering shrubs are all more or less overlapping in their time of bloom. Some four of them, obviously, are vines—clematis, trumpet-creeper, virgin's-bower and trumpet honeysuckle—but they serve the purpose of shrubs on our garden walls.

We have here about the cottage some twenty-six varieties of trees, some of which are most lovely in bloom, and sixty-four kinds of flowering shrubs and vines. These bloom, as a rule, for a fortnight or more at a time or longer than that, providing some colour every day for nine months of the year.

It should also be remembered that we have listed here no flowers, no annuals or perennials as such, but flowering shrubs and trees and vines only. Roses—climbers, tree, and floribunda—we have indeed included under shrubs, for they are a part of our permanent planting.

## WISE CHOICE

It is in February that the choice of shrubs should be made. March and April are planting months, but in February we are close enough to spring to get the feel of it in our bones. The wise gardener looks ahead through all the coming months of spring and summer, autumn and even early winter, and by deciding what he can afford to spend and selecting wisely for variation in time of bloom, he can extend his period of bloom miraculously.

This planning will fit any budget, for even one or two new shrubs at a time soon change the over-all picture. The elimination of some that are in too great number helps almost as much.

## BALANCED GROUPING

We have found that it is wise to buy, when the budget can stand it, a balanced group of shrubs at one time. So we try to decide what a particular corner or nook needs—shrub and background and sides as well. We select the shrub first, for that is to provide the keynote, the colour of the picture. Then the background, evergreen where possible. It may be a single rose-bay rhododendron or a little hemlock tree or English ivy for a wall already there or firethorn pleached or espalier'd on the wall, of all things most lovely in the fall. Some of these shrubs show colour in themselves, but basically it is their green that we want. Flanks are essential—and again we need green to accentuate the central shrub that gives the colour. Yews, low hollies, laurel, leucothoe, inkberries—the choice is endless, but obviously we have not limited ourselves to evergreens alone. However, if evergreens are used, the bleakness of winter is far less noticeable.

February is the month for planning, for looking ahead. It is also the month of hope. Thrust of bulb or stir in the aspens, the first, faint flush of colour on the hills, tell us, as they have told man through the ages, for whose pleasure they are and were created.

## FEBRUARY CHECK LIST

February is primarily the spraying and pruning month, in spite of a January start at this work. The time for dormant spraying of miscible oil or lime-sulphur is as early as temperature will permit—that is any day after New Year's, January or February, above 45 or 50 degrees.

Oyster-shell scale, tent caterpillar eggs, cankerworms, gypsy moths, aphids—all can be destroyed now, or at least their eggs can. As with all dormant spraying, keep in mind the pine and spruce trees, hackberries, witch hazels, lilacs, and other shrubs as well as fruit trees.

Do not put off pruning fruit trees beyond February if you can help it. Grape vines should also be cut back now, if that has not been done earlier.

Be sure to start seed flats now, even if one or two have been started in January. February is a good time for seeding annual phlox, dwarf marigolds, ageratum, and especially sweet alyssum in flats. Remember they need plenty of sun, but not much heat. Too much warmth makes seedlings leggy.

It pays to sterilize the soil of seed flats to avoid damping off; or treat the seeds themselves. Any seed store will recommend dependable preventatives made up commercially.

Do not make the soil in the seed flats overly rich; use loam and peat-moss, half-and-half.

Trim back leggy house plants in February, if they have responded too keenly to the gaining light. Try to keep them low, but do not sacrifice any more blossoms or buds than you must.

February is the prime month to lime the lawn. It gives the lime a chance to sink in before feeding and real growth begin. Take care that no lime is allowed near the acid-soil shrubs such as rhododendrons, laurels, azaleas, hollies, leucothoe, *Pieris japonica,* and the broad-leaved evergreens.

This is also an ideal month to enrich the lawn with any reliable grass food. Follow directions carefully as to the exact amount to go on per square foot. The amount varies somewhat with the plant food used. If the lawn thaws and freezes, so much the better. That will work the plant food deeper.

A sprinkling of grass seed pays off well if scattered on the lawn in February, but of course do not attempt to roll grass now. The frost-roughened surface is exactly what grass seed needs. Spring rains, later, will work it in.

Bone-meal and pulverized cow manure, as a first refresher, can go on beds and borders if the weather be mild enough to remove winter cover. Usually, however, it is safer to wait.

February, if we have planned for it, can be rich in early blossom out of doors. Snowdrops, snowflakes, winter aconite, blue myrtle, English daisies, heartsease, winter jasmine, the Christmas roses—really the tally is often most heartening.

Indoors, do not forget to keep up a supply of flowering branches —pussy willow, forsythia, bush honeysuckle, flowering quince, and the fruit tree blossoms as well.

Finally, complete plans and check lists now. Sap is stirring. Spring does not wait.

# CHAPTER III

# MARCH

## *The Now-or-Never Month*

If February be the planning month, the tree and shrub month, surely March is the lawn month, the tidying-up, the hard-at-it, down-to-earth month. Snow still may come to us—even a serious blizzard—but none the less things are growing now and our Hobby-Horse has the bit in his teeth for fair. Mud has not left us, of course, but March winds can do a lot of drying.

These same March winds and a March sun often play hob with evergreens, the broad-leaved rhododendrons and the laurels, parching them unmercifully and burning their leaves as they give off their precious water content. Boxwood, also, can be badly damaged by the winds and sun of early spring. That is why these shrubs are best covered by burlap on frames, especially young plants, although the shelter serves to keep off heavy snow and damaging ice as well. Usually the sunburnt mountain laurel and the rose-bay rhododendrons are not seriously injured and recover tone with increasing shade and spring showers.

### THE LAWN

By March (in our garden, at least) it is high time to start work on the grass, if that has not been seen to in February. March is usually the better time for this as the ground is drier. Lime, as has been said, must go on early before real growing starts. A good rain soaks the lime in well and then that danger is past. Next the lawn must be fed.

Too many people take grass for granted. If they do, they get grass all right—crab grass, fall grass, plantain, dandelion, all the valerian they may not want, but of good grass a sadly diminishing return.

March is, of course, the lawn-feeding month. Most commercial fertilizers are good. All contain the three essentials: nitrogen, phosphate, and potash, well pulverized. No amount of chemical fertilizer, however, can do good if humus and organic matter are lacking in the soil. We have found that a mixture of cow manure and bonemeal, reinforced with some chemical compounds, does the trick. Even better (say, every other year) we use mushroom soil, the rich mould that mushroom growers have for sale. We get ours from Kennett Square and put it on about one inch thick, for good measure. We have used as much as one ton of it on an area of 500 square feet. How the grass does spring up! And what a glorious healthy green it is after that treatment. Organic fertilizer, also sold commercially, is sometimes made from sewage disposal material and constitutes an excellent organic feed for grass as it will not burn it. The odour, however, while harmless, is not very pleasant for a few days. The important thing to remember is that all lawns must be seen to in spring if good grass is expected later. It must also be kept in mind that September is the real time to *start* work on next year's grass.

Prior to liming and feeding and seeding, lawn surfaces naturally must be well raked, and all dead, matted, winter-killed grass removed. A rather deep raking also breaks up the top crust left on the ground by winter storms, thus enabling both lime and fertilizer to sink in more rapidly and more deeply.

## GRASS SEED

Once the lawn has been prepared for re-seeding, it is well to sow early and catch the benefit of spring rains. In seeding, it pays to go to a thoroughly reliable dealer and buy the sort of seed best suited to the areas in mind. There is a great difference in grass seed prepared for sunny places, shady places, much-used spots and so on.

Seed is extraordinarily costly these days and none of us can afford to waste it. Try to seed the right sort in the place where it will do the most good and, above all, be sure that the ground has been properly prepared beforehand. Considerable attention must also be given to the type of grass sown, regardless of whether it be shade or sun seed. Many mixtures contain too much clover. This never results in a satisfactory lawn. Others stress blue grass, which is better. Often a good deal of rye grass goes into the seed. This makes a splendid showing in the spring, especially if the ground has been well prepared and the soil fed. Later, however, the rye burns off and bare patches appear, for this seed is really an annual. Bent-grass, though expensive, is the most economical in the end, for it seeds densely, makes sound roots and lasts from year to year if cared for. A lawn must also be rolled after seeding to press down the seed as well as to level off winter scars.

## WORKADAY MARCH

Until one tries it, it is hard to believe how much must be done in March to prepare for the spring, now so close at hand. The planning stage has passed. It is work now in earnest. Note how February chores, in spite of preventive efforts, keep sliding over into March.

4 March—cut down a stray mulberry tree in the east hedgerow so that the flowering shrubs in the border there can have a better chance. Picked up leaves and sticks and fallen branches about the border plantings. Weather still cold.

5 March—snow crocuses now out in front garden.

6 March—cleared up more of the shrubbery.

7 March—planted in the lower garden bed one *Berberis verruculosa;* one *Azalea mollis;* one *Azalea ledifolium album;* two *Rhododendron carolinianum;* and two andromeda. Winter jasmine now in bloom.

9 March—first snowdrops up in driveway bed—our warmest spot, as it faces south and lies in the shelter of the library wing. Planted three inkberries; one mountain laurel; and one Japanese andromeda in the myrtle patch under our kitchen window.

10 March—cut down white pine in east shrubbery. It never had recovered from the ice storm of the previous winter.

11 March—ordered 500 pounds of pulverized cow manure and 300 pounds of fertilized peat (peat and cow manure mixed), plus one bale of Swedish peat-moss. Yellow crocuses and blue spring crocuses now in bloom. Also the snowflakes sent us years ago by a friend from Glen Isle, that most lovely place in the Great Valley where flowers have been cherished for generations. Our very first Christmas rose, as has been said, came from Glen Isle, and it is blooming bravely still.

14 March—dormant spray on fruit trees. It should have been put on in February. Miscible oil was used. This is splendid against unhatched eggs, scale, and the witches-broom which is a bane of the old hackberry.

15 March—limed all lawns. Lime is usually put on a little less than half a pound to the square yard. Planted three winter jasmine by the library wall; one weigela, *Florida rosea,* in the south border. Moved it later, as ill-placed. This is not a very useful shrub at best. Planted 7 additional rose-bay rhododendrons and one hemlock in the east boundary shrubbery, where we needed to thicken our screening a bit. The older Japanese andromeda shrubs, planted some years ago, are now in bloom.

16 March—moved a wintergreen barberry and a trumpet-creeper to make room for some climbing roses soon to go in at that particular spot. First daffodils in bloom.

17 March—St. Patrick's Day—raked leaves from the side of the drive banks. Much sand and gravel had matted the winter creeper there. Sand had been spread after each storm on our very steep driveway and a lot of it had been churned on to the bank. Blue periwinkle blooming beautifully—no winter damage there. Planted two beauty-bushes and three pink flowering almonds. Transplanted one white lilac to lower border. Removed all salt hay and winter cover from beds and borders—except from the roses.

20 March—removed burlap coverings from the more tender shrubs that had needed such protection during the winter. Raked wall garden borders. Cow manure on roses. Also on the myrtle and euonymus both sides of the drive. Bale of peat-moss scattered on the east bank of drive. One hundred pounds of pulverized cow manure also put on drive banks. Snowdrops in blossom everywhere. Blue and gold crocuses in bloom—front garden terrace. Winter jasmine blossoming by library wall.

## TREASURES FROM TIROL

22 March—painted three weathervanes, two of them from the Tirol in Austria. One stands on top of our lych gate, where, in May and June, the red ramblers clamber high. He is a magnificently proud chanticleer, black bodied, crimson tailed and crimson combed, matching the climbing roses, obviously very old and obviously hand-made by some clever craftsman in the Tirol. Through the body of this weathercock, a stray bullet drilled a hole in one of the last skirmishes of World War II. The shot was fired by an enemy rearguard as they fell back towards the mountain fastness of Pyramidenspitze and the Hinter-Kaisergebirge high above Kufstein-am-Inn, Goering's much talked-of Redoubt that never materialized. The bullet hole still shows above our peaceful roses.

The other weathervane tops a little tool-house at the far side of the cottage. It also comes from the Tirol—a marvelous little man with Tirolean hat and a feather at the back of it and a great burgomeister pipe in his mouth, the tobacco in which he is tamping down with his hand. Over his shoulder he gaily carries a great Tirolean scythe and a strong-tined farmer's rake. He wears the *lederhosen* of Tirol and stockings, bare-kneed, of course. He is our pride. He, too, is clearly home-made and very old. Each spring these vanes are painted and oiled so that they turn readily to the breeze.

There were also painted on this day three old inn signs from the Schwarzwald in Germany, now hanging on our garden wall and by the tool-house pent. One of them is interesting indeed, consisting of six horseshoes varying in size from two that would fit a pony to a pair that would shoe the largest Percheron or Shire. During the war, shells destroyed the inn completely where once they had hung before the door, but the sign of the travelled road was retrieved from the ruins and now adds interest—and some memories—to our garden.

The ivy about our door lamps is clipped back a bit and the lamps repainted each spring. Year ago these lamps were used on our dog-cart with tallow dips in them and many a mile we have driven behind them.

Also on 22 March all the gardening tools were cleaned and oiled, as they had been in the fall. The little shrine that holds a statuette of St. Francis and his birds was tidied up and the back of it painted a rich, clear blue to set off the white porcelain of the figure. It stands in the far corner of the garden in an angle of the wall, a curved stone bench beneath it. Two porcelain birds were restored to their stance on the rim of our shallow millstone fountain.

23 March—put 150 pounds of pulverized cow manure on the roses, on the front garden bed, drive banks, and upper garden borders. Set out the large pottery flower pots that flank the steps leading to the lower garden. Still the ground is a bit too wet to fill them with earth. Put pulverized cow manure on the *Enkianthus campanulatus.* It has grown well for years, but never blossomed—too much shade. We'll move it one day. Raked and cleaned along the southwest wall from the potting shed to the garage.

24 March—tidied the road bank carefully, for the Christmas and wood ferns are there and will push their shepherd's crooks up through leaf mould later. Filled seven large pots with rich earth (bone-meal, too), ready for the violas and pansies that will soon bring their golden colours to them. These pots are used on the low wall of the driveway bed as well as to flank two pair of steps that lead down to the lower garden from the terrace. Now in bloom: Christmas roses (still a few left), *Pieris japonica,* crocuses, snowdrops, snowflakes, winter jasmine, winter aconite, blue myrtle, *Daphne mezereum,* and daffodils.

25 March—Lady Day—planted one hundred plumbago by the fountain in the walled garden. Hope they do well there. Their blue flowers in August and the fall should be cool and lovely. Put last winter's leaves on the compost pile—a most essential adjunct to any form of gardening but too often overlooked, especially in these days of chemical fertilizers. Organic matter is the foundation of gardening just as it is essential to all sound farming. Burning leaves—most leaves at least—is like burning dollar bills. Two tons of mushroom soil on grass under the apple trees— a shaded spot, of course, and usually in need of plenty of lime and plenty of feeding.

26 March—finished raking borders—thirty or forty great baskets full of rotted leaves to go under the rose-bays where they save the needed moisture in the soil. Transplanted eight clumps of privet, heeled in all winter after a driveway hedge had been removed, to the slope below the twin Norway spruce trees—where the privet, unclipped, will soon reinforce a screening needed there northwestward. Planted two of the tall-growing firethorns against the east wall, to be espalier'd there. Man never quite forgets the gift, the miracle, of the growing world he sees reborn each spring. Deep in his heart he knows that neither is he that planteth anything, neither he that watereth, but God that yieldeth the increase. Put in one *Taxus Hicksi,* two abelias *grandiflora* and four little-leaf Japanese hollies, *Ilex crenata microphylla,* by the parking place.

44

27 March—many more crocuses out—blue, yellow and the most striking white ones with the golden centres. Staked out the trace of a new myrtle planting between the parking place and the rose-bays that bank our southwest wall.

28 March—put a trowel full of aluminum sulphate 6 to 8 inches from the stem of each leucothoe shrub, for it needs an acid soil as do ink-berries and all hollies. Clipped back the frost-bitten stems of the flori-bunda roses. Daffodils now blossoming everywhere.

30 March—planted three Christmas roses; also one clump of yellow iris in the upper border. *Forsythia spectabilis* now in blossom, east border. Planted two bittersweet vines, mindful that they must be well curbed. Set out violas and pansies in the large garden pots.

31 March—wild violets out. Carried up all the garden chairs and benches from the cellar and scrubbed them. Put 50 pounds of grass seed on the lower garden lawn. Spread wood ashes from the fireplaces about the peonies in upper borders. Set out 4 primroses, 18 heartsease, 15 violas, and 20 pansy plants in the terrace border. Put 100 blue myrtle plants and 100 lily-of-the-valley pips in the new border by the parking place traced out for them a day or so ago. Bedded the plantings with plenty of peat-moss. Blue squills, now out by the hundreds, colouring all the myrtle on the bank. It was not our purpose to have given so much space to the chores of March, but they are so varied, yet so constant, year by year, and always so essential, that no account of March in the garden is complete without them.


## BLUE SQUILLS

The squills have the look of soft blue smoke drifting low above the green, reminding us of the drifts of the bluebells, *Scilla non-scripta,* under the great trees at Kew, surely as lovely a sight as any spring can offer. They come there in Kew Gardens before lilac time when, as Noyes tell us, "the cherry trees are seas of bloom and sweet perfume." And, indeed, they are. Yet the bluebells, which he does not mention, pluck at one's heartstrings more surely than all the flowering trees in Christendom. They do not seem to grow and root solidly as other flowers grow and root—these bluebells *float* in delicious pale blue clouds across the glades. The squills in our myrtle, oddly, have this same drifting, cloudlike quality about them in spring. Only a few of these were planted years and years ago, their bulbs set out in early fall deep in the myrtle before the door of our cottage. They have spread and multiplied amazingly there with no attention whatever except for the peat that has gone on the myrtle each spring. The blue of the squills and the blue of the myrtle are different in shade, of course, but they do not snap at one another as some colours do.

It should be noticed that the flowers now blooming have tripled in kind since February. Eighteen sorts and many of these in great profusion, have come in March. The bare look of the garden has gone now, as the ground begins to dry. Bed and border and grass, too, will not—at least should not—look so disconsolate again until next year's February brings its chill to all it touches, yet, withal, its promise of the spring hard by.

## THE CARRY-OVERS

Of course, a certain number of March flowers are carry-overs from February, some of them even from January. The myrtle for example, has been gaining in bloom for over two months now, only in March it is literally starred with the clearest, purest blue. Christmas roses first opened in December and are now in their fourth month of bloom. Surely we are in their debt, for no other flower does so much to redeem winter for us and to keep a tiny corner of spring in our hearts.

The Johnny-jump-ups, now blossoming, come to us in January some years, but not always. There is an element of chance there and mild weather. Yet in lucky years we have had them in January, February, and, of course, nearly always in March. Winter aconite has carried over from February. It is a very early flower, small, vivid gold in colour, and full of life. We regard it as a must. Winter aconites should be planted as bulbs in early fall (say, September) and they should be set out in clusters as generously as the budget will stand. They are too small a flower to make any sort of a show-

46

ing by themselves, but a dozen or so clumped close together under the green of a Christmas rose are lovely. They look well also when backed by the low-growing cherry laurel.

It seems almost impossible to overcome a tendency in many gardeners to plant everything in rows—especially bulbs—like well-disciplined hills of corn. Too few can be persuaded to plant naturally —in drifts, as nature does. Winter aconite is never a formal garden plant. Daffodils should not be either. Surely they can not be expected to dance in rows, and thrill our hearts with pleasure. So we try to group our winter aconite, as much as we can, to gain the massed effect of its early gold. *Daphne mezereum* is our fourth February carry-over. It holds its tiny pinkish-red bloom a long time and, although a small shrub and not a very hardy one, it is so filled with the spirit of spring that we try very hard to keep it. It is temperamental, killed apparently not so much by winter cold as by its own humour at the moment. We love it, nevertheless.

The fifth hold-over from February is the winter jasmine. This shrub is never spectacular, but when found growing high on some south wall, perhaps flanked by holly, its golden blossoms can be a sheer delight. Here, we have none on our walls, but low-growing by the drive and on our bank where, year by year, they keep the faith and blossom as early as any.

In February, of course, we usually have the crocuses—all sorts and colours—and they, too, hold over into March. The pale blue and the lavender snow crocuses come very early and then the yellow. And there are the so-called spring crocuses—the most lovely blue-and-gold sort.

Snowdrops are still another February gift to March, but snow-flakes with us, at least, often come a little later, nearly always in March, and most glorious they are. How we wish we could plant and plant them each fall. In an average year, we try to put in 100 snowdrops, 100 snowflakes (the *Leucojums* are expensive), 100 snow crocuses, and 100 giant-flowered crocuses. All these are match-less in March and some hold bloom from February on until April.

The only other carry-over from February is the Japanese andromeda. Naturally, these earlier blooming shrubs and flowers are far more generous with their blossoms in March than they could possibly be in February.

## DAFFODILS

It is the fresh bloom, however, that puts the final seal of spring upon March. Usually daffodils come first. They have been valiantly poking and thrusting up through their coverings since the start of the year. We have never seen them open here in February, but always, in March, some appear. In a mild March they bloom with us by the hundreds.

Each fall we try to plant them to the limit of our budget, so bewitched are we by their loveliness in spring. There is nothing shrinking about daffodils. When they open, all the golden treasuries of all the golden ages are with us again. Who could resist them?

Last fall we put in 12 Covent Garden, 12 Golden Harvest, 12 King Alfred, 24 Giant Trumpet, 50 Mixed Medium Trumpet, 50 mixed Red Cupped, 100 Special Mixture, and 100 Narcissus *Poeticus* and Poetaz; also, we planted 50 sweet-scented jonquils. Four hundred new bulbs. We had lifted several hundred more old bulbs in the early summer and dried them. These were planted anew in the upper borders and clumped here and there along the little wild-garden path among the rhododendrons. All of these, new and old, gave us masses of bloom in March.

Each year we put our new bulbs in the lower garden beds and the borders about the cottage itself. The lifted bulbs we set out not only in the upper borders and by the rhododendrons but everywhere on the drive bank where they blossom in the green euonymus there. Later, they are still blooming when the Virginia bluebells, *Mertensia virginica,* and masses of *Phlox divaricata* join them. The three of them—daffodils, bluebells, and phlox—in the winter-creeper vines, transform what once was a dry and barren slope into cool and coloured beauty. But now, in March, only the daffodils, with here and there some jonquils, are in bloom.

## FORSYTHIA

Matching the yellow of the daffodils and aconite and crocus, the forsythia—the gay golden bells—whatever variety it may be, is never far behind. We try to limit ours severely in number, for the forsythia bloom does not last very long and it seems poor economy of colour to have it all at once, with most of the flowering a year ahead. Besides, our space is limited. At one time we must have had a dozen bushes and more here, some of them the weeping, *suspensa,* and the high-arched *intermedia.* One at a time, lovely as they were, we culled them out, keeping only a few where they serve their pur-pose best, giving life and glorious blossoms when and where we need them. Shrubs flowering at other times of the year have re-placed the forsythia we sacrificed.

## WILD VIOLETS

Wild violets, touched with red, must have been growing on the place since it was a forest glade. We have a time controlling them, for they are great spreaders and nothing seems to kill them. Always a few clumps are left purposely, in the south border, and always their blossoms show in March, opening with the earliest of the bulbs there. They are quite indestructible and scatter themselves like mad unless ruthlessly culled. However, we should miss them were they gone entirely.

## THE VIOLAS

We always plant our violas in the richest soil we can find to fill the pots on the low terrace wall. This soil is well broken up, then reinforced with bone-meal and pulverized cow manure worked thoroughly into it. One should never let either of these fertilizers touch the roots of the plants—or of any plant, for that matter. They

49

should rather be mixed with the soil, a little below where the roots will come on planting. And the soil, so fertilized, should be well watered before each plant goes in.

*Viola tricolor hortensis* includes what we generally call a viola, as well as the heartsease (Johnny-jump-up), the pansy, and the violet. All four are related and show it in both colour and form. They give us a glorious succession of blue and white and gold— bright as the sun on the garden wall, rich as the deepest velvet in texture—well on to July.

The viola group are perennials actually, but in our climate they will not winter outdoors unless sheltered in some way. Many gardeners sow pansy and viola and Johnny-jump-up seed in early fall for next year's bloom, treating them as biennials. Whether home grown, as they should be, or bought as blossoming plants in spring (a far more costly procedure), they are altogether lovely. Even a small cold frame will pay for itself times over, if one grows flowers from seed in it.

In late June or early July our pansies, so gay in March, usually are past saving, but this is not true of the violas which we transplant at that time elsewhere and so have their colour with us through most of the summer. Pansies require cool weather, whereas the violas, with their large golden flowers, will stand a surprising amount of sun and heat. They must, however, have plenty of water and good drainage. The secret of bloom lies in constant clipping. Without it, pansies and violas and heartsease soon grow leggy.

## THE PRIMROSES

Primroses, a March flower with us, are set out in the terrace border each year; but others, transplanted long ago to the upper garden, have blossomed for years in spring and now and again in the fall, when the English daisies also respond to cooler weather and take on new life. The English primrose, called *Primula acaulis* or *vulgaris,* is not so easy to grow here. The cowslip, *veris,* and the oxlip, *elatior,* are varieties of it. Many hybrids of these early primroses, however, are now grown everywhere, but there is something most appealing in the simpler, earlier forms if they will but grow.

Like the violas, primroses require rich, well-drained soil. All are quickly killed by too much sun. In fact, they ask very little of it. A bit of sand mixed in the soil helps with drainage. *Primula polyantha,* one of the hybrids, and *Primula veris,* are not too difficult to grow. Without the primrose somewhere about, how could it be spring at all?

> "—pale primroses
> That die unmarried, ere they can behold
> Bright Phoebus in his strength—"

What with raking and rolling and liming and feeding and seeding the grass, filling the garden pots, scrubbing and painting terrace chairs and tables, turning on outdoor taps, cleaning the fountain, setting out the bird baths, wondering whether or not to risk a frost and lift the cover from bed and border, March is over before we know it—and still our chores half done.

## THE ICELANDIC TERNS

Back of the little fountain in our lower garden there is a brick-topped wall, completely covered with ivy now, and climbing roses and clematis. On this, near the fountain, the ivy has been cut away so as to leave a clear space where two arctic terns in flight have been made fast to the wall, framed, as it were, like medallions, by the circle of ivy about them.

These terns are of glazed pottery, most beautifully formed and coloured. While stationed in Iceland for several years at the start of the last war, we could not help but be thrilled by the variety and the abundance of bird life there, especially of water fowl. The beauty of the golden plover, the matchless grace of the arctic tern, formed pictures never to be forgotten. The terns, somewhat resembling small and agile seagulls, though infinitely more graceful and beautiful, leave Iceland each fall. Just where they go is a question. In the spring, they return year after year on the same day—a miracle, like the swallows of Capistrano, that never fails to amaze us. There is a lake in Reykjavík, the capital, called Tjörin. To it, far back through the centuries, the terns have come on 11 May. The golden plovers, whose return is watched for as eagerly in Iceland as the terns', are said to be the most widely traveled birds of them all, migrating in winter far into the South Polar Seas.

## THE REYKJAVÍK POTTER

The arctic terns on our wall were made by a potter in Reykjavík. I was lucky enough to find two of them hidden away among his gear and also two life-sized white tiercels (gerfalcons), the national bird of Iceland, and two little models of the ptarmigan, one in winter plumage of the purest white, the other in the brown and speckled colouring of summer.

All these statuettes were exquisitely modeled and coloured from life, really most lovely things yet not shown for sale—just laid away to be discovered by chance. The cost of them, when they were sold, was more than reasonable. Packed in sawdust, they survived the voyage home, escaping U-boat and bomb as a good many ships from Iceland did not. The terns have been on the garden wall, hovering above our fountain for years now, bringing back golden memories of the North—the great snowfields or jökulls, the glaciers, the plunging falls of the Gullfoss.

## BORDER EDGING

March is a good month for resetting the edges of borders, if winter frost has pushed them out of plumb. As a rule, natural edges of blossoming candytuft, the perennial *Iberis sempervirens,* or the annuals, *amara* and *umbellata,* or the annual dwarf sweet alyssum seem more desirable to us than an edging of tile or brick. In our upper garden, the borders are always edged with seeded flowers. We have used in addition to candytuft and alyssum, borders of strawberries, thus gaining the triple advantage of early and beautiful foliage, the colour of the blossoms, and the delicious fruit in season. Edging plants are endless. Blue ageratum is always useful. So are begonias and white myrtle and the vari-coloured rose-moss or purslane, *Portulaca grandiflora.* This last, though, needs watching, for like all the purslanes it will run riot easily. Ours came to us as a gift from friends at lovely Fairhope Cottage across the river. Bugleweed, *Ajuga reptans,* also spreads rapidly, but if controlled gives a border background of the deepest green with tall blue spikes of blossom in the spring. One year we set out eighty-odd plants of the ajuga just from the year's overflowing of the original planting. It makes delightful ground cover. In any case, natural edging is easy to obtain and the variety is without limit.

## TILE EDGING

If, however, the beds are small or more formal in design, it may be desirable to provide a permanent edging. In our lower garden, for example, two small crescent-moon beds curve out on either side of the millstone fountain. It has helped to tie these flanking beds into the millstone, as it were, by an edging of weathered bricks set slantwise in the familiar dog-tooth pattern. We tried for a long time—and are still trying—to find suitable red tile (the curved-topped thin sort) so as to make a low scalloped edging of the kind found in so many Colonial gardens, especially in Virginia. So far we have not been able to get what we want.

One advantage to the brick edging is that it cost us nothing. Also, it saves the flower verges from a lawnmower wheel each time the grass is cut. On the other hand, the grass close to the bricks must be hand-clipped, as the mower cannot reach it. One wins—and loses.

We have used this same brick edging on the verges of our terrace, above the lower garden, where there are two very narrow borders adjoining a low stone wall that separates the terrace itself from the pachysandra that covers the slope to the walled garden below.

In both places the permanent edging seems in harmony and traces, though unobtrusively in colour, the outline of the beds and borders. Especially in winter our lower garden beds, bare of spring bulbs and summer flowers, are strengthened by the warm colour of the bricks that edge them. March is the time to reset them, if they need it.

Actually, in these lower beds the bricks serve their purpose in winter, but by midsummer the inner edging of *Phlox divaricata* has almost hidden them. When the phlox has given us its sweet, cool blossoms of blue it is cut back, as low as the brick edging, but then sweet alyssum takes its place until fall.

This brick edging also ties in with the brick coping on the garden walls, the brick pillars that carry the lych gate, and the brick ends of the wall that frame the green wicket gate. Our garden steps are also flanked by low stone pillars, eight inches, perhaps, above the terrace wall and these are topped with brick. Window sills of the cottage are of brick, harmonizing with the coping of the walls and the edging of the garden beds below. It seems to make a pattern.

## CHANGING A BED

Should the outline of a bed or border need altering, March is the latest month this should be attempted. One might suppose that a border, once designed properly, would stay put, but this is not always so. Several times here we have had borders that served their purpose well for years. Then, little by little, trees or shrubbery in their rear have cut off more light and air—flowers breathe, you know, like most of us—so that the backs of the borders, once well out from the shade, sooner or later seemed overhung with it. Pruning is only a temporary relief, and applies to shrubs, for trees must grow to their natural size.

Last year, one of our perennial borders was moved several feet forward, the same curve of its outer edge being reproduced and a corresponding distance at its rear given over to encroaching shade. This sounds easy, but it is not, for most of the permanent planting of phlox and peonies, day-lilies, iris, and the like had to march five paces to the front and be re-rooted there. Most of this work was done in the fall before the daffodil and tulip bulbs were in. In March, however, the new edge of the border was more sharply defined with an edging spade and the ground worked over for the earliest possible seeding of sweet alyssum. We tried mixing alyssum with candytuft this year for our new edging and the result so far has been worth it.

## THE FOUNTAIN

Mention has been made of our little fountain and the March chore of preparing it for spring. It really should not be called a fountain at all—that smacks of the views and the vistas that are not here and never could be. The fountain is more of a splasher, if there be such a thing, homemade years ago by a kind friend who cannot possibly know what pleasure he gave us; probably he has forgotten that he made it at all. We have not.

The base or bowl consists of an old millstone, hollowed out perhaps two inches, maybe a little more, on the upper surface. This stone rests flat on the ground. The square hole through the middle of it has been sealed in solidly with cement and through this cement runs a narrow bronze tube extending upward about one inch above the surface of the stone. The cap on top of the bronze tube is pierced with a very small aperture. The lower end of the tube, below the millstone, is threaded to an ordinary copper pipe which crosses the garden, underground, climbs the slope to the terrace and eventually joins the water system of the cottage. Here, by means of an outside tap on the side of our wall, the fountain can easily be turned on or off. Alongside the millstone, itself, sunk in a little box underground, is a petcock for draining the pipe and the fountain in winter and so avoiding destruction by freezing.

If the hollow in the stone be empty when water is turned on, a thin stream is shot upward into the air as high as the dogwood tops behind the wall—twenty feet, at the least. If, however, a pail of water has been poured onto the millstone before the fountain is turned on, covering the protruding end of the tube at least one inch, then the splasher really works. The jet, instead of being forced high in the air, is curbed now by the weight of the water above it, and a splashing, cheery tossing of water occurs that can be regulated and kept at any height desired. Three feet make the bravest showing. Best of all, as we pay for our water—and dearly—nearly all of the fountain's splash comes from the same water tossed up again and again by the pressure of the jet from the tap. Amazingly little fresh water is used and none of it is wasted, for what overflow there is serves to freshen our mint bed hard by.

We wish that the fountain's donor could count the happy hours he has given us and that he might know how deeply we have cherished his gift through the years—just as we have cherished the snowflakes from Glen Isle and the rose-moss from Fairhope.

It is, in truth, "the nameless, little, unremembered acts of kindness and of love" that bind the world together and give meaning. How dull man's pilgrimage would be without them!

## MARCH CHECK LIST

Things move fast in March. Already it is time to seed annual poppies out-of-doors, as well as other earlies such as larkspur, sweetpeas, and candytuft.

The cold-frame is more useful than ever now, for by March all sorts of annuals can be seeded there or in seed-flats. Petunias, zinnias (always dependable), annual phlox, ageratum, stocks and cosmos and calendulas—the list is a generous one.

Chrysanthemum clumps should be divided now and some of them put in the cold-frame where they will respond rapidly to the added warmth and protection. Other perennials to be divided in March include phlox and hardy asters. Plumbago plants may be set out now. Bugleweed can be thinned a bit; it is a great spreader.

One of the gravest dangers in March is uncovering beds and borders too early. It is equally harmful to leave heavy winter cover on too long. The wise gardener takes a little cover off at a time, thus affording some protection against winter throwbacks, yet allowing an increasing amount of air and light to work through the cover and encourage sturdy growth.

Do not forget that March is the month for fertilizer on beds and borders and lawns. Bone-meal, pulverized cow manure, fertilized peat, mushroom soil, or one of the complete compounds such as "5-10-10," are useful. A better preparation for the lawn is "5-10-5."

Be careful *not* to roll the lawn when the ground is soaked. Grass roots need air to breathe. Rolling, ill-timed, will seal this off with a surface far too hard. Remember every lawn needs lime and feed in late winter. March is the time for it. Do not overlook organic fertilizer while you are at it. Above all, rake the surface of the lawn deeply to aerate it.

A light dusting of aluminum sulphate about the acid-soil shrubs is useful, especially where leaf mulch has not kept the soil sufficiently acid. February, however, is a better month for this.

The compost pile, after a winter's matting down, needs a good forking over. Also, March is the month to work the compost into the soil where you plan to seed or plant later on. Winter mulches should also be worked into the ground at this time. In cultivating, do not go at all deep or the new shoots of perennials, still below, but near, the surface, will be injured or destroyed.

March is really the last month for pruning and dormant spraying. It is likewise the best month for transplanting trees and shrubs before the sap starts moving. While at such chores, check over any winter losses that need to be made good. Usually, a rose or so calls for replacement. Be careful not to uncover roses too early.

If your boxwood and other evergreens have been shielded from winter winds, leave the cover in place through March. Early spring sun can do considerably more harm than January cold.

Above all, tidy the garden for spring. Clean and oil all garden tools that need it. Do not forget to sharpen the lawn-mower, sickle, shears, clippers, and the rest. Straighten up brick edges of paths. Re-lay flagstones if frost has tilted any of them.

Bloom in March should include snow crocus, winter jasmine, snowdrops, snowflakes, Christmas roses, leucothoe, first daffodils, blue periwinkle, andromeda, winter aconite, *Daphne mezereum*, early forsythia, blue squills, heartsease, grape hyacinth, early violets, violas, pansies, primroses, cowslips—each of them a token of the bounty to come.

CHAPTER IV

# APRIL

## *The Month of Fulfillment*

The first three months of the year are largely, as far as gardening is concerned, the preparing months, the hopeful months, though they have their rewards that mount with a warming sun. The actual planning time with most gardeners is, of course, a year before their plans are made effective. April, however, is the fulfilling month and all things answer to her call. May and June will pour their gifts before us in richer, more lavish profusion, but we have so much beauty about us, such wealth of colour and of scent, that we may too easily take some of it for granted and miss the miracle of the flower in the wonder of the mass. In April it is not so.

### "NATURE'S FIRST GREEN IS GOLD"

Colour is here—in many ways the fairest of the year, so clear and so pure is April's burnished gold. The scent of early cherry blow, peach and pear, is never matched till April comes again. April is the month of noticed, thanked-for beauty. We see the swaying trumpet of a daffodil and note the detail of its gold and white as we rarely stop to catch the detail of a single flower later when all the world's abloom about us.

It is the same in the woodland. We thrill at the hint of a thrusting bloodroot, the white gleam of windflower, or the lavender of an early cranes-bill. We kneel to trace the scent of shy arbutus under leaves and all of April's magic plucks our hearts at the sight or the scent of a single flower.

It is now too, that we look for our trees and shrubs to play their part, the dogwoods, flowering crabs, sweet almonds, azaleas and the rest, each in its own particular setting and place, heralding the joy of spring, for beauty walks with happiness of heart.

## APRIL'S BOUNTY

April brings us with her showers and her benison of sun—pansies blue and pansies gold; apricot violas, rich in colour; heartsease; cherry blow; with apple blossoms soon after and the Seckel pear; English daisies; wild violets; Dutch hyacinths, the hybrids of *Hyacinthus orientalis;* the vivid, intense blue of bugloss, *Anchusa myosotidiflora; Arabis alpina*—surely no wall could be complete without the sweet scent of Alpine rockcress in the spring and the charm of its flowering. There are, of course, trumpet daffodils and jonquils—the many strains of narcissus and double narcissus (*leedsi, Barri, Narcissus jonquilla*) blossoming now by the hundreds; *Mahonia aquifolium,* the holly grape; blue squills (*Scilla nonscripta* and *sibirica*), carrying over from March; pachysandra, now blossoming also, but so unobtrusively that we often fail to notice it. Flowering almonds, *Prunus amygdalus glandulosa,* are lovely; and bush honeysuckle, *Lonicera tatarica;* bugleweed, the crocuses —early *imperati* especially; *Phlox divaricata;* bleeding hearts, *Dicentra spectabilis;* the earliest of the tulips—DeWet with its early bloom and Murillo, the Darwins and the Cottage and the Breeders, most of these the old-fashioned sort. Then there is a wild anemone or so; Japanese barberry—its flowers are tiny, not always noticed, yet how rich they are with promise of scarlet colour in the fall; wintergreen barberry; Japanese andromeda, still carrying the bloom that came to us over a month ago; leucothoe, another carry-over; and the forsythia. The azaleas are perhaps the most spectacular of our April glory, *nudiflora, kaempferi, mollis* and *ledifolium album.* We see rare colour in the flowering crab; the dogwoods, *Cornus florida* and *paniculata; Wisteria sinensis;* the silver-bell tree; and the viburnums. Not overlooked are the strawberry vines or plants—whichever they are—that form an edging to the beds in our upper garden; white lilacs, Syringa; and lavender lilacs, old-fashioned ones, these, tall shrubs that have been with us from the start. And still the primroses—sun-shy, but brave in the face of a late frost if it comes. A real delight are our dwarf roses, five inches tall at the most, yet a blossom or two already showing. Then there are the Virginia bluebells. How these do spread, covering the east bank of our drive with swaying clusters of pale blue, with here and there a rose-pink blossom, a hint of the mile on mile of wonderland when the bluebells —some call them Virginia cowslips—come to the Perkiomen in spring and touch the reaches near Audubon's old farmstead with a magic that must be seen to be believed. And, of course, the white shad-bush, so delicate, yet so sure of spring, in bloom almost before its pale green leaves are out. We like the older name of shadblow, used in the country here.

April with us averages between forty-five and sixty different kinds of blossom on shrub or tree or flower—well over twice the number that comes to us in March. Of course, it is the great tree-like viburnums and bush honeysuckles, the azaleas and the trees themselves—dogwood and crab, cherry, pear, and apple—that give the splendour. It is, however, the flowers of April, even to the smallest, that really win us. The primroses during frost, the rockcress, the daffodils and tulips, the bluebells and the heartsease—these are April's heart.

> "If all the year were playing holidays
> To sport would be as tedious as to work."

April is our workaday month all right. It is our setting-out month for one thing. Cold-frame or greenhouse, no matter how small, roadside vendor or our own winter window, all will soon be ready to yield their treasures to outdoor bed and border. We must not be too keen though, for frost lurks in the sudden chill of many an April night and nurtured plants are easily nipped. Even those hardened gradually, as they should have been, in the cold-frame, have to be moved with care. Yet move them we must, for it is April's moisture as well as April's sun that gives the root growth needed. We are contending, indeed, with the uncertain glory of an April day, and cannot take too many chances.

## CHORES

April plantings include:

2 April—50 pansies; 10 apricot violas; 60 English daisies; 7 bleeding hearts, in the terrace border.

5 April—10 coral bells, *Heuchera sanguinea,* in lower garden beds.

6 April—heartsease above the ha-ha wall; 10 English ivy plants by the log-guard at new parking place.

7 April—3 small English hollies, male and female, in the terrace border.

8 April—3 English ivy cuttings, rooted indoors in winter, now set out on north wall of garage; 14 columbines, *Aquilegia canadensis* and *alpina,* below the ha-ha; 6 foxgloves, *Digitalis purpurea* and *alba,* in lower garden beds; 12 violas; and 36 pansies in garden pots.

9 April—4 yellow rambler roses on the kitchen trellis and library wall—2 Golden Climber and 2 King Midas; 4 floribunda roses in lower garden beds—2 Betty Prior and 2 Yellow Pinocchio; 2 tree roses on the terrace—Goldilocks. Set out 16 strawberry vines in border above the ha-ha as an edging.

12 April—12 more Christmas roses in the lower garden beds. Transplanted 2 more from upper garden to the lower garden beds. Twenty-six Shasta daisies in our south border; 200 blue myrtle; 100 lilies-of-the-valley in new beds by parking place.

14 April—planted 6 sweet williams, *Dianthus barbatus,* in lower garden beds.

15 April—set out 6 White Supreme dahlias; 1 Dee-Dee; 7 Joe Fette in east border. This was earlier than usual for dahlias. Four primroses by the garden steps.

16 April—planted 4 dwarf roses—Oakington Ruby and 4 rosa Rouletti in terrace border; 20 larkspur, *Delphinium,* in lower and upper garden beds—Giant Loveliness; Giant Happiness; Glorious; Freedom; Desirable; Delightful; Enchantment; and Gayety.

17 April—planted 6 Peruvian daffodils in lower garden beds. Also, 12 gladiolus and 12 montbretias, *tritonia.*

18 April—planted a Chinese chestnut tree at the end of the upper garden. Set out 9 Virginia bluebells on east bank.

19 April—planted 11 floribunda roses on east border, 1 Donald Prior, 3 Rochesters, 1 Geranium Red, 1 Permanent Wave, 1 Pink Bountiful, 3 Yellow Pinocchio, and 1 World's Fair.

20 April—planted 4 pots of small-leaved English ivy on wall by the tool-house of the lower garden.

21 April—transplanted one Goldilock tree rose to upper garden and put a new Goldilock tree rose in by the terrace walk. Planted 2 white arabis beside the fountain.

25 April—planted 2 virgin's-bower on the west wall; 2 clematis; 1 trumpet honeysuckle; 1 matrimony-vine; and 2 bittersweet on new post-and-rail panels by the parking place. One Virginia creeper; 1 bittersweet on garage wall.

28 April—started a small herb garden in the terrace west border. Set out 3 sweet marjoram, *Origanum majorana;* 3 comfrey, *Symphytum officinale;* 2 camomile, *nobilis;* 2 rosemary, *Rosmarinus officinalis;* 2 rue, *graveolens;* 2 sweet lavender, *Lavandula officinalis;* 2 sage, *Salvia officinalis;* 2 lemon verbena, *Lippia citriodora.*

30 April—planted 2 climbing hydrangeas, *Petiolaris scandens,* on the library wall.

## A BUSY TIME

It can be seen that April is a busy month, in fact, the busiest of all, when it comes to setting-out or transplanting flowers. It is a hurried month, also. We may be thankful that everything does not come at once. Thank God it is a bit too early still for much seeding with us outdoors. The poppies and sweetpeas are best sown in fall or by March at the latest, but candytuft, sweet alyssum, and portulaca go in with us during April. Little else. For the rest, seeding belongs rightly to May.

Planting and transplanting flowers already well established is a chore, however, that will not wait. Often when we have set out some plants—even the hardy violas and pansies—we have to cover them against the killing power of late frosts. Newspapers, a bit of burlap stretched on sticks, an upturned basket or so, almost anything will do as long as the more tender plants are covered on a threatening night. Rain does no harm. It is the dry, windless frost that kills.

April is also the time for dividing the clumps of chrysanthemums that are sure to have doubled in size since last spring. It is well to separate the new growth at the edges of the old clump and then set out the best pieces as new plants.

In April we cultivate all beds and borders, breaking up the winter's crusts and trying not to chop the heads off bulbs already in blossom or the later ones still spearing from the ground. We weed beds and borders, plucking up great spreading clumps of grass that seem to have sprung up overnight where no grass was before. We put aluminum sulphate around (but never touching) the rhododendrons, laurels, and azaleas, one trowel full to each plant. We feed our roses—the climbers, floribundas, tea-roses and tree roses—following directions carefully as to the amount to be used per plant. We spray the evergreens—the white pines, Norway spruce and the rest —for scale. If we have the time, we even gild the squirrel on the weathervane that tops the garage. He is always eating a golden acorn, that golden, greedy squirrel, and setting a bad example to his livelier brethren who do their best throughout the year to eat our strawberries, cherries, the pick of the apples and all the Seckel pears they can gorge. Always we intend to shoot them—but always that is to be tomorrow. Finally, serious frost no longer a danger, we turn on our garden taps.

Planting or transplanting should take time. Too often, however, we care for a plant all year, rejoicing in its beauty, looking forward to its bloom next year, then jeopardize the very life of it by hurry if we have to move it. Roses especially must be planted properly. The commonest mistakes—there are two very serious ones—have to do with preparation of the new site and the ill treatment given the roots of the plant being moved or set out.

## PLANTING ROSES

In April, if new roses are going in, we try to make sure that the hole for each rose has been dug deeply—at least two feet or more below the surface. Also, the hole is made several inches wider—at least five or six—than the spread of the roots. If drainage seems doubtful, the hole is dug even deeper and a layer of small stones or coal clinkers is put in. In any case, we nearly always include at least one stone at the bottom of the hole. Then a generous mixture of bone-meal and pulverized cow manure, 1 to 3, and some peat-moss —all of them *well worked* into the loose soil—is put at the bottom of the hole, but never left in one lump of fertilizer there. On top of this we put some fresh soil, well crumbled and fine, but not mixed with bone-meal and manure. The hole is then treated to half a pail of water which is allowed to sink down into the fertilized earth below.

When new roses first arrive we put them—roots, packing, and all—in water. It is usually fatal to rose bushes if their roots are allowed to dry. They must be kept from the air, either by their moistened wrappings of moss or by actual soaking in water—that is, a soaking of their roots, not their canes. In no case, however, should the plants be kept over twenty-four hours in water.

We do not expose the roots of our roses to the air for more than a moment or two, for they are kept in water until the hole for each has been prepared. We then lift them out of the pail, one at a time, nip off any broken roots, spread the roots as wide as they will naturally go, taking care that no roots are entangled with others—and place the rose upright in the hole awaiting it. Rich earth, but not freshly fertilized, is next poured in evenly round the roots and the lower stock of the plant, one handful at a time. When the hole seems filled, we tamp it down hard. This is important, for it will lower the level several inches, but it also steadies the canes of the new rose bush. Most important, also, it serves to press out air channels and pockets in the soil, which, if neglected, can easily dry out the tender roots before they have a chance to take hold properly, thus retarding, injuring, or killing the plant. After tamping, we pour in more water, generously, and let it sink in. Finally, the hole is filled in up to the top and above it with loose earth, the richest we can find, but not mixed with fertilizer and not tamped down. This earth is heaped up higher in April than we intend to leave it later. The mark on the plant itself where the earth reached in its former bed is easily seen. That is the level where new earth should be kept —except for the additional inch or so at first planting.

## MULCHING AND WATERING ROSES

Safely planted, the roses are given a mulch of peat-moss, dampened, but not soaked, two or three inches heaped about the stocks and spread for a foot around them. The peat conserves moisture and keeps the ground from baking and crusting in the sun. It also prevents the growth of weeds. This peat, however, must be stirred up from time to time and kept porous or it may form a mat almost as smothering as the hardened soil. Nothing could be worse for the plant. We are likely to forget sometimes that in April there is little or no shade, even from the leaves of the smallest plants and that the exposed surface of the ground can be burned by an April sun more seriously than in the hottest days of summer, when ground cover and shade are abundant. We try to soak new roses well down to the roots once a week in dry spells—and April, in spite of its showers, can prove dry as well as warm.

## FEEDING ROSES

As soon as the first tiny leaves open and we know that the rose is living, we scrape aside the mulch of peat-moss and work in two or three tablespoonfuls of commercial rose feed, getting it well into the topsoil in a circle about six inches out from the canes. The plant is then well watered again, a slow and soaking watering, and the peat is replaced to keep the moisture from evaporating at the surface.

This first feeding nearly always comes in April or in the early days of May. Later, we feed several times more—always after first blooming and, perhaps, two or three times during the summer, especially with the floribundas that bloom from early summer to frost and often well beyond. There seems to be scant need for spraying or dusting in April, but by May we try to maintain a once-a-week schedule of spray or dust to keep our roses in trim. We use the well-tried commercial spray and powder, prepared by the firm that sells us our roses as well as our rose feed. It has paid to use none but the best.

The safeguards of planting roses—the care in preparing the soil, the spreading of the roots, and so on—are, of course, equally essential in any other planting. We try to apply these simple rules of common sense whenever a shrub or bush or sapling goes in. And nothing—flower or shrub or tree—is ever planted without some enrichment of the soil with bone-meal or cow manure (usually both) and a little peat. The sand pail also is used, for some sand worked into the soil, along with the fertilizer, tends to keep the ground friable, especially if it be at all heavy to start with.

It is in April that we must select and order seed, though it is better if this has been done in February or March. Indeed, such flowers as pansies, violas, heartsease, and sweetpeas are a chore for early fall, as has been said. In April, however, we are looking toward June and high summer. In the days of hired gardeners, it was easy to be lavish in plans as well as in planting. A friend of ours in Dorset—that most delectable of counties on the south coast of England, where the climate is kind—once thought that his outlay was frugal when he devoted five acres to roses. He does so no longer!

## GREEN BORDERS

One answer to this—and it seems a permanent answer, for the spacious days are as far away and as unlikely to return as are the Hanging Gardens of Babylon—one answer that works, at least, is the permanent green border which calls for little care and labour, with planned spaces in it for blossoming flowers. These can be kept to the limit of anybody's budget. It is astonishing how small these spaces may be and how modest may be the clusters of flowers in them, planned for colour and a succession of bloom yet giving the effect of a mass of blossoms from one end of the border to the other.

In our lower garden, we once had flowers and only flowers. Eventually these beds called for more time than we could possibly give to them. Besides, in winter, they presented as bleak a sight as well could be till the glory of the bulbs in spring redeemed them.

Necessity has changed all that and, as it often does, for the better. We have turned two-thirds of each bed into permanent planting—the evergreen shrubs have already been listed—English holly; holly *osmanthus;* Chinese holly; cherry laurel; leucothoe; and *Berberis verruculosa.* These form a low background green throughout the year. Pruning so far has kept each shrub at its proper height. Two English hollies flanking the fountain are being allowed to take on their natural height. Three or four azaleas (the lovely orange-coloured ones) were added two years ago and so far are not too large. The ends of both beds were trimmed off with bugleweed. Around the millstone fountain are plumbago, wild mint, and European pennyroyal. All begin to show now in April.

These shrubs have combined to make the beds in the lower garden green and keep them green. Back of them is the high garden wall also green the year round with English ivy. And the slope from the terrace to the lower garden is deep with pachysandra—likewise green all year. The garden, when seen from the terrace or from the large window of the library overlooking the terrace, presents as green a picture as one could wish. Outside the wall it is backed with hemlocks and interspersed dogwood.

## COLOUR

To give colour, we plant the open spaces in front of the shrubs with bulbs for spring—daffodils, jonquils, and narcissus and tulips. These are also clumped here and there between the shrubs and even back of them where a narrow path of flagstones winds around between the rear of the beds and the base of the garden wall. Blue phlox comes into flower with the tulips. This phlox came as a gift sent to us years ago from the gardens at Spring Bank where old box hedges scent the air in spring and roses are a dream to remember.

After the daffodils and tulips have gone and the bulbs have been lifted for drying, the spaces left vacant are filled with such low-growing plants as dwarf French marigolds, *Tagetes patula;* verbenas; sweet williams; white vinca; dwarf blue ageratum, *Houstonianum latifolium nanum;* white begonias— faithful summer and winter, never resting, a gift from nearby Chilton; fuchsias; a few geraniums from our winter window (as are the begonias); and coral bells. Toward the rear of the beds are the taller bellflowers, *Campanula glomerata dahurica;* the foxgloves and the delphiniums. Here and there between the green of the cherry laurels are snapdragons, antirrhinum; and calendulas and zinnias—the dwarf sort only, in our lower beds where everything except the foxgloves and delphiniums has been scaled down to harmonize with the low shrubs and the size of the garden itself.

Along the narrow path in the rear are English daisies, pansies, violas and, seeded now in April, sweet alyssum. Between cracks in the flagstones are all sorts of rock-loving plants—low thymes, veronicas, saxifrages, and the rest.

In the middle of each bed, where sufficient space has been left for them, are two floribunda roses—a pink Betty Prior and a yellow Pinocchio. They give height as well as colour to the beds and do not seem to overpower the low blossoming flowers at their feet. Planting of this sort assures us of green beds all winter and a profusion of colour from April until November or later.

## SEED ORDER

So each year, we try to keep our seed list down. Usually, the lower beds, having priority, are set out with small plants, not seeded, when the bulbs are lifted. Always the upper beds are seeded. Our April list includes:

*Zinnias* (White Gem, Tiny Tim, Pixie, Lilac Gem, Goblin, Snowdrop, Scarlet Gem, Mexicana Miniature, Tiny Cupid, Lilliput Pompon, some mixed colours of the Pompons, some of the Canary Yellow and the Golden Gem); *Larkspur* (Early Giant Hyacinth-Flowered Mixed,. Imperial Double Mixed, Tall Branching Double-Stock Flowered Mixed,. Ground Branching White Wonder, Salmon Wonder and Dark Blue Wonder); *Snapdragons* (Avalanche, Eldorada, Majestic, Rosamond and Mixed Colours); *Sweet alyssum* (Carpet of Snow); *White Candytuft;* *Cornflowers* (Blue Boy); *Aster-Pompon* (Mixed); *Heliotrope* (Mme. Bruant); *Mignonetta* (Golden Sunset); *Portulaca* (Salmon); *Gaillardia* (Dazzler and Goblin); *Wallflower* (Extra Early Single—Mixed); *California poppies* (Sweetheart, Delightful, My Favorite, and Golden Red); *Iceland poppies* (Gartref Art Shades, Sandford Giants, Coonara Pink,. Yellow Wonder); *Bachelors-Buttons* (Mixed); *Sweet Rocket; Cosmos* (Radiance); *Calendula; Strawflowers; Coreoposis* (Golden Yellow);. *Scabiosa* (Salmon Pink); *Hollyhocks* (Double Mixed).

These seeds are ordered well in time and so are in hand by April. Also, by April, a chart has been made showing where the various seeds are to be sown in beds and borders. Markers of plastic, very reasonable in price, are prepared to save time later. They are essential, for otherwise we are sure before long to be digging up what we have so carefully and prayerfully seeded or seeding something else in on top of it.

## DAHLIA ROOTS

By April, also, old dahlia rootstocks should be looked at and any new supply ordered. The old roots have been lifted in the fall after frost has bitten the plants and then stored all winter in our garret where it is dry and cold, but not too cold for them to keep properly. Though apparently dormant, these rootstocks sprout a bit when it draws toward spring. April is a good time to see if all are alive, for replacements, if needed, must be ordered at once. It is important to keep dahlias marked, whether they be old or new, for it is necessary to know the variety so as to tell the colour of their blossoms ahead of time—useful information in planning pattern of bed or border.

## EAST BORDER

Once our seeds are on hand, we check the plan for each border.

As said, the lower beds are essentially a green garden. Our east border is much the same, only it is a long curving border rather than a bed. Once it was planned and treated as a perennial border, all flowers, until, as with the lower garden beds, economy of effort became necessary. Accordingly we removed most of the flowers, saving the best of them. The rear boundary of the border was then planted with peonies (all of them white varieties, Le Cygne and *officinalis alba plena*); inkberries; cotoneaster; mountain laurel; *Rosa hugonis; Azalea mollis;* a *Taxus cuspidata;* some yellow iris here and there. In short, we made our east border almost as much a green border as the lower beds, except that the spaces left for annuals, toward the front of the border, were much larger and more in number.

Here and there along this border floribunda roses were clumped in groups of four or five, set against a background of permanent green which actually enhanced their beauty. At the back of the border, among the green of the shrubs there, are some of the perennials we saved—masses of white *Phlox decussata* (Fiancée and Mary Louise)—we had weeded out all the magenta ones long ago; a few hollyhocks, also white; a wild pasture rose; clumps of golden day-lilies (Fulva, Margaret Perry, and Thunbergi mostly) which are being added to each year for their midsummer colour and cheer; the blue hounds-tongue, so quick to spread, from the old borders at Hawthorne. In the cooler recesses at the back, wild violets, lilies-of-the-valley, English daisies, heartsease, and the primroses—low-growing treats that we must seek out behind the more pretentious giants of the border in front.

All these unite to form our combination of a permanent flowering-shrub border, a green border, a perennial border, plus the seeded annuals in the spaces left for them. The colours of the old perennial border have not been unduly minished. Our east border is edged by strawberry vines and candytuft—an odd mixture, but highly satisfactory to the palate and the eye.

## SOUTH BORDER

The south border is nearly all an annual planting, backed as all beds and borders must be, by some perennials. Ours are white peonies (Duchesse de Nemours, Festiva Maxima and Crystola), iris, day-lilies, some monkshood, bleeding hearts that do well here, Shasta daisies, chrysanthemums, and all the dahlias. We also have a few floribunda and two old monthly roses that have been blooming each year since our cottage was built.

It must not be supposed that there are no disappointments along our garden path. Seed catalogues are luring and their pictures irresistible. Results, however, seldom quite answer to our hopes. How could they? "A man's reach must exceed his grasp or what's a heaven for?" One year we innocently seeded enough larkspur to fill the whole border. But we had seeded carelessly on ill-prepared soil and far too late in the spring—after the bulbs, the tulips and the daffodils, were out of the ground. A single plant of larkspur appeared that year—just one—to mock us. In our ignorance we had not realized that these larkspurs were perennials and should have been seeded the summer before and transplanted. Or that at least they should have been seeded very early in the spring and on properly prepared ground.

Another year we seeded too far in the shaded rear of our border, where even the sturdiest zinnia was hard put to survive. Still again, we forgot to cut off the seed spikes of summer phlox—the white Miss Lingard, *Phlox suffruticosa,* and others. Of course, these re-seeded themselves and next year the newer growth began to revert to the old familiar magenta we had thought we were through with for good. Time, however, teaches us a lot. It is a stupid gardener indeed who does not learn to profit by his mistakes. Occasionally, however, by some lucky chance of soil or sun or seeding, April plantings and April seeds surpass our hopes and bring to summer a glory and a colour we had not dreamed of nor deserved. Our Virginia bluebells have done this, taking kindly to our bank. So have the scillas. The old-fashioned stand-bys—blue cornflowers, marigolds (tawny-golden in the fall), ever-faithful zinnias, strawflowers, verbenas, calendulas, bellflowers, cosmos—these never fail us. No doubt we use too much. Who can but love a friend?

## OUR UGLY GULLY

One problem that defeated us for years was a gully—water-scoured and scourged in rain, bone-dry in drought—that dropped steeply some twenty or thirty feet from the level of the upper garden to the road below, just to the east of our driveway. An eyesore it was to greet us. Nothing would grow there, not even screening weeds. The gully was shaded deeply, overhung by white oaks, swamp maples, and other trees still left us from the original forest. A wild dogwood or so was there, giving colour in the spring. The place could not be wholly without hope.

We tried at first to save the gully from the foot where it showed the most, working upwards, from the road itself, putting in a ground cover of euonymus, then a low screening of *Taxus cuspidata.* That helped a little, but not enough. Above the line of yews, not growing well in the shade, nothing would grow save one or two hardy mountain laurel and a rose-bay rhododendron or so, near the top. Then in April the thought came to us that we had seen in the woodlands gullies like ours, flooded and dry by turns but never wholly bare. Always something seemed to grow in them—wild shrubs of some sort, sweetfern, blueberries, maple viburnum—and wildflowers, too, in spring. If cultivated plants would not thrive in our gully, perhaps wild ones would.

In April, just as the woodlands were greening, we began to reckon up what might be accomplished by way of a wild corner, no matter how small it must be. So plans and estimates were made. Work started later and much of the planting since then has been done in the fall, but it was in spring that we first visualized the possibilities of transforming the gully.

Really the work was simple and should have been thought of years ago. We needed to prevent erosion by heavy rains, so as to conserve moisture on the steep slope, and we needed to restore some richness of topsoil and leaf mould to replace that washed away. Rock went in first—weathered stones, big 200-pounders dug two thirds of their bulk into the ground so as to hold there regardless of weather. These, we hoped, would safeguard soil pockets where plants could root and hold soil in their turn.

After the rocks had been put in place as naturally as we could site them, here and there, from the bottom of the gully clear to the top, we dug in the richest topsoil available, in the lee, as it were, of each protruding stone and above it as well. We then covered the whole slope with a mixture of leaf mould, peat, and well-rotted sawdust, hoping that some of it would be kept in place by the stones.

While thinking of all this in April, we remembered that bracken grew wild in many of the woodlands close-by; it might do in the gully. Besides, it carried us back to the steep cleaves and combes of Dartmoor and the lovely sharp steep valleys of the Exe where foxgloves are like fairyland and the bracken grows as high as the points of a warrantable stag—a royal with his rights, as they say of the red deer. So we headed our list of plantings with bracken.

Then came the other ferns—the wood fern and the Christmas fern mostly. For flowers, we turned again to our woodlands for guidance. When we had made our list and the time had come for planting, we put in alumroot, not showy, but yet so typical of our dry woodlands from early summer till August; New England asters whose purple flowers are the glory of our glades in fall; wild bergamot, hoping for the lavender blossoms that brighten many a sunny slope all summer; red baneberries, both for the grace of their cool white bloom in earliest spring and the richness of their scarlet berries in the autumn; white baneberries for their strange white berries tipped with purple; butterfly-weed, another lover of dry banks and roadsides whose orange flower heads are as bright with colour as any we could possibly find; wild carnations, the tiny Deptford-pinks, lovers of the sun; wild columbines—the rock-bells—not so fond of the sun, red flowers, incredibly graceful, the very spirit of the spring; Jacob's-ladders, also liking more or less damp feet, whose blossoms are lilac in colour and last from May to August; jack-in-the-pulpits that everybody looks for in the moist woods of early spring; cone-flowers, for their tall golden bloom that lasts from July through September; Virginia bluebells; wild blue phlox, a tiny flower, not eight inches in height, that gladdens woodland slopes all summer; white snakeroot; spiderwort, purplish blue, low-growing, leafed like an iris and blooming from June on; white trilliums, an early comer, blossoming in April and May; blue lobelias; and the cardinal flowers, filling the low, damp meadows with colour—blue and crimson—from July to frost.

All of these wildflowers we have known and loved. Most of them we had found growing in the dry places, in open glades or roadsides by a wood or on a sunny slope where trees were not too thick. For this reason, we counted on them for our gully, where it was sure to be dry at best. The others—the lobelias, columbines, Jacob's-ladders, jack-in-the-pulpits, bluebells, and trilliums—which like moist places and shade, we planned to tuck in by the coolest rocks and in the deepest shade.

Planning can be the rarest fun—almost as much as the planting itself—for it is in anticipation even more than in reality that we give rein to our hobbies and really let them gallop! Finally we decided to help both moisture and soil by spreading every available basket of leaves and leaf mould we could spare on the level spaces at the top of the gully.

So we piled the leaves deeply there, when they had been raked in April from nooks and crannies and lifted from where they drifted during the winter. Since then each fall we have put more leaves there above the gully. Two feet deep they often are at the start, but by spring they have sunk down to a soft brown carpet that, as a matter of fact, forms a path that first gave us the idea of continuing the wildflowers and the ferns of the gully on along the little opening winding between the rose-bay and the laurel to join the lawn and the flowers of the upper garden above.

The complete change in the moisture content of the gully and of our euonymus bank to the east of it has been amazing. Instead of dry, parched earth where nothing grew, the new rocks held the rains. The gain in moisture has favoured growth, so it was not long before wildflowers began to appear. Each flower made root and since it is by roots, even the tiniest roots, that soil and moisture are held, once vegetation had started the happy cycle gained new heart —the greater the ground cover, the greater the moisture, and naturally growth in return.

Where seeds of wildflowers come from, God knows. Probably for years they lie dormant in unfavourable or impossible soils. A few spring flowers came first to our gully: May apples, like opening umbrellas—we had planted none and had never seen them there; false solomon's seals—the wild spikenard; a clump of goldenrod here and there in fall. All of them apparently have been made possible by the richness of the leaf mould piled so thickly above and by the moisture that is the key to it all.

Later, of course, the rocks and the lower planting of ferns and bracken transformed the place completely, but the leaves at the top were the start and their cost was nothing. Loosestrife, a gift from Cherry Lane, was the first wildflower planted. It has begun to spread already.

Our friends who have given us so generously of their own gardens would be surprised if they could see how their gifts have multiplied here, bringing to our cottage borders a beauty that is deepened by the memories that sweeten them.

God's world calls to us through all the year, of course. In deepest winter and in earliest spring, we are the happier if we harken. Many are fainthearted when February winds or the driving sleet of March drown out the first challenge of the spring. But now—

> "when proud-pied April, dress'd in all his trim,
> Hath put a spirit of youth in everything,"

how dull are they who pass such splendours by. For those, the lucky ones with eyes to see and hearts to heed, April swings wide the gate that March has set ajar.

## APRIL CHECK LIST

April is a good month to give periwinkle a generous scattering of peat-moss. This soon works down and serves as a useful mulch for the roots, keeping them cool and damp in summer.

Christmas roses need spring feeding, now that their period of bloom has passed. Bone-meal, worked into the soil five or six inches out from the plants, is excellent.

It is not too late to feed a lawn with "5-10-5," four pounds to 100 square feet, but February and March are far better for this.

If the garden has delphiniums, watch the clumps for the earliest sign of spring growth, then spray promptly with a commercial cyclamen-mite control. Keep this up weekly.

Spray peony shoots with Bordeaux mixture against peony-blight. Repeat weekly till May.

April has never a dull moment. Finish transplanting trees and shrubs—May is too late. Tender shrubs are likely to be winter-killed if moved in the fall. Such trees and shrubs as silver-bell, redbud, holly, magnolia, dogwood, and the lovely rowan tree are best moved now.

Remember even March was not too early for some outdoor seeding such as sweet peas and candytuft. Larkspur, portulaca, sweet alyssum, annual poppies should be seeded now, as well as the California poppies.

April is late for dormant spraying and early for blossom sprays, but just the time for battling the birch-leaf fly. Commercial sprays designed for this purpose are available at any seed store.

As always, keep the garden tidy. April is the time to get rid of leaves that have packed themselves under hedges and been matted into the stalks of shrubbery. Their removal is difficult and injurious to plants if left until the shrubs are in leaf.

Do not move plants or seedlings from the cold-frame the first warm day. April often has killing frost or even snow. Many things, however, can be set out such as pansies, violas, English daisies, bleeding hearts, coral bells, hen-and-chickens, heartsease, columbines, and foxgloves. It is an excellent time to set out English ivy, all the roses, Christmas roses, Shasta daisies, primroses, Virginia bluebells, rock-cress, blue myrtle, sweet williams, and larkspur. Lily-of-the-valley pips may be planted this late, though they do better if planted in the fall.

If the month be warm, dahlias may be risked, but the ground must be warm before the roots go in. Peruvian daffodils, gladiolus, montbretias, stonecrop should also be planted now, as well as virgin's-bower, climbing hydrangea, trumpet honeysuckle and the old-fashioned matrimony-vine.

Do not forget the herbs. April is the month for sweet marjoram, comfrey, camomile, rosemary, rue, sweet lavender, sage, lemon verbena, and the rest.

As in March, cultivate beds and borders lightly. Finish separating chrysanthemum clumps. It is not too late for aluminum sulphate about (but never touching) rhododendrons, laurels, and azaleas; a trowel-full per plant, but always well out. Feed all roses, then mulch them well.

Plan for a succession of colour and blossom through summer, fall, and winter. It can be attained.

Do not neglect the possibility of a wildflower corner. It affords endless delight and costs little.

In April, among other things, look for the earliest cherry-blow; peach, pear, and apple blossoms; the wild bloodroots, windflowers, cranesbill and arbutus; flowering crabs, dogwood, sweet almonds, flowering quince, silver-bell, spiraea, azaleas, pansies, violas, heartsease, English daisies, primroses, violets, hyacinths, bugloss, arabis, daffodils, jonquils, Virginia bluebells, bugleweed, blue squills, crocuses, tulips, *Phlox divaricata*, Japanese barberry, wintergreen barberry, Japanese andromeda, leucothoe, wisteria, the virburnums, bush honeysuckle, and mahonia. How blessed we can be in spring!

CHAPTER V

# MAY

## *The Merry Month*

May is the month of the leaf. Light has been heartening us for almost half a year now. By Twelfth Night we knew that the days were lengthening. At Candlemas, if we were keen of eye, the stir of spring was there to see. March winds brought the snowdrop and the jasmine, the snow crocus and the opening daffodil. April, for all its lingering frost and treacherous nights, soon turned the woodlands and the orchards to a fairyland of blossom, gay with the tiny gold of the spicewood, bright with shad-blow and dogwood and the bloom of apple and pear. Housman knew that when he sang—

> "And since to look at things in bloom
> Fifty springs are little room,
> About the woodlands I will go
> To see the cherry hung with snow."

### LEAF ON BOUGH

Yes, the leaf belongs to May. Not until May does the forest really deepen and veil her glades in a mystery of filtered light, fresh vaultings of green that stir the woodland memories and wake some instinct of the race we did not know was there.

Our greens at Christmas—the mistletoe, the ivy, the holly, and the tree—all of these are rooted in a woodland heritage. But this is forgotten till the forest calls us as it always does in May—most surely and most sweetly in May—and then something buried deep within

79

us answers. We long for the sight of the opening leaf, the green mazes of the glades that must lead over the hills and far away— just where we never know, nor very much care; Sherwood's as good a name as any.

In our garden it is the same. April brings colour and our hearts warm to it, but May adds the life of leaf on bough and the welcoming play of shade and shadow. Always there is life in May, intense and vivid in every leaf and flower, answering the call of the warming sun.

In the old days, people lived closer to this. They had to and were the happier for it, lacking the soul-slaying horror and futility of the modern town which is at best a warren compared to what the green world could be.

## MAY DAY MORNING

Men once saw and felt firsthand the moving cycle of the year. They read the meaning so richly broidered there. Chaucer in his day watched them pay observance to the spring.

> "For May wel have no slogardie a-night,
> The seson priketh every gentil herte,
> And maketh him out of his slepe to sterte."

Nearer our own day, Emerson sensed the same sweet tenderness: "What potent blood hath modest May!"

## APRIL BOUNTIES STILL WITH US

May, with most of April's blossoming still with us, is quick to add fresh beauty and a sea of colour all her own to our walls and borders. Tulips are at their best, the daffodils and jonquils passing. Who could weave in words a tulip's beauty, the high, sharp ecstasy of form and colour, vivid chalices of flames and purest, sun-kissed gold? Azaleas are as generous as in April. The lilacs still remain.

It is not by chance that we find a lilac bush, if nothing else,

80

beside the ruins of almost every abandoned farm. Even when the forest has crept back to claim its own again and only a cellar pit remains, there surely a forgotten lilac will bloom in spring. What stories these lost lilacs could tell!

In addition to the carry-overs just mentioned, there is many another, such as the wisteria. Once we had it all about our garden walls, before time and ivy had mellowed them, but now we have restricted it to an arbour or lattice-work of its own where it gladdens its corner in spring. Violas, pansies, and heartsease, of course, are in flower from April and will carry over through June. The bush honeysuckle holds its flowers well into late April and early May. We have an old shrub of it here that has grown almost into a tree; it is larger than most of the dogwoods, pruned through the years so that its three stems grow upward from one root, then bend in graceful arches to right and left like the three handles of a great loving cup, shading one of the bird-baths that stands against the east wall, flanked by the firethorns that we hope to espalier there.

*Cotoneaster horizontalis* usually blossoms, with the clematis and the coral honeysuckle, in April or May. Its flowers are inconspicuous but, like the barberry's, they bear a promise of more colour later when the fall brings the berries. Clematis (both the purple and the most delectable white) varies—now April, now May. Coral honeysuckle, *Lonicera sempervirens,* usually waits until May for it grows on our garden wall inside, it is true, but facing the north. How vivid it is, so gay and vibrant in colour against the green. Sometimes, however, it is an April carry-over. Winterberry, *Ilex verticillata,* blossoms in late April or May. The silver-bell tree and the viburnums hold over from April well into May, as do the columbines, the English daisies, bridal-wreath, and lilies-of-the-valley. Blue squills always carry over into May; there are few flowers we cherish more. Barberry comes in April or May, as do the cherry-blow and the blossoms of pear and apple and dogwood. In late springs, the viburnums and the silver-bells come more often in May than in April. Always they are lovely. The golden-chain tree waits for the weather—one year April

81

and the next May. Whenever it comes, it brings us beauty.

May and April merge so gently when it comes to blossom on tree and shrub and flower that it is hard to say just what belongs to each, but by and large the flowering shrubs, the fruit trees, and the bulbs —save tulips—are April gifts, while roses and most of the flowers come in May.

## VIRGINIA BLUEBELLS

The bluebells have a fairly long range between the first blossoms that come in April to the last at the end of May, but the individual flowers do not hold long once they have come to flower. Soon after blossoming, the foliage wilts so that by June almost all trace of the plants has disappeared; just a yellowed leaf or two is left to show where they have been. These bluebells, or cowslips as they are often called in the South, are amazing shifters-about. They can be planted carefully as you will in one spot, where they are wanted for their colour in spring, but if they do not particularly like that spot, they will move on somewhere else of their own accord. Wherever they go, we love them and we respect their freedom of choice. After all, it's their *pied à terre* that is at stake more intimately than ours.

In late spring, the leucothoe opens as often in late April as in May. The holly-grape shows its yellow clustering flowers on the bank sometimes as early as mid-April, but always by May.

## MAY BLOSSOMS

In the east and south borders, early peonies open—all white now, as we have said. They are definitely a May flower, not an April one. Calendulas are a May flower, too. In the lower garden beds, sweet williams come in May; and the early snapdragons.

*Rosa Hugonis* comes to flower in mid or late May with us. And then come the blue flags, the iris. And the gold ones as well. Petunias (we always like the white ones), verbenas, blue ageratum, primroses, early marigolds—all give colour that April cannot match.

## THE ROSES

The floribunda roses are early bloomers, but rarely so early as our oldest roses—the month-by-month, old-fashioned sort that bloom almost from frost to frost. Indeed, they cut into the frosts of spring at times as well as into those of fall. Amazing old friends they are.

By the end of May, the tree roses are out—Goldilocks. They are soon joined by the climbers—some of them scarlet old timers; others King Midas and Golden Glow; and the sweetest of them all, a very old climber, yellow just tinted with pink, that has blossomed here from the start. The first rose is an event with us; usually the first is in bloom by mid-May. In lucky years they may last until December.

Other mid-May blossoms include the pink *Diervilla* and the *florida rosea;* the early golden day-lilies; and the *Deutzia lemoine.* The lilies are low and gay, the deutzia a great towering shrub. Both blossom at the same time and near together, forming a border bloom and a background planting, and both of them breathing of May. With them the laurel comes—unless it has been lured to flower earlier by a sun more kind than usual. We have masses of laurel here, its pink and white blossoms a thing of beauty and a joy forever, at the terrace end and in the east border and here and there among the taller rose-bay rhododendrons that keep the purlieus of our cottage green all winter. The laurel is striking in flower and lasts well, especially if May has proved showery and mild. Heat in spring is hard on all the earlier shrubs and flowers, causing their blossoms to fall.

## MORE MAY BLOSSOMS

In May the firethorn is blooming and it brings us a double gift, for now the white clustering blossoms are cool and graceful against their own foliage, while in fall their orange-tawny berries are a delight.

The first sweet alyssum, seeded in March or April, begins in May to cheer our borders with a foam of dainty white that soon overflows the brick edging of our lower garden beds, and forms an edging of its own in the upper garden beds. Best of all, we'll have it with us until frost. Carnations—the early sweet pinks, Irene and Silver Mine —come to flower in May in our terrace border, while above the bank of the driveway the mock oranges, Philadelphus, are white and sweet with scented blossom, against a cool background of hemlock and rhododendron and laurel.

The ajuga comes into its own now, in May, sending up straight spires of blue (a deep and glorious blue it is!) six to eight inches high. Strawberries are in flower usually in early May with us. The cherry laurel, so sure a green in every glossy leaf, blossoms in mid-May. We could not do without it in our lower garden where the beds are always green. The English holly blossoms also in May—its tiny, waxlike flowers hugging the stems where the rich scarlet berries will come later and add to our Christmas cheer.

In the little terrace bed below the library window on the south, the wintergreen barberry has added its golden blossoms to the azaleas and the tulips and the hyacinths still gaily in flower. In the lower garden beds, the coral bells are sending up great slender stems from their leaf mass to carry the coloured chimes that sway so far and so delicately above the green.

By the terrace steps the *Daphne cneorum* has blossomed and is filling that corner of the garden with a scent that no other flower can equal in fragrance. The beauty-bush never fails us in May. The Chinese holly blossoms occasionally, though not every year. When it does flower, it is in the month of May.

Foxgloves raise their stately belfries here and there in bed and border as May draws to a close. No other flower carries one more surely to a Devonshire lane where, wise men, so they say—

> "Have watched the moonlit fairies as they sung
> And tolled the foxglove bells;
> And oh, how sweetly, sweetly to and fro
> The fragrance of the music reeled and rung
> Under the loaded boughs of starry May."

The foxglove bells are rich in memories, gladdening one's heart through the years. Children love them. Poets understand—and sing of them most sweetly.

## HERBS

Late among our May blossoms are the lemon verbena, the first of our herbs; and thyme, low-growing, whose scent must have opened men's hearts ages before a young lad of Stratford, the glover's son, roaming Charlecote woodlands and the lane that led to the thatched cottage at Shottery in leafy Warwickshire, noticed such things and remembered later the wild thyme, the woodbine, and the musk-rose, to bewitch a world that has almost forgotten the quiet beauty of a country lane, the loveliness that heals the fever and the fret.

Wild thyme in spring still blows as sweetly. It takes a poet, though, to see the vision in a flower and save for us the passing miracle of beauty and of scent.

## THE ROCK PLANTS

Rock plants are opening fast in May, snuggled deep in the cracks of the flagstone paths. The first to show are the *Veronica pectinata,* with deep blue flowers; the *Potentilla verna nana,* whose small gold blossoms are a joy in April and May; *Arabis Sturi* with its white flowers; *Veronica repens* with pale blue flowers; *Antennaria neo-dioica,* often called pussy-toes, silvery-white in colour; *Draba si-birica* whose flowers are yellow; and the low *Phlox subulata Britoni,* the smallest of the *Phlox subulata,* scarcely two inches high.

Old fashioned stonecrop begins to flood our dry-stone walls with gold in May. Once years ago my friend and I, trudging on the hills with haversack and thumb-stick a hundred miles from home, came at sunset to a little farmhouse in the lee of the Blue Ridge. We put up there overnight, and shared in a supper and a breakfast that neither of us will ever forget, so glorious and so abundant were they both. In the morning we stopped to admire the garden path all gay with country flowers. The goodwife, finding that we loved such things and knowing that our long tramp was nearly over, filled a flat basket—a garden frail it really was—with stonecrop and the rest, their roots well guarded in damp moss, saying that we could pick them up, as a gift, as we passed the farm on our way home by car. We did so and planted all she gave us. The stonecrop is still living. No other flower in our garden carries kinder memories of wind and weather on the hills.

## HOME GROWN

Geraniums and the shrimp-plants, the miniature roses, all the pots from the winter window are set out fairly late, often in mid-May. Cold, even without frost, is hard on them and retards bloom unless they have been acclimated gradually. We begin, as do most people, by putting them out during the day when sun can nourish them, and taking them indoors at night for a while. The shrimp plants, strange, dragonlike affairs that have a fascination all their own, are quick to blossom outdoors and keep it up until frost kills them.

The fuchsias, once called Ladies' Eardrops—how lovely the old names are, so many now forgotten—purple and crimson, pink and white, some almost all white; the begonias, aptly named wax plants for their glossy leaves, in all shades of pink and white (we do not favour the scarlet and crimson, but love the white begonias best, especially the graceful sort from Chilton that carry their flowers in cool sprays above the lushness of their leaves); these and many more are the products of our winter window and proud we are of them. Indeed, our terrace border is gay all summer with last year's slips and nothing else, save for a few petunias to help things on at the start. If the slugs and the snails get the better of these petunias later, we do not replace them, for the faithful begonias, apparently immune to bug and blight, are sure by then to have filled the border with a colour and a bloom that is as cool and as cheery on the hottest day as could be wished.

## SEEDED ANNUALS

In the past we depended far too much on potted annuals set out to fill our permanent borders—a costly and a somewhat uninteresting way of doing things. Now we have changed over completely, in the upper beds, to seeded annuals, among the green planting and perennials already there. Each year, of course, we have added a few perennials where they are needed. But our annuals now are largely seeded, reinforced by plants that are the result of the previous summer's slips, begun in August and pampered through the winter in our warm south bay where they flourish.

## MAY SEEDING

Seeding, of course, is the main chore of May—only it is not rightly a chore. It is work all right, and hard work, to do it properly —preparing the soil, getting in the seed, taking care that the seedlings receive sufficient water if nature has not turned on her taps— but none who has dealt with sowing, earing time, and harvest, can be an atheist at heart. The first gardener of all, so we are told, was not puzzled. He knew very well Who it was that walked in His garden in the cool of the day. There is nothing surprising about that. We can know it also.

## FIRST THINGS FIRST

In May seeding, three things are necessary. First, to make sure that the soil is ready. It must be moist, yet dry enough to break and crumble readily when a handful of it is lifted and pressed in the fist. If it forms a heavy lump and will not pour through the fingers, we must wait a bit till sun has sweetened it. To be sure that the soil is friable, we must work it deeply to remove unbroken clods below the surface. Where possible, it should be spaded a foot deep and fertilizer worked in. Sometimes we spread well-rotted cow manure, when we can afford that luxury, on our borders in the fall and work it in with fork and spade in spring. In any case, ground to be seeded must be fertilized and made fine before the seeds are sown. Bone-meal and pulverized cow manure in a 1 to 3 mixture which is reasonable in cost, along with some peat-moss, are easy to work in with a trowel where seeding must be done in small spaces among perennials.

The second thing to consider is the seeds themselves. It helps in germination if seeds are soaked overnight, but never longer, in saucers of fresh water. They should then be allowed to dry until they no longer stick together. To ensure an even spreading of the seed—and this too often is overlooked or passed by as a bother—a little dry sand should be mixed with the seeds.

Later, when the seedlings have sprouted and are above ground, we must thin them out a bit. That is always necessary, but the sand and seed gently rolled together in the palm of the hand, then sown, are sure to remedy some overcrowding at the start.

The third requirement is depth of seeding. Tiny and delicate seeds, buried deep in the best of soil, are hard put to germinate. Yet time and again we find ourselves raking great layers of earth over them and tamping it down to boot as though we were planting corn or beans. Of course, this retards tiny seeds at best and well may kill them. On the other hand, to cast seed by the handful on the surface of the ground, then leave them there is asking for the sun to burn them, the rain to wash them away, and the birds of the air to eat them for breakfast, lunch, and dinner. St. Matthew, St. Mark, and St. Luke tell us all about that. Seeds have not changed their ways much since their day and are not likely to change much in ours. Naturally, a thin coating of soil must cover them, smoothed with a pat of the hand or the tap of the trowel or the flat tines of the rake, but the danger of there being too much earth on top of the seed is usually greater than the danger of there being too little.

Many flower seeds, especially the large ones, are not—and should not be—broadcast in this way; rather they should be planted, seed by seed, several inches apart. This is always the case in small areas set aside for annuals. The pellet seeds, available everywhere, have been designed to make it easier to plant individual seeds well apart. If they are used, they should scarcely be covered with earth at all, for the covering of the pellet provides the seed with the protection and the initial nourishment it needs, until it begins to sprout and send down its own roots. Water it must have, as must all freshly sown seeds.

Of the three considerations to be given to seeding, the most important, obviously is a sound preparation of the soil. Lacking that, the best of seed is wasted.

In May, we plant all the seeds listed as made ready in April. And we try very hard to mark what we have sown. In spite of care in this, strange bedfellows sometimes appear where two seedings have gone in the same spot.

## DAY BY DAY

Dates reflect weather and hence have interest.

2 May—28 gladioli bulbs in lower garden beds.

5 May—planted 9 Hemerocallis (the day-lilies) below the ha-ha wall —3 Enchantress, 3 Dumortieri, and 3 August Pioneer. Also, 10 mixed montbretias by the fountain. Seeded Golden Sunset mignonette to flank the little herb bed on the terrace. Seeded heliotrope (Mme. Bruant) below library window; it did very poorly there—too much shade. Seeded sun-moss (the portulaca-single and double mixed, and Double Flowering Salmon), in the flagstone walk. This was easily two months too late. Portulaca should be seeded in early March. Some of the loveliest anywhere, over at Fairhope, is always seeded in the fall and thrives amazingly. Seeded candytuft along the base of the west wall. This could have been done in April, but snow crocuses, spring crocuses, English daisies, and some daffodils seemed to have taken up all the room then. Seeded in the south border—the varieties have been listed in April—larkspurs; wallflowers; California poppies—far too late really for them; Iceland poppies; bachelor's-buttons; cornflowers; more sweet alyssum and candytuft. Planted 2 Creeping Charlie vines by the garden steps and 4 more of them in the garden pots.

7 May—planted 6 *dianthus*, 3 Silver Mines and 3 Irenes, at either end of the herb bed.

8 May—planted 2 *Daphne cneorum* by the ha-ha steps; 2 *Thymus nitidus* flanking the terrace steps near the smallest pair of English hollies. Planted 22 other creeping plants in the stone paths, including *Thymus herba-barona* for its spikes of purple flowers; *Thymus serpyllum minus* with rose-colored blossoms; *Thymus serpyllum*, with purple flowers to come in July; *Thymus transylvanicus* with rose-pink flowers coming late and lasting until frost; *Thymus vulgaris argenteus*, blossoming in July and August; *Veronica rupestris nana*, with clear blue flowers in May and June; *Veronica spicata nana*, with blue flowers; *Verbena canadensis* with reddish-purple flowers, *Tunica saxifraga* with rose-pink flowers; *Teucrium chamaedrys* with lavender flowers; *Satureja calamintha*, with little purple flowers all summer; *Muehlenbeckia axillaris*, with tiny yellow blossoms; and *Antennaria microphylla*, silvery colored and lovely. Many of these were by way of experiment. Those we like we shall keep and allow to spread.

9 May—planted more rock plants in the stone-flagged walks—*Dianthus arenarius*, white flowered; *dianthus Brevicaulis*, with carmine flowers in May and June; *Dianthus glaucus compactus*, with bright pink flowers; *Gypsophila fratensis*, with clear pink flowers repeating in the fall; *Penstemon Davidsonii*, with purple trumpet flowers in June; *Veronica pectinata rosea*, with white and rose flowers; *Arenaria laricifolia*, with white flowers; *Mazus reptans*, with lavender flowers; *Geranium Pylzowianum*, with lilac flowers, *Thymus serpyllum lanuginosus*, the woolly thyme, with purple flowers; and *Achillea tomentosa aurea*, the woolly yarrow, with bright yellow flowers.

12 May—planted 24 dahlias in south border—2 Snow Clad, 2 Fairy, 2 Amber Queen, 2 Mary Mums, 2 Raleigh, 1 Red Robin, and 1 Bishop of Llandaff among them.

13 May—transplanted 56 bugleweed—from the lower garden beds to either side of the little path that leads through what we hope will be one day our wildflower garden.

15 May—planted 2 wormwood, *Artemisia absinthium*, in herb border.

18 May—planted 12 Christmas roses and 12 coral bells in the bed below the library window. A poor time, probably, for the Christmas roses.

20 May—planted 18 dwarf French marigolds, 18 blue ageratum and 8 white verbenas in lower garden beds. Seeded in south border: zinnias (White Gem, Tiny Tim, Pixie, Lilac Gem, Canary Yellow, Snowdrop, Scarlet Gem) and snapdragons (Majestic, Avalanche, Eldorado and mixed colours).

23 May—planted 3 sweet marjorams and 2 Helleborus viridis in the herb border.

26 May—planted 12 snapdragons; 12 white petunias; 8 calendulas; 8 sweet williams; and 12 verbenas in terrace borders and lower garden beds. Transplanted the English daisies, white violas, and some of the heartsease from the terrace border to the shady confines of the south border in the upper garden, where the rear of the border consists of permanent shrubbery that keeps that part of it green all year.

27 May—seeded sweet-rocket; cosmos; strawflower; dwarf French marigold; gaillardia; snapdragon; calendula; coreopsis (Salmon Pink); aster (mixed pompons); scabiosa; and zinnia. The kinds have already been listed.


## WEEDING

One of the chores that never ends in May is that of weeding. It is always a prime necessity but especially in spring. If dormant weeds are going to grow at all, they will begin in April and May. Sorrel and plantain, chickweed and dock nothing can destroy, but we can prevent their taking over entirely and reseeding. Obviously a constant eye for every weed that shows in May and the prompt removal of it mean a garden cleaner of weeds the rest of the year.

Yet it is amazing to see how one or two weeds always elude us and grow to giant size, usually in full view, passed over week by week, until some delighted friend twits us by asking just what sort of dahlia is that. Or is it a hollyhock? And how did we manage to get it so tall? Had the confounded thing but stunted its growth and really hidden under a peony or tried to escape detection in the shadow of the day-lilies, we should have spotted it months ago and yanked it out.

## WEED-KILLER

So far the best way to get weeds out seems to be old fashioned hand-weeding. In the lawn, however, it is different. Weed-killer, for plantain and dandelion mostly, goes on in May. How well it really works, we are not sure. Some weeds are destroyed—for a while— each year. A lot of good grass is also destroyed often, it seems, for good. We do, however, try to control such weeds in the lawn as we can by spraying and by prying them out by hand. That is a slow process, but it tells through the years and fewer and fewer are left to reseed themselves. Crab-grass is the hardest of them all to beat.

## MAY SPRAYING

Blossom spraying is always a May chore. In well-ordered orchards there are five such sprays given and all of them to the purpose. We content ourselves here with three—one dormant and two blossom sprays—and pray for the best. Usually our few apple, pear, and cherry trees, so treated, give us enough fruit to last our household from June until April or May. We cannot complain of that. Miscible oil, the dormant spray, is used against scale, of course, and unhatched eggs of other pests. Miscible oil spray is also excellent against witches-broom. Early May is the time for the blossom sprays.

In May our well-beloved hackberry is sprayed with DDT powder solution, for then the leaves are out. It is the underside of the leaves that seem subject to aphis attack. Our witch hazel is also sprayed at this time, for it, too, once suffered from blight. The DDT solution leaves a residue on the leaves that proves most effective. Whenever using DDT it is well to add a miticide, as DDT kills the natural enemies of the mites.

## THE LAWN

Lawns usually are ready for their first cutting in May. Many unwary gardeners cut too closely, encouraging crab grass and fall grass later and depriving the good grass of its own shade to guard the surface roots from sun. Too often, grass cuttings are raked up or caught in a container as the mower moves in its swath. This is the sheerest waste and robbery, for, unless the grass has been allowed to grow taller than it should before cutting, what is cut ought to be left where it falls to mulch and feed the young grass and to protect it from the summer droughts that are sure to scorch it later. Grass clippings are far too rich to be raked and thrown away. If they must be raked up, they are excellent to put about roses as mulch in hot weather.

Other tasks include the usual unpredictables that are always with us. Some are carry-overs from April. In May, bone-meal is usually worked into the soil near the canes of all the roses and about the bases of other flowering shrubs. All shrubs that will blossom next year on this summer's wood are pruned as soon as their blossoming is over. The forsythia is a good example of this; its blooming past, it must be pruned well back in May. Never give it the familiar crew-cut. Try to prune out the older stems, cutting them off near the root of the plant, so as to retain the appearance of natural shape.

## THE END OF THE HEDGES

Once we had long reaches of privet hedge bordering our terrace and edging the drive and a very long stretch of it outside the west wall. In fact, that particular hedge was there long before the wall was built. The cutting of all this privet—it needed a trim every fortnight in summer—involved a great tax on time and a deal of swinking to boot, if we may use the good old term for hard labour. One at a time the hedges came out. We replaced the terrace privet with a low stone wall, one foot in height, that has served ever since to keep the pachysandra in bounds on one side and the terrace flower border on the other. "Good fences make good neighbours," we are told.

The next hedge to go was the long one outside the wall, its removal hastened by several hives of yellow-jackets at the foot of the wall, where the angry bees were always lying in wait for the honest hedger—ourselves—to put a careless foot on their nests. Clad in shorts, the clipper lost that battle year by year. Besides, most of the west wall, outside, had long since been covered with English ivy, Virginia creeper, and virgin's-bower, far more lovely than the privet which really barred them from a proper share in the sun. So privet and some junipers were dug out.

The last hedge to go was that circling the turn-around in the drive. When this was enlarged to form a little parking-place, it was backed on one side by a planting of blue myrtle with three Japanese hollies growing in it, and on the other side by a panel or so of post-and-rail fence now covered with matrimony-vine, coral honeysuckle, and wild clematis. The parking edge was guarded by a length of telephone pole, stained dark in colour and soon covered with English ivy. Back of it we planted a beauty-bush, an abelia, and one taller yew to balance the hollies across the way. In spring the guard log is gay with pansies and violas growing along it on the far side.

## IVY

In May, the ivy must be cut back at door and window for it is growing now incredibly fast. The lower windows are simple, but our ivy covers the cottage to its eaves and over, so the upper windows and gutters are difficult at times. In a wet summer ivy can be almost as much bother as a hedge, but in winter it redeems everything with its welcome green, besides furnishing a refuge for birds in rough weather. We like to see them there. And green we are here in the worst of weather, with rose-bay and laurel and holly and all the broad-leaved shrubbery about us and ivy cheering every wall.

Wisteria, too, is a great May grower as well as bloomer and needs some curbing in spring and summer. It is also indestructible. Years ago we dug it out along our garden walls—dug it deep and wide with mattock, pick, and spade, till the last traces of root, so we thought, must have been grubbed up. Yet every year, some wisteria still appears by the walls—to be uprooted in turn. The perversity of growth is part of its miracle and delight. Two or three wisteria roots were taken up carefully, not torn in any way, when we removed the others. They were replanted at once with equal care in well-prepared ground, watered and fertilized. Next spring they died.

## THE WOODBINE

Woodbine by the upper garden steps needs plenty of summer-round cutting, but especially in May. What a pest this lovely vine can be if turned loose, yet how lovely and sweet-breathed it is if kept in bounds. It needs no tenderness in its control. One must be ruthless. We would not part with ours—not for all the curbing it demands and the trouble it causes.

## VIRGIN'S-BOWER

Virgin's-bower is another great spreader as are most clematis. Ours is constantly enamoured of the pink dogwood outside the west wall and tries to embrace it. A good shearing in May acts as a deterrent to that infatuation. The glory of the virgin's-bower in the fall, of course, makes up for everything. More clematis must be trimmed from the climbing roses in May, where the garden walls have been overplanted, but we cannot bear to cut down any of them. We must—one day. It is like shooting the squirrels—maybe tomorrow.

## CULTIVATION AND WATERING

Cultivation is needed in May—mostly a breaking up of topsoil after rain so as to form a mulch of dusty soil on top that will save moisture below. A four-pronged rake-hoe (sometimes called a cultivator-hoe), or the triangular warren-hoe is handy for this. Watering, too, is often but not always necessary in May. How we hate to see the ground dry out so early. Young seedlings especially must be kept moist, for the protection that comes to them from leaves is inadequate in spring. Care is needed in watering; only the finest spray and that used gently will serve where seedlings and young flowers are concerned. Almost always in watering too much is put on the surface too quickly and not nearly enough allowed to soak in slowly. It is the deeper roots of flower, tree, and shrub that need the moisture—not so much the surface roots. By watering the surface rapidly and in great quantity, much runs off. What moisture remains tends to draw roots towards the surface, whereas everything possible should be done to have them work deeply into the soil where they are protected from surface heat and burning.

## STAKING

All phlox, some of it almost ready to bloom with the laurels and much of it lasting successively, till frost, must be staked in May. Light stakes serve. Too often a garden in spring, before much growth has been made, presents the appearance of a log palisade, so heavy are the stakes set up to support the lightest flower. Even tall and heavy dahlias do not require hop poles.

## DRYING BULBS

One of the last chores in May is the lifting of the earliest bulbs. These must be dried in the sun, then stored in a dry, dark place, where fresh air can reach them and prevent moulding. We save many hundreds of bulbs this way each year so that by now it would be hard to reckon the number that bloom for us in the spring. In time, old bulbs, whether lifted and separated or not, pass their prime and cease to bloom, but the leaf growth continues. It is wise to watch for these in May and dig them up. They have served their turn and now only cumber the ground where something else could grow.

## EARLY ROSE CARE

First dusting of the roses for mildew and blackspot should be given in May. It pays to start in time and then keep it up. The roses are also given their first commercial feeding in May. Some bone-meal and cow manure may have been worked into their beds earlier in the spring, but usually roses set out in April, as well as the old ones, are given their first rose food when the tiny leaves begin to open in May.

## TIDYING UP

This is a good month, too, for checking such things as frost-loosened stepping-stones and the laying of new ones if you need them. Later, vines and flowers will make this more difficult; earlier, the ground may not be firm enough for proper setting. As soon as frost is out and the ground drying, they should be seen to.

May is our last chance to remove dead leaves from the pachysan-dra and euonymus and myrtle. Oak leaves tend to hang late—well into the spring—and so must be gathered months later than the usual raking in fall. How odd it is that the word "fall" is not used in England. Perhaps that is because America was deeply wooded when the settlers came to it and the fall of the leaf most noticeable where everyone lived in a forest clearing. In any case, some leaves must be gathered even in May and the pachysandra always attracts them. Red maple seedlings leap up everywhere in May and must be pulled out or all our banks would soon be maple trees. Wild parsnip also has a way of springing up in May among the myrtle. It can be a miserable pest there unless removed whenever it is seen.

## THE GULLY

It was in May that we got to work in the gully, putting in the great stones and planting it with 150 Christmas ferns, 50 evergreen wood ferns, and 50 bracken. We planted a redbud, *Cercis canaden-sis,* on the bank above at the same time.

One of the delights of gardening is the never-tiring cycle of seed and planting, and withal, constant change and variation, so that from one year to another we never know what dreams may come or how altered our plans may be.

For a long time we never got around to transforming the gully. We worried about it—that was all. Yet now we have it deep with fern and bracken and half-concealed glimpses of weathered stone where moss has begun to form on them. Moisture is holding well there. Once we had no intention—had not even thought of—a wild garden. Yet now the wild columbine and baneberry, loosestrife and lobelia, jack-in-the-pulpits and wild spikenard have made a showing, with plenty more to come. The bluebells are opening in the euonymus by the drive as well as in the wildflower corner. The false Solomon's-seal has put in its appearance. Here and there a few dogtooth violets are showing among the bugleweed, almost lost among the blossoms there. They remind us that they should be moved to the other wildflowers where they belong. One day that chore will be attended to. Already the May apples and the wild geranium are with us—just to show that the wildflower corner has come to life.

## WINDOW BOXES

Window boxes (balcony boxes they are really) that have been fastened to the railing of the balcony above the library window, are filled in May with pink geraniums and trailing periwinkle vines that extend by midsummer almost to the terrace below.

## EDGING

If there be time for it, some edging may well be done in May, cutting the turf off sharp and clean where it joins a bed or border. If sweet alyssum or candytuft has been seeded, this edging should have been done earlier. Separate shrubs, however, can well be edged in May. It givs them a neat appearance and also makes a hollow around the plant that will catch spring rains when rain is needed. We try to mulch most of our shrubs, as we do the roses, with peat-moss. Newly planted shrubs are always mulched and kept watered. It is their first summer that tells.

### FIRST FRUITS

Best of all, in May we pick our first ripe strawberries and the cherries—great red and gold ox-hearts—that tempt every bird and squirrel for miles around. All *we* can hope for is a share.

May is in truth the merry month, the richest in the year, if we will but share the joy she spreads before us. How tragic it is and how sad that we have lost something far more precious than we know since the days when man found peace of heart, and merriment as well, in May—when, as Stowe puts it:

"On May-Day in the morning, every man would walk into the sweet meadows and green woods; there to rejoice their spirits with the beauty and the savour of sweet flowers and with the noise of birds, praising God in their kind."

### MAY CHECK LIST

May is the month of blossoms, for many of the early blooms still linger, while newcomers add daily to our delight.

Pansies, violas, and Johnny-jump-ups should be picked steadily, for the more they are picked, the more their blossoms will appear.

It is time now to make the foliage of daffodils and other bulbs that have passed their flowering as inconspicuous as possible, but never cut the leaves back until they have withered to the ground. They may, of course, be tied together or pinned down, thus taking up less room. The space so released should be seeded promptly with whatever you wish in the way of annuals. A touch of bone-meal will help, as bulbs have already fed heavily from the soil.

Remember in May to keep well watered all trees and shrubs that have been moved earlier in the spring. This will encourage new root growth and offset the shock of transplanting. This watering must be kept in mind well through the first summer.

Pest and disease appear fast in May. Be on guard against them. A nicotine sulphate sprays helps control oyster-shell scale. Do not forget to add soap. The usual mixture is 1 to 2 teaspoonfuls of nicotine sulphate and 1 ounce of soap per gallon of water. Lice, lacebugs, and aphids are controlled by nicotine or rotenone. Blackspot and mildew call for Bordeaux mixture.

Mid-May is the time to move indoor plants out-of-doors, but watch the weather. It is wise to break them in to the change by giving them a bit of midday sun as a starter. Do not risk them out-of-doors during early nights in May. Indoor plants must have a chance to harden.

As plants go out-of-doors, watch for slugs and snails and combat them with some form of slugshot.

May is obviously the seeding month. Keep in mind preparation of the soil, soaking of the seed, and proper seeding itself. Do not overcrowd. Mix seeds with a bit of sand for more even distribution. Watch for the proper depth of seeding. Avoid seeding too deep as well as not deep enough for germination. Do not broadcast all seeds. Large ones should be planted individually with reasonable spacing.

Put in gladioli corms if this has not been done in April. Hemerocallis and montbretias may also be planted. It is time now for setting out such plants as dianthus, *Daphne cneorum,* and all the flagstone lovers—the thymes, veronicas, verbenas, gypsophila, penstemon, dwarf phlox, pussy-toes, *Sedum acre,* and the rest. Get the last of the dahlias in now. Transplant ajuga from where it has spread too widely. The cold-frame may have ready for transplanting petunias, calendulas, and sweet williams. Coral bells, ageratum, verbena, lobelia, and the like may be set out-of-doors safely now.

Seed heliotrope, portulaca, wallflowers, Iceland poppies, bachelor-buttons, cornflowers, more sweet alyssum and candytuft. Seed zinnias, large and small; also snapdragons, dwarf marigolds, sweet rocket, cosmos, strawflowers, gaillardia, coreopsis, asters, and scabiosa.

**Weeding has come and will be with us till fall. The more weed-**

ing now, however, the less later on.

Blossom sprays continue in May. A DDT powder solution helps against aphids. Remember to spray witch hazel and hackberry as well as fruit trees. Consult a good orchard man about your blossom sprays.

In mowing the lawn, never set the blades too low as is often the case. Two-inch grass is not too high.

Prune spring-flowering shrubs as soon as their flowering has passed.

Ivy and wisteria need some control in May or they will get out of hand. So will virgin's-bower.

Remember that by May the soil needs some cultivation. Get stakes in for dahlias, phlox, and other tall plants that will need them later.

Lift and dry bulbs when their leaves have withered. Feed roses after first bloom.

Open your eyes to the magic about you.

# CHAPTER VI

# JUNE

## *The Happy Month*

John Masefield, Poet Laureate of England, never spoke more truly than when he said:

> "Best trust the happy moments. What they gave
> Makes man less fearful of the certain grave,
> And gives his work compassion and new eyes.
> The days that make us happy make us wise."

June *is* the happy month—just as May is the merry one. There is a difference. We work hard in May, but there is a gaiety about it, a lightness and a joy, that come to us from a realization that the promises of spring have been fulfilled. The year has reached its freshest, fairest peak of bloom and blossom. Leaf and bud and every flowering, fragrant spray seem created to delight us. Of course, our hearts are in the trim.

By June, however, the first rapture of the new green year has passed. Like the mountaineer on high rock, far above the headwall of some difficult peak, he must—if he would live—descend to the heavier air of the valley, once he has thrilled to the ecstasy above.

June is a month of unutterable, inexpressible loveliness, but some portion of our anticipation has passed with the consummation of that beauty. It is a month of conflict also, for we must fight to hold the beauty that we have. There can be no settling on the lees, no deceiving ourselves that our labours are over just because each bed is at its prime.

102

## APHIDS

The very lushness of early summer, the abundance of tender stem and leaf invite attack everywhere from the most inveterate of June foes—the aphid. Unless we counterattack, irreparable damage will be done.

The aphid, sometimes called aphis, is a tiny plant louse that devours new sprouts and stems and the tips of shrubs with unbelievable greed. Aphids come in hordes, covering the stems completely and sucking the fresh juices from them. Few plants can resist them unaided. We watch for the first appearance of aphids, then spray the infested stems and leaves with nicotine sulphate. This is not always sufficient to destroy a serious infestation. If it is not, we use our own fingers to squeeze them off the shoots, crushing them as the hand moves up the stem. Or we use a bit of cotton dipped in alcohol and scrape them off the stem with that.

Our male holly, the little potted plant we had just transplanted out-of-doors this year, was badly attacked in spring by aphids, but recovered nicely when sprayed once with nicotine sulphate and given the hand-squashing treatment. Usually, the nicotine sulphate spray will turn the trick.

## MILDEW AND BLACKSPOT

Dusting for mildew and blackspot on roses has been mentioned in April and May, but it must be continued through June. Indeed, every week is not too often. In spraying and dusting roses, directions for whatever is used must be followed explicitly. Both sprays and dusts can easily burn the foliage of rose bushes if applied in quantities greater than recommended or in stronger solutions.

Roses are not the only plants that suffer from mildew in June, though climbing roses seem particularly sensitive to it. Lilac and phlox are both attacked and should be dusted with flowers of sulphur. This is sure to help them and need not be repeated for weeks unless the mildew reappears, as it may, in humid, damp weather.

We use powdered sulphur dust in June on almost all our growing plants—roses, marigolds, delphiniums, foxgloves, and the like. Sulphur is especially useful when rust attacks hollyhocks.

## SLUGS AND SNAILS

A humid spell in June often results in countless hordes of snails and slugs that will, if unchecked, destroy a border almost overnight —for it is at night that they do their greatest harm. Petunias and all plants having succulent stems fall easiest prey to them. We try to aid ours by setting out little piles of commercial snail bait designed to attract and kill them. The trouble with most snail-control preparations is that they contain a high percentage of arsenic or other poison and cannot be risked where children or pets are about, for they are not dusted or sprayed lightly but are left in considerable quantities in each pile. In the old days, circles of lime were sometimes laid around plants subject to attack by snails and slugs. This kept at least some of them at a distance and was not dangerous.

## FUNGUS

For fungus control we rely on the old-fashioned Bordeaux mixture—copper sulphate and hydrated lime and/or powdered sulphur. Both are effective. Our campanulas, and especially the old-fashioned Canterbury bells, do not suffer so much from insects as they do, now and then in a wet season, from stem rot. This is usually caused by injurious fungus in the soil. The cure is to cut away what is diseased and burn it. We sometimes forget that there is not only injurious fungus growth but also beneficial fungus in all living soil. It is only when damage is being done that fungicides must be used.

## THE BATTLE JOINED

June, high June, is surely the month of battle. The greater the glory of flower and shrub, the sharper the assaults made on them by insect pests and disease. Experience, however, teaches us what to expect and forewarned is, at least to some degree, forearmed. Insects, we soon learn, depend on chewing or on sucking as their mode of attack. The chewers go for the tender leaves, the flowers, and the stems. They include borers, caterpillars, and beetles. Those that suck go for the sap or the juices of stem and leaf. These are the aphids, the leafhoppers, white flies, the thrips, and the scale insects.

## THE CHEWERS AND THE SUCKERS

We combat—or try to—the chewers with insecticides—rotenone and other preparations serve admirably against them and have the very great advantage of being nonpoisonous to men and animals. The old-fashioned Paris green sprays and arsenate of lead are effective as stomach poisons against the chewers, but they are dangerous especially if children are about. Rotenone can also be used successfully against the sucking insects as can pyrethrum. A nicotine sulphate spray, however, is our most usual recourse against the sucking insects. Some soap in the mixture helps make it stick. It is well to remember that insecticides are always of two sorts: one that acts as a stomach poison when eaten by the insect; and the other a contact insecticide that destroys the insect by reacting on its body. By and large the chewers require a stomach poison such as rotenone, pyrethrum, Paris green, or arsenate of lead. The suckers are best controlled by contact dusts or sprays such as nicotine sulphate.

## CAUSE AND CURE

Of our June flowers, blue ageratum may suffer from the so-called white fly. If so, spray with nicotine sulphate. Sweet alyssum is attacked by the flea-beetle. Rotenone or pyrethrum is an answer to that. Calendulas are nearly always a prey to the aphids. We use nicotine sulphate.

## PINKS AND CHRYSANTHEMUMS

The pinks and carnations in our borders suffer once in a while from a plague of red mites, usually called red spiders. Nicotine sulphate or rotenone soon puts an end to that. Rotenone is also a great help in keeping aphids off the chrysanthemums. Red spider and chrysanthemum midge are at least discouraged by nicotine sulphate. Powdered sulphur will offset mildew on chrysanthemums. Bordeaux mixture or any fungicide helps against leaf-drop and rust.

## COLUMBINES

Lindane is a good thing to use against leaf-miners on columbine. Once a plant is infected, however, it must be dug up and burnt or you will have the same trouble next year and worse.

## DAHLIAS

Dahlias are subject to the chewers as well as to borers and to what is called the tarnished-plant bug. They are sometimes attacked by mildew as well. Dahlias are lusty growers and need plenty of fresh air about them as do all plants susceptible to mildew. Insecticides will care for the chewers and the tarnished-plant bug. Borers in a dahlia stem must be located, then removed with a knife, care being taken not to slit the stem any more than is necessary. Sulphur dusting offsets the mildew, but good ventilation is a necessity.

## DELPHINIUMS

Delphiniums and larkspur are lovely in June, but the cyclamen-mite can do irreparable damage as can the red spider and the thrip. Plants should be treated when they need it (or before) with a spray or a dusting of insecticide—rotenone or pyrethrum is as good as any. A dusting of sulphur or of a miticide such as Ovotran or Aramite is always a help against the cyclamen-mite. Black-rot at the crown can be prevented by a spray of Bordeaux mixture. Mildew is also offset by flowers of sulphur, our favourite remedy against all mildews.

## IRIS

Borers and soft-rot are the plague of the iris and they support one another. Borers may be controlled by destroying the infected rhizomes entirely. This is sometimes a necessary, though ruthless, remedy. A sulphur dust on the rhizomes is said to help. We have never tried it. What the borer begins, the soft-rot completes. Superphosphate and lime worked into the soil will help to control soft-rot.

## MARIGOLDS AND PANSIES

Marigolds, in June, are often stripped almost clean of their foliage by leaf-eaters and are attacked on the stems by aphids. An insecticide spray or dust will soon restore them. The aphids also have a try now and then at our pansies and violas as do the ubiquitous leaf-eaters. Again an insecticide spray or dust is the answer. Sulphur dusting is the cure for stem-rot in pansies, if it appears, but we have not had trouble with that so far.

## PEONIES

The leaf-eaters—the chewers—are fond of peony leaves, but can be restrained by rotenone or any other insecticide that acts as a stomach poison. Peonies are also subject to what is called Botrytis blight. This may attack young plants in early spring or full-grown plants in June or later. Bordeaux mixture or some other fungicide must be used promptly. Nicotine sulphate is useful against stem scale.

## SUMMER PHLOX

Perennial phlox is lovely in the garden. Early varieties bloom for us before June has really started. In the doldrums of midsummer we could not do without the great cool masses of it (with us always white), so fresh it is and so luxuriant against the background of the green borders. One of its banes is leaf-spot; mildew is another—both damaging the leaves from the ground up. Sulphur dusting, begun early and continued, is the answer to both. A stomach-poison insecticide helps control red spider and the leaf-eaters. Mildew is all too often encouraged in phlox by careless gardeners who tie them too closely together in tight bunches when staking, thus cutting off the free passage of air and ventilation they must have about their stems. This is true of all staked flowers—they must be able to breathe.

## PRIMROSES

Primrose leaves, from spring on, are subject to slugs and snails. The quickest remedy is snail bait. Insecticide spray or dust will soon rout red spider and aphids.

## JUNE ROSES

We have already spoken of roses. In June, we have to contend with aphids. Rotenone, pyrethrum, nicotine sulphate, or any reputable rose spray will help control them. We use a commercial spray or dust—alternating according to the weather—against aphids, rose bugs, rose chafers, chewing caterpillars, and the other chewers.

Choice between a dust or spray is largely a matter of preference. Dusts are sometimes hard to manage in high wind; however, sprays may wash off in heavy rain. After rain or heavy dew, we generally use a dust. In very dry weather we are likely to change to a spray. As for Japanese beetles, nothing seems to do much good against them except picking them off and crushing them to death, and they can be spry. Borers in rose stems can do a lot of harm; the stem attacked must be cut off and burned. Bordeaux mixture, powdered sulphur, or a commercial spray or dust are useful against black-spot as well as against mildew. We have used all three in a single season. Pruning is the remedy for brown canker in rose stems, once it is detected. Sulphur dust is a sound preventive. In addition to dusting and spraying, one must feed roses three or four times during the summer, always after each round of blossoming. And they must be kept well watered and mulched.

## NEVER SAY DIE

To catalogue these plagues of insects and disease—something attacking every bud and flower, something chewing or sucking or boring—and to list long tallies of spray and dust designed to repel these foes, make it difficult to believe that anything can survive. Yet the contest adds a certain zest to gardening and is never a matter for despair. Usually we have to hunt on hands and knees for insects on healthy flowers, but never are we put to this in seeking blossoms. Borders are massed with colour in June.

We have, of course, a lot to do in June when it comes to fighting garden pests. The reason is obvious. We like green peas for dinner when they are fresh and tender. The insects relish just as keenly their leaves and stems tender and succulent, and they find them that way most often in June. Later, plants grow tougher hides and make shift for themselves. It is unquestionably true, however, that insects feed most hungrily on weak or sickly plants—injured ones or those that show a deficiency or a lack of proper balance in the soil from which they grow.

Spraying and dusting, weeding and cultivating and watering, guarding each day against some new attack—these are one side of the ledger and they would indeed be depressing if that were all there was to it. The other side, however, squares the balance and a profit to boot—new flowers showing day by day, bed and border aglow with beauty. Always the miracle is new, just as each spring is really new to us, fresh in wonder and new joy.

## THE MOUNTING CADENCE

1 June—snapdragon in flower. Impatiens blossoming. Laurel in bloom.

2 June—picked ripe strawberries, quantities coming on now. Loosestrife opening its gold in the wildflower corner. Also comfrey in our

little herb bed and lovely white peonies in the south border. The ants that crawl all over the tight new buds will do no harm.

3 June—Canterbury bells in blossom. Pansies, violas, and heartsease still as fresh as ever. Geraniums in blossom, some of them Martha Washington. Heal-all out in the wildflower corner and by the upper garden steps. Also wild spikenard among the ferns and in the euonymus vines on the east bank. Lantanas, white myrtle, blue ageratum, and dwarf French marigolds in bloom.

4 June—white petunias and white carnations blossoming.

5 June—phlox *subulata* out. The sweet-bay tree, *Magnolia virginiana,* in flower.

7 June—inkberries and honeysuckle out. Also Japanese holly. Climbing roses in blossom. Sedum, delphinium, and campanulas out.

9 June—more and more laurel in flower. Mock orange also and most sweet it is.

11 June—calendulas in flower.

12 June—stocks in blossom; also Shasta daisies. Tree roses are blooming (Goldilocks). And the floribundas—Betty Priors and the rest.

15 June—fuchsias now blossoming. Sweet alyssum flowering everywhere in the borders.

17 June—yellow day-lilies in flower. Marigolds (Naughty Mariettas) and white begonias out.

19 June—hydrangea out; pinks in blossom.

20 June—sage out in the herb border. English holly in flower. Cornflowers, blue vervain, and hollyhocks out. The rose-bay rhododendrons are flowering now—great masses of them.

21 June—Midsummer's Eve—we wonder if the bonfires still flame on the hills in Britain as they used to do. Are Puck and Robin Goodfellow remembered any more? And all the Little People of the tors—pixie and elf and what-you-will? This is the night one must save a handful of ashes from the Midsummer Fire and cast them on the garden for luck as they do in Roscommon—the surer to win a leprechaun's favour. With us, Midsummer's Eve Fire, of course, though small. Partridge berries in bloom.

22 June—tiger lilies out.

23 June—white regal lilies opening.

24 June—astilbe in blossom—a gift many summers ago from a dear friend at St. David's.

28 June—cosmos flowering and the first of our dahlias.

30 June—larkspur and coreopsis and nierembergia (the cupflower) in blossom.

## HIGH SUMMER

Through all this lavishing of blossom, there is a carry-over from May, varying with new bloom each day to prove that spring has yielded pride of place to June with all the glories of high summer in her train.

June is, of course, the month of roses. They overshadow all the rest: climbers on our walls and trellis, tree roses on the terrace, the floribundas and old-timers in the borders—what dreams of colour they can give.

With them are June's great shrubs, more glorious, if that be possible, than the dogwoods and viburnums of May; for it is in June that the mock orange, the rose-bay, the mountain laurel and the sweet-bay magnolia are at their bravest, past all describing against their full-leaved verdure. Some 123 different varities of bloom had come to us last year by June—and half the year still to go.

## THE IMPORTANCE OF COLOUR

Colour is most important in a garden, especially during the summer. Early spring takes care of itself with its predominate gold and white and a good deal of clear blue. Later come the pinks and whites of the first shrubs and fruit-tree bloom. By June, however, we have a good deal more choice with the flowers—annuals especially. The shrubs of June are mainly white and pink-and-white. That is the background note.

In our climate, June is reckoned a hot month. July and August are even hotter, with a humidity that has to be kept in mind. It seems

111

a mistake and a needless one to fill midsummer borders with scarlets and crimsons, heavy blue and the magentas so loved through suburbia. Such blossoms add to the heat by their fiery or smothering colours.

We base all our summer colour on the cool greens of our permanent planting. How could anything look more fresh and cool than the leaves of a Chinese holly, glossy and sleek as a seal's head when he climbs from his pool to a rock? Against such green we plan primarily for white—white and yellow and some clear, light blues. Only here and there, do we encourage a red floribunda for its contrast. A touch of scarlet or crimson or brick-red has its place—if it be a *touch*—but white and gold for us, with some cool blues and a bit of pink. The more white against green, the better.

## WHITES FOR MIDSUMMER

For white, we have in June masses of mountain laurel in the permanent borders and on the terrace. Its blossoms are, of course, pink and white and most delectable at that, but the effect is white. The laurel carries us back to many a cool green glen in the Smokies, riding from Cataloochee, or climbing high by the Duck-Hawk Rock and the Chimneys. With the laurels we have the first of our white phlox. It outlasts the laurel, for by selecting phlox with a little thought, we can find varieties that will blossom all summer. Many are fragrant as well. *Phlox suffruticosa*—Miss Lingard—is a wonderful grower that provides the purest white bloom from late May until frost. Fiancée and Mary Louise are also sure stand-bys in midsummer—both a cool white.

Some of the hybrids, *Phlox Arendsi,* have the advantage of blooming first in early spring and then again several times during the summer, if cut back. They are lower-growing than the regular *decussata* and somewhat taller than the *divaricata*—from both of which they have been evolved.

Another all-summer white that brings its cool touch to our bor-

112

ders is sweet alyssum, already mentioned many times. Even in the dog days it stays fresh and cheery.

As good, but not always white in colour, the candytuft plays its part from spring till fall. Now and then some white candytuft will show other colours—pink or lavender or even red. Most of it is white, however, the same fresh colour as sweet alyssum's Carpet of Snow or Little Gem.

White regal lilies—*Lilium regale* or *regale album* or white Show Lily, *speciosum album,* are wonderfully cool against a background of green. White delphiniums, especially *grandiflorum album;* white myrtle; white petunias; verbenas; white geraniums; white fuchsias; white begonias; white hollyhocks; and white roses such as the Summer Snow floribunda; white dahlias, Snowclad or Snowsprite or White Fawn; Shasta daisies; white impatiens—until we began to look for them, we had not the faintest knowledge that so many white flowers were available for midsummer. And, of course, there are far more than we have listed.

### COOL GOLD

Yellow and gold are also cool in colour and we use them wherever we can among the whites, though not quite so generously. Goldilocks tree roses; yellow Pinocchio floribundas as well as Rochester and Holiday (though that is a combination of orange-yellow and pink; Goldilocks floribundas; and the climbers, King Midas and Golden Glow—all bring a wealth of purest cool gold to border and trellis. Day-lilies; cosmos; coreopsis; yellow iris; early French marigolds; lantanas; calendulas; many of the miniature dahlias, such as Yellow Gem; the zinnias and the chrysanthemums that come later—we could not count the golden bloom that carries the colour of spring on through the hottest days till frost.

### THE BLUES

We do not have many blues in our early summer garden: some

light-tinted larkspur in June; blue ageratum; hounds-tongue, the cynoglossum; and bellflowers, always most lovely. There are not many more. Blue, particularly dark blue, is too heavy a colour for our humid weather. What we really need is clear, fresh, sharper blue of something like chicory, opening with the sun as it grows in every country lane. We have not found much of that colour in our garden in June. White and gold and the lightest blue—these are our dependables in heat.

## JUNE ODDS AND ENDS

As in every month, the odds and ends go on, quite apart from fighting June blights and insects, June heat and even June floods. That may be why we enjoy gardening so much—never an idle moment. And surely never a dull one. For example:

Thinned out pansies that were crowding each other. Thinned out and transplanted some of the earlier seeded zinnias where they had grown up too thickly in the lower garden beds. In the upper borders there was plenty of room for them. Also transplanted some ajuga from the lower beds to the upper garden borders. How this does spread and how lovely it can be in flower.

Cut back tulips and daffodils. This is always a bad practice for it starves the bulbs below ground just when they need most to store up food through their leaves above. Bulb leaves should be left on until they are completely withered, for then—and only then—the bulbs are ready to be lifted without harm. To save space in crowded beds or borders the leaves, still green, may be bunched together and tied, but they should not be cut off. Bulbs, when lifted in June, are dried all day in the sun before they are stored for the summer.

## TRANSPLANTING

It has been claimed that small plants like iris can be moved readily in June, but that shrubs and ferns and trees cannot be safely moved so far along in summer. This is probably true in the case of

114

trees and the larger shrubs, but we have successfully moved large rose-bay rhododendrons without damage. One thing is certain—all plants moved must be well watered all summer.

Seeded the grass under the apple trees. June is late for this, but often after a cooling rain a little seed, broadcast and tapped lightly in, may help out with the weak spots.

## JUNE PLANTING

Planted Shasta daises, chrysanthemums, plumbago, white petunias, and carnations in the lower garden beds, together with stocks, a few blue petunias, and dwarf phlox. Put in the dahlia bulbs (roots, they really are), old and new, in the south border. In the driveway bed, which is a small one, planted a few lantanas, white verbenas, and geraniums. In the east border found time to set out blue lobelia, heliotrope, and some snapdragon. Marigolds and white begonias were put in the terrace border where they always do well.

## JUNE SEEDING

Seeded candytuft and Golden Sunset Mignonette and Violet Queen sweet alyssum as border edgings. Even in June a surprising amount of seeding goes on. Seeded zinnias in the upper garden beds —Crimson Gem, Lilliput White Gem and Golden Gem, Salmon Rose, Canary Yellow, Burnt Orange, Fantasy, Autumn Tints, Giant Crested and Double mixed. Also Pompon and Mexican Midget and some creeping zinnias. Seeded also in upper borders: scabiosa, geums (Lady Stratheden), gaillardia (Dazzler and Goblin), snapdragon (Majestic, Rosamund, Eldorado and Avalanche), calendula, cosmos, and hollyhocks. Seeded wallflowers in the garden beds.

## CLIPPING AND PRUNING

In June, the arborvitae bushes—we have but two of them now— are clipped. The ivy also must be given its second clipping from

115

about the windows and doors of the cottage. Masses of wild honeysuckle and woodbine outside the south wall now and then become entangled with upstart poison ivy. It is a June chore to cut the honeysuckle back. Gradually we are killing out the poison ivy with weed-killer. Unless the roots are destroyed, however, it is useless to hope for success.

We are not likely to regard June as a pruning month, but actually it is insofar as shrubs are concerned. Once they have finished their blooming, it is time for us to decide which ones must be pruned at once so as to grow next spring's blossoming wood during the summer, and which ones should be left unpruned so as to give us the glory and the colour of their berries in the fall. Last June, for example, we pruned back the mock orange after its flowering. It had grown luxuriantly and was taking up more than its share of sun and air in our limited garden. We cut back a *Rosa Hugonis* that had blossomed, but which was spreading a bit too widely. Then we pruned the bridal wreath as soon as it had finished its flowering. As for the shrubs that bring us berries in the fall, they must be left strictly alone after their blossoms have gone. The cotoneaster is an example of this. Sometimes they call it the hollyberry. Its charm in the fall would be sadly missed were it pruned in June. So would the firethorns, the barberries, the viburnums, and many others.

### TREE PRUNING

Speaking of pruning, the normal time for pruning trees is, as everyone knows, in the fall or winter, when the leaves are off and the sap is no longer in the branches. Maple trees, however, as well as walnuts and the birches are the exception and must be pruned in June or midsummer because at this time they will not lose much sap. In the dead of winter, when most trees are dormant and should be pruned, the maple and the walnut and the birch cannot be pruned or they will bleed excessively, for their flow of sap occurs at that time rather than in summer.

## WATERING

A really appalling drought began last June and held well into October. So, at the very start of summer, our watering began. Flowers as well as grass and shrubs need water at least once a week in summer. Shrubs can stand drought a little longer. If there be no rain for a week, we try to help matters out with sprinkler and hose or with the cloth hose that permits water to soak in slowly and easily all day long. We usually water the upper garden first, where most of the seedlings are. All summer long we keep at it, if we get no rain, taking each bed by turn, week after week. It is amazing how quickly summer weather dries out ground.

We have found that saplings, shrubs, and ferns really need regular watering badly through the first and second summer after they are planted or transplanted. After that, they are able to fend for themselves in anything like normal weather. Rhododendrons especially must be watched for two years, or even longer, after planting, if they are in a place that is exposed to the sun or where the ground slope tends to dry out quickly. When their leaves begin to droop, it is a danger signal that should be heeded at once or a fine rhododendron may be lost. To watch a thirsty rhododendron recover almost as it drinks is surprising. We put the hose near the roots of ours, its nozzle on a bit of board or a shingle so as to prevent its washing away the soil or channeling the ground; then we turn the water on in a good steady trickle, letting it flow that way for as long as twenty-four hours. Such a slow soaking reaches to the lowest roots of the shrub and will store sufficient moisture there a long time if a good mulch of leaves is maintained all about the bush, as it should be.

Evergreens (other than the so-called broad-leaved sort) perhaps because they have no deciduous leaves with which to signal thirst are all too often overlooked in summer and allowed to suffer seriously from drought. This, though not apparent at first, will do them great damage and in the end can destroy them. Watering of evergreens is essential unless they are well-established plants.

## WEEDING

Another chore that repeats from May and keeps up through June is weeding. Weeding is particularly a June essential for weeds are in the ascendant then. As with the watering, we take each bed and border by turn. Once last June a little shower—the last real rain we were to have for many a month—made our weeding easy, for it enabled us to get the weeds out roots and all. Nipping the stem off a weed at ground level really encourages growth, yet that is what happens when weeding is attempted in dry weather with the soil baked hard—unless it has been well cultivated. In that case, it will not need weeding anyway. Not only do we weed all the beds and borders, but we also weed the myrtle and the euonymus on the bank, if the wild parsnips have showed up.

## MULCHING

The broad-leaved evergreens such as the rose-bay rhododendrons and mountain laurel must be protected by leaf mould and mulching because their roots spread very close to the surface of the ground, that is, the small feeder roots do so. These tiny roots must be given moisture and that can only be maintained near the surface by mulching. We use most of our white-oak and pin-oak leaves, when they fall, for this purpose. Also all the white pine, Norway spruce, and hemlock needles we can spare from about the roots of such trees. A good thick mulch each year, four or five inches of it, will keep the rhododendron roots cool as well as moist. Furthermore, the oak leaves especially and the pine needles tend to give the right acidity to the soil. After all, that is nature's way of tending them in their own cool forests. It is worthwhile to look about us a bit, then use our wits, reproducing as best we can the sort of habitat from which each shrub or flower originally came.

## WEED-KILLER

Control of weeds in the lawn is a never-ending task. We attack the plantains and the dandelions regularly with commercial weed-killer, but that always seems to kill a lot of grass as well. Perhaps we make our solution too strong. We also use weed-killer now and then to keep down the grass that sprouts between the cracks of the flag-stone paths. Our new rock plants, however, are beginning to take care of most cracks. That will be one chore the less.

## SPRAYING AND DUSTING

Many of these chores are, of course, a repetition of work done in May. The spraying and the dusting of roses and other flowers, for example, begin in May and must be repeated through until frost. As a matter of fact, we spray for aphids even as late as November. Roses are fed usually four times during the summer. Always we feed them after a round of blossoming.

## THE COW BELL

In addition to all this, there are the mixed chores of June. We paint the dowsers by the lych gate. We clean the great cowbell from Tirol that hangs under the lych gate roof. This bell is a huge one, of the heaviest metal, beautifully embossed with figures of the saints, its tone ringing and lovely—not in the least like the usual metallic clack of a cowbell. The weight of it is appalling. How any cow could bear such a burden on her neck we do not pretend to know, but bear it a good cow did. And not on level pastures at that, but up and down the unbelievably steep alps of Tirol. This particular bell had two collars: one of tough leather, four or five inches wide, for everyday wear; the other, also with wide leather as a base, covered with embroidered silk—a really magnificent piece of work. This latter was worn on feast days only, when cherished cattle shared in the festivities. The Feast of Corpus Christi in Tirol is celebrated everywhere with pageantry and colour and the deepest devotion. We are proud of our bell in the garden lych gate.

119

## TIDYING UP

Some of the work that must be done in June might well surprise one new to the vagaries of gardening. Borders are edged. Then they are cultivated. This begins in May and must be repeated until all seeding has been completed and the open spaces are too full of seedlings to permit further cultivation. We stake and tie up the peonies and stake the taller hollyhocks as well. We dust our first powdered sulphur on the delphiniums and on the roses. Once a week is none too often for this in June when mildew and blackspot are rampant if the weather is at all damp or humid. We put a good mulching of peat-moss on the dahlias, now sprouting nicely. That always helps them. Indeed, as we have stressed before, we try to mulch all other plants that need it.

## ONE REWARD AT LEAST

June brings us one gift that offsets all the labour and the strife that in reality make it the Happy Month. Our strawberries are ripening in earnest now and toothsome they are, as they grow along the borders of the upper garden. With them come the cherries—quantities and quantities of ox-hearts. As always, we share these with the birds who have a fondness for the strawberries also. There seems to be enough for all.

## ST. ALBAN'S DAY

June is above all the month of roses and doubly so in a personal way, for it was in June that roses played a part in one of those strange, inexplicable quirks of fate that change our lives, yet leave the reason for it beyond our knowing.

On Sunday morning, 18 June, during the last war, while stationed in London, I had decided to attend matins at the Guards Chapel in Wellington Barracks, near Birdcage Walk. It was a glorious day—clear, pleasantly warm, though not a trace of heat—the sort of day that makes June June, in London or the world over. Too fine a day, I thought, for staying in town. Why not go to the country and leave the Guards Chapel till another day? After all, it was not far from where I was billeted.

So, half-way through St. James's Park, I turned back. I'd have a look at St. Albans' Cathedral and the Norman work I had heard of in the transepts there. And near-by Verulamium—the ancient Roman city mostly under sod now—where the splendour of mosaic pavements recently unearthed would add to the enjoyment of a Sunday out-of-doors. St. Albans was only twenty miles from London. But the Chapel . . . I had planned for that particular service; why not go to it, then to St. Albans afterwards, for lunch?

Again I turned and walked toward the Mall through St. James's Park. And again I turned back—three times in all. It was ridiculous. St. Albans it would be. And St. Albans it was. Now I had not the faintest notion that the day before—June 17—was St. Alban's Day. I had no idea at all who St. Alban might be, but I found out before the day was over.

The little town that has replaced the Roman Verulamium, now a borough in Hertfordshire, was ready and waiting, it soon appeared, to pay honour to Britain's protomartyr—the Roman Centurion, St. Alban, who in the third century was beheaded there for proclaiming his faith in Christ. He was, so I learned, the first known martyr in Britain.

Arriving before luncheon, I had a chance to see what is claimed to be the oldest pub in England—the Red Lion—still going strong after eight hundred years. Better still, I had a chance to sit in the Bishop's garden near the Cathedral, after I had seen the Roman pavements and the Roman wall. Waiting there for Evensong among the Bishop's scented roses where the Bishop's bees were humming and the savour of the blossoms in the sweet June sun came like a breath from paradise, I noticed more roses. Everybody seemed to have them, armfuls or single sprays or perhaps a single blossom, but every man, woman, and child that passed the bench where I was

121

sitting had a rose of some sort. And still I did not know why—not until a great procession began to near the Cathedral and move slowly through the precincts toward the door.

Thousands upon thousands were walking there preceded by a Crucifer and the Lord Bishop. Choirs were there, parish choirs and parish clergy, priests and people, from all over the diocese of St. Alban—and every person there carried a rose. I had never seen such a sight before and never shall I see the like again unless I return to St. Albans on St. Alban's Day, for it was his Feast they were celebrating.

When I joined the procession entering the Cathedral, I was the only one in all those thousands lacking so much as a single rose. I had not dared raid the Bishop's garden. But I had not reached the great door of the nave before my neighbours in the procession had pressed some of their own roses upon me.

Never have I dreamed of such colour: roses red and gold and pink, scarlet roses and roses of the purest white, tea-roses and rambler roses—the old, sweet sort that grow in cottage gardens and clamber to the thatch—all of them obviously home-grown and picked this Sunday morning for St. Alban. For that is why we were carrying our roses down the long Cathedral aisles, our lines parting at the chancel and passing the high altar, right and left, so as to enter the Chapel of St. Alban beyond it. Here, so they say, is the spot where the saint was beheaded. And here arose the rude wooden shrine that grew through the centuries into the Gothic glory of the Cathedral about us. And here, too, once rose the great chantry above his tomb—a chantry sadly marred in the religious wars. As our two converging lines reached the tomb, each of us, old and young, tossed our gift on the martyr's grave—an incredible sight, for the blossoms soon were piled high above our heads and each of them a country rose.

As we filed from the chapel and back again to the nave for Evensong, an old man walking beside me said, "It's good to be remembered sixteen hundred year like 'im—so they say. I don't begrudge 'im a rose o' mine."

122

I did not either, though no rose was rightly mine. When all had returned from the chapel, and the nave and the transepts were filled to overflowing, the Bishop in his mitre stood at the altar steps and repeated, as has been done each year through the centuries, St. Alban's gallant answer to his accusers when pressed to recant:

"My name is Alban. I am a soldier of the Christ."

To hear that ring like a challenge on this, the anniversary of his death, and to see through the arches of the chancel the unbelievable masses of roses covering his tomb, the gift of all these good people (country folk, for the most part, but many of them soldiers and sailors and lads of the R.A.F., who had come to pay a debt) made Evensong at St. Albans like no other I had known. Nor ever could know.

That night I returned to London to learn that a bomb had struck the Guards Chapel during Morning Prayer, plunging through the roof and exploding on the floor of the nave. The Chapel was, of course, destroyed. Two hundred and one persons—all, save two, in the Chapel at the time, were killed outright.

I had come almost to the door of the Chapel, then turned back. Three times I had hesitated, then chosen St. Albans. The roses there I can never forget. Nor the courage and the challenge of the saint still honoured and still loved because he dared to speak the truth—and die for it.

The modest roses about our cottage in June bring that amazing Evensong to mind and give meaning to the age-old prayer as we work among them.

Prosper Thou the work of our hands upon us, O prosper Thou our handy-work.

## JUNE CHECK LIST

June is probably the gardener's busiest month. Everything happens and everything must be attended to, it seems, at the same time.

Avoid leggy plants by pinching back their tops now. This applies to annuals such as zinnias (although a little later), and to chrysanthemums now.

Keep on pruning spring-flowering shrubs after their flowering, but do *not* prune those whose berries are colourful in fall. Maple, walnut, and birch trees should be pruned in summer; never in winter.

Keep moisture near the surface of the garden by repeated and thorough watering and especially by mulching. Roses, peonies, dahlias, and delphiniums are great drinkers. Do not forget to soak the evergreens and all newly transplanted trees or shrubs. Mulching conserves moisture as nothing else can. Never slight it.

It is time now to divide and set out the spring-flowering perennials such as iris, primroses, and alyssum.

Weed, then weed some more. Weeds destroyed in June before they can go to seed are destroyed for good.

Finish staking begun in May. Make no stake heavier or more conspicuous than is necessary for the plant it is designed to support.

Do not forget to feed your growing plants—annuals as well as perennials. Any complete plant food will do. Before feeding, cultivate lightly to give the food a chance to work into the ground.

Also, give lawns a June feeding. While you are at it, get rid of early crabgrass by hand-weeding in small areas and by careful spraying with a recognized commercial preparation over wider areas. Remember lawns have as many enemies as flowers; to thrive they require regular care.

June enemies and your allies against them in every garden include: aphids (nicotine sulphate); mildew and blackspot (powdered sulphur or commercial spray or dust); rust, leaf-drop, and fungus (sulphur powder or Bordeaux mixture); slugs and snails (lime or snail-control compounds).

124

Guard against the chewers with insecticides such as rotenone. For the suckers use rotenone, nicotine sulphate, or contact dusts. White flies, red mites, and chrysanthemum-midge are checked by nicotine sulphate; for flea-beetles, red spiders, and leaf-miners use rotenone, pyrethrum, or nicotine sulphate. For cyclamen-mites and thrip use rotenone or pyrethrum. Sulphur dusting helps control soft-rot, stem-rot, and leaf-spot. Bordeaux mixture is useful against Botrytis blight in peonies.

Spray or dust roses weekly in June. Rotenone, pyrethrum, nicotine sulphate, or any reputable rose spray work wonders.

Keep in mind the five June chores of spraying, dusting, weeding, cultivating, and watering.

Adhere to some colour scheme in your garden. Be ruthless when it is violated.

Remember the coolness of the summer whites—mountain laurel, white phlox, candytuft, white lilies, white delphiniums, white myrtle, petunias, geraniums, fuchsias, begonias, hollyhocks, roses, Shasta daisies.

Gold, also, is a cool colour, offered us generously by golden roses, yellow day-lilies, cosmos, coreopsis, iris, French marigolds, lantanas, calendulas, dahlias, zinnias—how rich the list can be if planned for.

Keep picking and thinning out pansies. Lift and dry the last of the tulips and daffodils, if they have withered to the ground.

It is not too late for plants to go in: Shasta daisies, chrysanthemums, plumbago, petunias, carnations, stocks, dwarf phlox, lantanas, verbenas, geraniums, lobelias, heliotrope, snapdragons, begonias, and marigolds.

Candytuft, mignonette, sweet alyssum, zinnias, gaillardia, scabiosa, wallflowers, geums, calendulas, cosmos, and next year's hollyhocks may be seeded now, although most of these should have been seeded earlier.

Finally, keep the garden tidy as possible. Watch edging of the borders. Try to prevent disorder from piling up.

# CHAPTER VII

# JULY

## The Month of Change

"I do hold it," Francis Bacon assures us, "in the royal ordering of gardens, there ought to be gardens for all months of the year; in which, severally, things of beauty may be in their season. . . ." Surely we cannot cavil about that. Isn't it precisely what we are trying to do in our own garden? ". . . And because the breath of flowers is far sweeter in the air (where it comes and goes, like the warbling of music) than in the hand, therefore nothing is more fit for that delight than to know what be the flowers and plants that do best perfume the air."

Bacon, by the way, lived at St. Albans, scarcely a mile from where we saw St. Alban's Feast of Roses. He goes on to speak of his favourites for scent—the violet in April (and of its second blossoming at Bartholomewtide in August), and the muskrose which he rates next to it in sweetness. With us, July—indeed all summer—is hard on scent and even the freshest spring is not too lavish with it.

### SWEET SAVOURING

We get colour in July—plenty of it—and some sweet savouring from midsummer phlox or bee-balm or the herbs, but something in our drier climate and more prolonged heat defeats scent, save that from a few flowers like the *Daphne cneorum* and some of the shrubs like mock orange. These, rightly, belong to May and June. Our loveliest blossoms in May and June, the most scented months of the year, bear no resemblance at all in fragrance to those that sweeten an English lane. Some of our roses are mildly fragrant it is true, but not richly so.

A breath of the wild thyme, once tasted on an English heath, clings to our hearts forever, And

> ". . . will you e'er forget
> The scent of hawthorn in the sun or bracken in the wet?"

We must not scorn our own July, however, for it can be surprisingly rich in beauty, charmed by bloom and blossoms that content us. Midsummer is truly lovely, in spite of lack of scent and a heat that must be matched by watering. It is, of course, the month of change. High summer has passed. The sturdier blooms of August, the hint of ripening fruit, the first, sweet mellowing of the year— these come later, but meanwhile July gives us a quiet beauty all its own.

## THE CHANGING CYCLE

July reflects the period of the seasons' changing cycle. The glories of June, full blown, have yielded to a stage of calm and rest, an easing off, when gardens seem to relax a bit, dreaming through the drowsy heats of noon as though taking fresh heart for the splendours that will come in fall. If we recognize this breathing spell and appreciate its need, we can enjoy our gardens in July as keenly as in any other month, especially if we have planned our flowering cadence with an eye for coolness and colour. There need be no lack of either.

## JUNE CARRY OVERS

This year our borders were more than gay with carry-overs from June. Floribunda roses were at their height, as were all the roses except the climbers whose real months are May and June. Sweet alyssum, candytuft, white phlox, calendulas, blue ageratum, early marigolds, geraniums, petunias, lantanas, verbenas, white myrtle, fuchsias, snapdragons, foxgloves, begonias, honeysuckle, bell-flowers, Shasta daisies, madonna lilies, cosmos, early dahlias, coreopsis, hollyhocks, astilbe, impatiens, shrimp plant, *Beloperone guttata, Daphne cneorum* (the sweet-scented garland-flower, now re-blooming), rosebay rhododendrons, bleeding hearts—all these and more bring rich memories of June deep into July.

## JULY COLOUR

During July fresh bloom includes matrimony-vine, moth-mullein, fleabane, and heal-all in the wild-garden; and scarlet pimpernel, butterfly-bush (so aptly named, for it is gay with attendant butterflies from dawn till dark), hydrangea, abelia, chrysanthemum, rose of Sharon, cornflower, day-lily, trumpet-creeper, midsummer phlox, heartsease (still going strong since January), wild thyme, tree-roses (now in their third blooming of the year), viola (also in bloom since the earliest spring), a spray or so of wisteria (re-blooming or late blooming, as it always does, six weeks after the rest of the vine has podded), portulaca, columbine (a few late-flowering plants below the ha-ha just to remind us of spring again and mock at July heat), stonecrop (also late), lemon verbena (this *does* give us plenty of scent as do the wild mint and pennyroyal by the fountain), sweet william (cut back and now re-blooming), trumpet honeysuckle, hounds-tongue—some sixty different kinds of flowers in bloom despite the heat and the drought of a warm July. We could do worse than that.

## SOAKING-HOSE AND SPRINKLER

Watering comes high in the July list of priorities. Chrysanthemums especially are likely to stand in need of it as are other plants that make their leaf growth in the summer and blossom in the fall. Lawns as well as shrubs must be watched in midsummer droughts and watered thoroughly. One rule holds: water once a week in unbroken droughts. Water slowly and deeply; never yield to the easier surface sprinklings, no matter how frequently they may be given.

Surely, we cannot deny midsummer its gift of quiet beauty, vouchsafed us when lawns are parching and the leaves of the rhododendrons droop in the sun. Soaking-hose and sprinkler are essential now. We must remember always that a plant or shrub well soaked, slowly and steadily, deep to its lowest roots, will profit far more from such a watering than from half a dozen surface sprinklings that do more harm than good. Mulches must be maintained in July, for nothing so conserves moisture and keeps the ground surface cool.

## DUSTING AND SPRAYING

Although July may pause a little in the exuberance of its bloom, our battle against plague and pest affords us little rest. It is true that sound weeding in May and June will relieve us almost entirely of that chore in July. It is also true that proper dusting and spraying in June will make our pest control less insistent in July, for we should have succeeded by now in keeping most pests in reasonable check. Mildew and blackspot, however, will be with us still unless we keep at our spraying. The suckers and the chewers and the borers, the caterpillars woolly and the caterpillars smooth, the termites and the millipedes so fond of plant roots, these and countless others have not all been destroyed. One gain is that our plants are tougher. The secret of it all, of course, is to dust or spray regularly —once a week at least with roses. It is well to bear in mind that insects and most other destructive pests often breed cosily in rubbish piles. We must see to it that the garden and its environs are tidy. The place for rubbish of all sorts is a bonfire.

## THE SHRUBS IN JULY

Shrubs are often overlooked in the matter of pests, as are some of the perennials which we can too easily take for granted.

We must not devote all our attention to the obvious needs of our roses and our favourites among the annuals. It pays to have a look in season at everything, shrubs included. July usually gives us a chance for this.

## FLOWERING ALMONDS

Flowering almonds—we have two lovely ones—are sometimes attacked by borers. These must be removed or the branch tips will first wilt, then die, thus destroying the whole plant. The defense is to keep an eye on the shrub and cut off the damaged branch when it is attacked.

It is the shrub itself we must try to save. A little care will soon disclose the borers that are doing the mischief. Most often, of course, they attack the stem of the shrub near the ground, as is the case with fruit trees and saplings. We have used hairpin wire to locate these borer pests.

If scale has attacked flowering almonds, they should be sprayed with the same miscible oil used against scale on fruit trees. This is work for early spring, not July. But borers must be guarded against all the time.

## ROSE OF SHARON

Rose of Sharon, the shrub althea, which blooms from July almost till frost, falls easy prey to the Japanese beetle, for its blossoms are at their early best just as the beetles are swarming in hordes from the ground. Rosebuds, hollyhocks, Virginia creeper, and rose of Sharon seem to attract the Japanese beetle more than all else here. When we had grapevines on the place, they suffered even more severely. It seems impossible to check the ravages of these tough-shelled devils, but a stomach-poison spray may help a little. Starlings do a good job at it. Once we watched a hardy fellow eat twenty-five beetles without a pause. A robin near-by was doing his best all the while to keep up, but apparently he had to crack each beetle's armour a bit before swallowing and so make two bites of it. The starling, less fastidious or more greedy, just gulped and kept on gulping—a beetle a gulp. What a meal!

## THE AZALEAS

Azaleas suffer at times from so-called lace-bugs—one of the sucker family. Nicotine sulphate is a good insecticide for them, so a spray should do the trick. A damaged leaf looks like openwork lace—hence the name of this particular pest.

## CLEMATIS

Clematis must be protected against fungus and also against mildew and the borers. A good dusting of powdered sulphur will soon remedy the fungus as well as the mildew. Remember that the damaged area is nearly always close to the ground with clematis. If borers have attacked the stems of clematis, above the collar, they must be spotted and removed.

## THE FLOWERING CRABS

So far, our flowering crabs have fared well, but these lovely trees are often attacked by borers as are most young fruit trees unless watched. A wilting of the leaves betrays the presence of borers. Crabs, like all fruit trees, should be sprayed for scale in early spring, but July is as good a time as any to have a look for the borers. Should fire-blight appear in midsummer and the leaves of a flowering crab wilt or die, cut off all infected branches and burn them. This must be done with all infected parts of trees or shrubs or flowers, else the infection will continue to spread, year after year. Aphids, too, have a fondness for flowering crabs. If they show up, a nicotine sulphate spray is the answer.

## THE DOGWOODS

We check our dogwoods for borers usually twice a year: once in spring when we are spraying and checking other trees, and once in the fall. There always is a lull in July, however, when it does no harm to have a look at them. Dogwoods are so prized that it pays to watch them. If borers are present, the wilt of the foliage and a general lack of tone in the trees will soon be noticed. Borers must be pried out of their channels with wire or hairpins and the holes they have made should then be disinfected and plugged with a bit of tar. Borers are found at the base of dogwoods, well dug in under the bark.

## EUONYMOUS VINES

Our euonymous vines covering the banks on both sides of the drive, have thriven well for years with no particular care. There is, however, a scale that attacks some euonymous, sucking the sap from the leaves and from the stems. If this scale is present, the vines should be sprayed with miscible oil when the trees are sprayed in the spring, then sprayed again, in full foliage, during July or August.

## THE LILACS

Lilac, for a shrub that persists so long by ruined farmsteads, seemingly indestructible, is subject to all sorts of ills when nurtured and cosseted in our gardens. Oyster-shell scale is inevitable if spraying is neglected, and it will kill the healthiest lilac. A miscible oil spray checks this if given in spring when the plant is dormant. Mildew sometimes attacks lilac bushes even in midsummer. A dusting of powdered sulphur helps control this as does Bordeaux mixture or any other good fungicide. Borers have a liking for lilac stems, as they have for most shrubs that we specially cherish. They must be found, pried out, and destroyed. The lilac leaf-miner is another troublemaker. Like most leaf-miners and insects that suck the juices from plants, they are controlled by a spray of nicotine sulphate.

## LILIES

Lilies are attacked by, among other pests, aphids and the whole

132

tribe of chewers. Pyrethrum or rotenone, nicotine sulphate or any other suitable insecticide should be used when needed. Botrytis blight—a fungus disease—needs plenty of Bordeaux mixture. The trouble can easily be detected by the transparent spots it makes on the lily leaves. If the leaves appear mottled, the plant probably is suffering from what is known as mosaic disease. Such plants must be removed from the garden and burned. Too much emphasis cannot be laid on this point. Whatever the plant or whatever the blight, we must not leave infected leaves or stems lying about or our trouble next year will be multiplied past all measure. Stem rot in lilies is often a result of bruised bulbs. The answer to that problem is to plant only uninjured bulbs. Parts of bulbs superficially damaged may be cut away and the sound part planted.

## THE SWEET BAY

Our two magnolia trees, sweet bays, have escaped so far any serious attack by scale—a common enemy of magnolias. If scale has appeared on magnolia stems, however, a dormant spray of miscible oil should be used.

## RHODODENDRON SPRAYING

We have spoken of midsummer pests and the need for repeated spraying and dusting. Do not forget that rhododendrons are often subject to lace-bug attack on the under side of the leaves. A 50% wettable DDT powder is a useful spray for this, if repeated several times. Often nicotine sulphate is added. A 50% DDT is a sound remedy also for earwigs which are hard to find in the daytime but are great rovers-about at night. Look for them under something. They like the dark.

Until we check on them, it is difficult to realize how many garden pests do their damage after sunset. Slugs and snails are always night workers. The old-fashioned way to kill snails—perhaps it still is— was to pour salt on them and watch them dissolve almost instantly

into horrid slime. Thousand-leggers and sowbugs are busy at night.
Should anyone doubt the prowess of night prowlers, all he has to do
is look at a planting of, say, petunias, after one night's banqueting
of slugs and snails. Cutworms seem to like night work, too.

The answer, of course, is slug bait, spraying, and dusting. Insecticides do not stop working because the sun has downed. A dead slug
will.

## A STITCH IN TIME

It should be noted that with shrubs and their ailments much of
the remedy consists in early spraying. This clearly is a spring chore
—not one for July. It is, however, in July and midsummer that we
often notice for the first time that something *is* wrong with our
shrubs. Leaves wilt or die or blacken. Drought is frequently blamed
for these signs that all is not well. Too often the trouble goes deeper.
That is why July is a good month to check for borers as well as for
fungus blights and insect or mites that may be eating or sucking
the foliage. Such care holds good for the perennials—the lilies and
other bulb plants—as well as for shrubs. It pays to find what is
wrong and to find out before too much damage has been done.

The rules we found useful for flowers in June are just as useful
now for shrubs. Locate borers and pry them out. For the chewers and
the suckers use—and use in time—contact or stomach-poison insecticides (nicotine sulphate, preferably mixed with soap to make it
stick, or rotenone or pyrethrum); for fungus, stem rot, mildew, or
the like, use Bordeaux mixture or powdered sulphur; for scale, use
a spray of miscible oil. One must try it, to see what even a modicum
of care will do.

## STAKING

July is not lacking in other chores. If we have not staked our
taller annuals, that must be done now or never. Indeed, we are lucky
if unsupported annuals of any size have stood upright this long.

Dahlias should have been staked two months ago, in fact, when their bulbs were planted. Lilies usually need some support, especially the tall madonnas. Other annuals and perennials such as snapdragon, foxglove, larkspur, phlox, the taller zinnias, some of the marigolds, campanulas, cornflowers may need supporting. Our hollyhocks always do.

Bamboo rods, thin enough to do the job, are handy for most flowers except dahlias and hollyhocks. These require real staking. If the thin bamboo canes have been stained green, they will be quite inconspicuous. Indeed a little care can make them invisible from most angles. Thin wire rods are also useful. Staking annuals is as much a July chore as staking the earlier perennials in June.

## THE LAWN

Lawns can suffer from more ills than a dry summer. It is in July that the crab grass and fall grass begin to appear. The damage done to grass roots earlier by the grub of the Japanese beetle now shows up. Chinch bugs are at their height. This insect, known as the hairy chinch bug, lays its eggs in the grass. When these hatch, the chinch bugs begin to suck juice from the grass stems, working outward in ever widening circles, so that a lawn attacked by them is soon spotted with round areas of dead grass. Chinch bugs start work on a lawn in spring and will keep at it until frost unless they are checked. There are several remedies, but a lawn can be ruined in one season unless some effective check be applied in time. A nicotine sulphate spray is one answer. Or it may be dusted on the grass, which gets it closer to the trouble. DDT powder is said to be most effective, but we have not tried it here. Rotenone has been used by many gardeners—1% rotenone dust, 25 pounds to 1000 square feet. In applying any dust, it must be kept in mind that the hairy chinch bug is at work close to the roots of the grass so that the dust must be worked well down to the ground level, not just spread on the upper blades of grass where it can do little good.

135

## CRAB GRASS

Crab grass, so far, has defeated us. Year after year, we have a try at it, but also year by year we seem to kill more sound grass than crab grass. The approved treatments are legion, but most of the chemical compounds now sold commercially are based on potassium cyanate. All control depends upon a rigid following of directions for the particular compound used. That is where we make our mistake, year after year, trying to improve on directions. Potassium cyanate, properly used, will kill crab grass and should not injure permanently lawn grass (so they say) apart from a temporary burning at the tips. Indeed, it is claimed that it helps lawn grass by way of fertilizing it. Knotweed, mouse-ear chickweed, the various purslanes are also controlled by proper applications of potassium cyanate. A stronger killer, such as 2-4D, is usually needed to destroy dandelions and plantain.

## CAREFUL DOES IT

It must be repeated that the greatest possible care should be used in each application of these crab grass and weed controls, for lawn grass is a precious asset. A sound lawn, once ruined by an over-zealous dose of weed-control, is a costly luxury to replace. We speak in a chastened and contrite mood, for only this year, though well aware of the danger, we put on too generously an excellent commercial compound based on potassium cyanate—with appalling results. A chore this fall will be to retrieve some of that damage, but the lawn, for this summer at least, has been ruined. It is astonishing how many weeds find congenial lodgement in a lawn unless removed: chickweed, masses of yellow sorrel, heal-all, shepherd's-purse, dandelion, knotweed, lesser-ragweed, plantain, horse-nettle, buckhorn, quack grass, pigweed, curly-dock, low-mallow, bindweed, cocklebur, lamb's quarters, valerian—these are but a few.

Not everyone realizes that it takes as much effort, perhaps more, to maintain a lovely lawn as it does to grow flowers in a pleasing border. Pythium disease, brown-patch, snow-mould, dollar-spot, damping-off, mildew green-scum, slime-mould—these and far too many others can come to vex us. Most lawns suffer more seriously in hot, humid weather than at any other time. And July with us can be humid. We mow higher than usual—up to one and a half inches helps to keep the roots cool. Mercury compounds help somewhat with pythium disease and are also useful for combating brownspot. Snow-mould attacks bent-grass in spring. It, too, is controlled by mercury compounds. Dollar-spot nearly always occurs in periods of high humidity, but it is not limited to heat. Mercury compounds again are the answer. Damping-off kills freshly sown grass; there is no treatment that we know of except to reseed. Damping-off seems to be caused or to be increased by excessive flooding of the surface just as the young grass is beginning to grow. Mildew, green-scum, and slime-mould look worse than they are, for they do not appear to do any lasting harm. A deep raking often will remove them. Dry sunlight always helps, of course. Lawns need real thought in July.

## THINNING OUT

Watering, dusting, spraying, feeding roses, renewing mulch—all as needed—continue through July, but the seeding of annuals has mostly passed with June as has much of the transplanting. Zinnias and other seedlings may be thinned out now and planted elsewhere, especially after rain; that task depends upon their growth. Sometimes it is a June chore with us; sometimes a July one. Weeding, as has been said, should be well over by now. Only now and then must some overlooked intruder be plucked from bed or border. Grass, stray and maddening clumps of it, has a way of springing up in every sort of summer weather right in the middle of our best-loved flowers. The trick is to keep an eye on all beds and not let the vagrant grass get a start. In seeding a lawn it is amazing how far the grass seed will carry on a windless day. This accounts for some of the stray clumps.

Our gardening, like our blossoms, has reached a passive phase, if

137

such a word may be applied to anything so tense with life, so touched with the vitality of growing leaf and flower, so pregnant with promise of more beauty ahead, as is the sleepiest of gardens in the drowsiest of Julys.

## ORDERING AGAIN

One midsummer task that seems ahead of time, but really is not, consists in ordering fall bulbs—if this has not been done earlier. Note that we are speaking of autumn bulbs, not spring ones, that is, bulbs that must be planted in late summer so as to blossom this fall. Each year we put in some colchicums and autumn crocuses, *Sternbergia lutea,* and the true autumn crocuses, *speciosus albus.* We also order in July what seed we may need for our replenishing of pansies, violas, and Johnny-jump-ups. These, like the fall bulbs, should be planted in late August or early September, so July is the time to make sure that we shall have them when needed. And, of course, the biennial and perennial seeds should be on hand already.

## ALWAYS A CHALLENGE

It has been said, probably with some truth, that gardening knows no routine. Each day, month by month and year by year, the tasks that must be done are really fresh challenges because we are dealing with things that live and grow and change—not with automatons. Repetitions there must be, of course, but then repetition has been called the mother of learning. They should never bore one—too much loveliness is at stake. Note the odds and ends of an average July.

2 July—cut down and dug up the roots of two retinosporas under the dining room window, where they were cutting off too much light and dying back on the side toward the house. Replaced them by transplanting a lower hydrangea there. Planted ageratum, marigolds, and begonias in terrace border. Lantanas in the driveway pots. Set out fuchsias in pots by the tool-house steps. Thinned out some overly rank peonies in upper garden borders. Staked hollyhocks and phlox. Clipped

all faded blossoms from the roses and trimmed back the ramblers. Seeded sweet alyssum at the base of the lower garden walls. Found time to note that lilies, day-lilies, Peruvian daffodils (not really daffodils at all, *Ismene calathina*), and Deptford pinks had blossomed since the last check of bloom a day or so ago. Chrysanthemums, also, are opening, as are some of the dahlias. A busy day.

3 July—cut woodbine from around the barberry bush. Gave a mulch of peat-moss to the myrtle and euonymus on east side of drive—it is far too dry there. Weeded front bank. Thinned out strawberry vines along the ha-ha. Watered the crab tree transplanted this spring. Stained the new brick coping of the wall with a mixture of train-oil and tobacco, slapped on with a paint brush. The fresh brick looked too new. Planted in lower beds marigolds, white vincas, and fuchsias. Clipped ivy round lower windows and doors—is this the third time this year or the fourth? Scrubbed all garden chairs and tables. Birds will be birds. Noticed that the matrimony-vine and the wild moth-mullein are in bloom.

4 July—cut back firethorn that had been smothering a fine azalea in the upper garden. Set out some white myrtle there. Weeded new myrtle beds and put more peat-moss on them for a mulch. A little rain has helped. Blossoming today (that is, noted for the first time today): scarlet pimpernel, cosmos, trumpet-creeper, butterfly-bush, hydrangea, and masses of snowy rhododendrons. Took it easy—for the Fourth.

5 July—put more white myrtle, begonias, and some nephthytis plants in the driveway bed. Abelia is blooming and fleabane just opening now in the wildflower corner.

6 July—weed-killer on dandelions and plantain. Repainted the back of St. Francis' shrine in the lower garden. Cultivated upper borders. Reseeded some late alyssum in border edgings. Seeded—far too late—some extra zinnias and ageratum in upper borders. Began the yearly struggle against crab grass—and with a vengeance. Repentance came later. In bloom today: heal-all.

7 July—light rain today, but not enough. Put some grass seed on lower garden lawn and on the terrace. Fed the rhododendrons with a broad-leaf commercial feed. Continued to soak the crab grass with a good killer—far too good and used far too generously. Woe! Woe! *Eventus stultorum magister est!*

8 July—weeded all rhododendrons and shrubs along the east bound-

ary. Noted that 89 different kinds of flowers, trees, and shrubs have blossomed here since the first of the year.

9 July—Fed most of the roses and also dusted them with powdered sulphur. Gave the delphiniums, foxgloves, campanulas, and marigolds a dusting of powdered sulphur. Also, slug-shot on the roses.

10 July—put out some dwarf phlox in garden pots. Not too satisfactory.

11 July—watered lower garden beds and lawn. Crab-grass killer now beginning to show what it can do to grass—if improperly applied. In blossom today; midsummer phlox in the upper borders. Rose of Sharon just budding by the summer-house wall. How heartening this old-fashioned shrub can be. As children at Ardmore we used to trap bumblebees in its blossoms by closing the ends, then thrilled to the sound of their angry buzzing within the close-held trumpet of the flower.

12 July—seeded zinnias now in bloom. First chrysanthemums opening. Latanas and candytuft, of course, in full flower.

13 July—put out geraniums and more begonias in lower garden beds. Worked—though vainly—to repair the damaged lawn. We are told that though we should bray a fool in a mortar among wheat with a pestle, yet will not his foolishness depart from him. Surely, our folly has struck as deeply, for this is not the first year that we have killed our grass so. Watered ferns in the wild-garden gully all day—slow sprinkling. Put out snail bait to save our petunias from slugs and snails. It worked. The snails were soon in as sad a plight as our poor lawn is, but the flowers were saved. This time we followed directions.

14 July—more weed-killer on the plantains. Put on carefully, it is working. Dusted roses again—a shower had removed last week's sulphur. Worked some more on the sickly lawn. And sick it is.

15 July—more water on ferns.

16 July—watered upper borders. We are in a real drought now. Gave the damaged grass a hundredweight of organic fertilizer. Phew! But it was worth it. In the end, this really helped to heal the scars of our crab-grass crusade. Planted some hounds-tongue from Hawthorn. Now blooming: cornflowers, plenty of them; more and more marigolds (how lovely the Rose Gem and the Pink Blossoms are); masses of sweet alyssum and candytuft.

17 July—clipped back some exuberant yews and a Japanese holly or

so that needed a summer trim. Slug-shot on everything likely to be chewed or sucked. Hand-weeded crab grass from parts of the lawn not already marred by our weed-killer. Cultivated terrace borders, carefully, with a hand prong, as they are filled now with flowers. Staked snapdragons. In bloom: madonna lilies.

18 July—sprayed roses again. Gave the plantains and dandelions there a shot of weed-killer—most carefully, you may be sure. Dwarf zinnias opening every day. Trumpet-creeper out and nearly all the dahlies in bloom.

19 July—fed the floribunda roses.

20 July—transplanted some day-lilies from the lower garden beds to east border—weak spots will show up now and then and must be filled, even in midsummer. Watered lower garden beds and grass.

21 July—watered upper borders and also the ferns in the gully. One can see that watering is the main and the most repeated chore of all July. Calendulas blooming nicely in east border. The midsummer phlox is also lovely now and very fragrant. Francis Bacon would approve of that. Thirty-seven different varieties of flowers in bloom today.

22 July—put some wire-netting on the south wall to help the clematis there. Watered the euonymus on the east bank of the drive. Weeded ferns on the front bank. Set out twenty-two clumps of portulaca from Fairhope.

23 July—weeded the base of the lower garden walls. Clipped back ivy there and on the walls as well. The berries of the viburnum are well formed now. Sedum (stonecrop) is also blooming or rather re-blooming by the ha-ha wall.

24 July—made a level place for a bench beside the summer-house in the upper garden. We have a small gazebo there, as such arbours once were called—a pleasant place for tea, if one wants it out of doors, but under shelter.

25 July—Bordeaux mixture on roses and new trumpet-creeper that showed some mildew. New virgin's-bower also needed some of this. Watered all beds and borders. Fed such roses as needed it. Dusted slug-shot on roses, marigolds, and new virgin's-bower, for good measure. It can be seen that dusting or spraying or both is a weekly chore, whatever else is done or not done. Trimmed the trumpet-creeper on kitchen wall. Gave the wisteria its third trim this year. Cut back some bush-honey-

suckle that was fast overshadowing the new firethorns—those we are starting to espalier on the east wall. Plumbago now in blossom by the fountain and a lovely, clean blue it is. The new trumpet-creeper on the fence has also blossomed.

26 July—watered new myrtle beds as well as all grass and the new plantings of Japanese holly, beauty-bush, yew, and abelia by the parking-place.

28 July—kept on with yesterday's watering. Painted a new garden chair. In bloom today: hounds-tongue, foxglove (long since cut back and now bravely at it again), and *Daphne cneorum,* most delicious in scent. Surely no musk-rose, let alone the St. Albans violets, could surpass our daphne in fragrance, re-blooming now in the heat and drought of summer.

29 July—put in one golden-yellow chrysanthemum where we needed that colour in the east border. Chrysanthemums, even in bloom, can easily be moved in midsummer. Not many other flowers can—except seedlings, which can be moved at any time. Transplanted some white vinca and zinnias to the lower beds where the sweet william had left a place to be filled.

30 July—watered the terraces about the house. Put some new potted geraniums on the terrace wall. Transplanted some of our older ones to the lower beds. Clipped ivy about the garden lych-gate. Re-mulched all the floribunda roses with peat-moss.

31 July—watered upper lawn. Gave the little male holly a tobacco spray for aphids. Also wiped a good many of these pests off with alcohol and cotton and squeezed some from the stem by hand.

## A LITTLE AT A TIME

One can see that July—the month we have flattered as restful and relaxing—is not wholly one of idleness. Actually, the work done day by day sounds much more exacting than it is. A little work attended to when the need occurs, some work done every day, soon mounts to a gratifying total. It must be remembered that this is a very small place and that the beds and borders and shrubbery are in scale. It should also be remembered that there is no gardener employed, except for the man who comes for half an hour or so once a week in summer to cut grass. All other work we do ourselves. Naturally, we cannot spend all day in the doing of it, though that would be a pleasure indeed. Most of our gardening is a late afternoon affair, with Saturdays thrown in, during summer.

### THE MUSTS

In July the essentials are easy: roses and other flowers must be dusted or sprayed. We try to see that this is done regularly; rarely is it skipped for longer than a fortnight in the vital months of June, July, and August. Our goal is once a week. Watering depends upon the weather, of course. All other chores can wait their turn—and do. Gardening must never turn to a slave-driving scourge. A harried gardener is tragic.

### TEA TIME

In the July just described probably an hour or an hour and a half in the afternoons was the average time spent on the work and every moment of it a joy. To make it more delightful each day's work is broken midway in our labours, for a dish of tea, sometimes hot, sometimes cold. If cold, our mint bed adds to the savour.

### MORE CHORES

We have said that seeding ends in June. That is true, of course, for most annuals, but July is the prime month for seeding next year's plants—the biennials and the perennials. If started now, they will make sound growth before frost.

There are other July chores we have not listed. Strawberry vines are ready in July to be set out from the runners of old vines. Do not forget to mulch them well and give the new plants a fair start with all the manure you can spare, well dug in.

### KEEP THEM BUSHY

Another July chore is the pinching back of this year's annuals as well as a good many perennials so as to lessen height and increase bushiness, before they come to bloom. We nip back our zinnias in this way and the chrysanthemums and many of the others. Indeed, so regular is this work—a plant here and a plant there—that we have not listed it in our day-by-day work at all.

## DIVIDING IRIS

Iris should be divided now. Some iris is ready for this in June, but July is probably the more usual month. When dividing, watch for borers. Use only the best rhizomes—those that have grown on the outside of the clump you are working with. Make sure that each new plant has a fan or two of good sound leaves when it is transplanted.

July with us is a maligned month, its evil reputation enhanced by humidity as well as by heat. It is, nonetheless, a month of quiet, restful after the madder ecstasies of June. A month of looking ahead, as the early months of spring are. There is more green than colour in forest and field now, just as there is in our borders. How wise nature is to pause a while and give midsummer a chance.

## ANTICIPATION

The wonder of gardening and much of its joy is the anticipation we derive from it. Each consummation in the cycle of the year, perfect and complete though it be, ends not with satiety or any cloying of the loveliness about us; indeed, it does not end at all but rises to a new perfection, enriched with hints of what is still in store. All gardeners are aware of this rhythmic cadence.

Winter in its deepest snow speaks always of the spring not far behind. Spring in the fairest of its blossoms does not end with cherry blow. We feel in it the rarer delights of June and all the magic of high summer to come. Each season seems to reach a peak and end, but just before that end can come we sight new loveliness beyond and all our hearts are gay again with promise. This is particularly true of July.

## LOOKING FORWARD

Fruit-tree boughs bend low with apples and pears that, though unripe, are showing their metal now. In the borders, though it is but July, fall flowers are to be reckoned with—no bloom yet, but lots of promise. On the hottest, stickiest day we begin to cast forward a bit and see in our mind's eye the colours that soon will brighten the green of our shrubs when asters and mums and marigolds glow like freshly minted gold against the cooling dews of fall and virgin's-bower banks the wall with starry, fragrant snow.

We remember last year's glory of berry and fruit—dogwood and sour gum, viburnum, firethorn, cotoneaster, barberry, yew, and holly, and the vines of the bittersweet; how quickly and how surely we forget the doldrums as we picture the changes to come. Always, in a garden, there is a longing for what comes next, blended with the joy of what we have at hand. Tennyson's Ulysses felt it and found answer in his travels:

> "Yet all experience is an arch where through
> Gleams that untraveled world, whose margin fades
> Forever and forever when I move.
> How dull it is to pause, to make an end,
> To rust unburnished, not to shine in use!
> As though to breathe were life!
> Life piled on life were all too little."

A gardener knows exactly what that means. Our travels may not take us to the garden's end, but travel we do through the ever-changing beauty of God's year. We, too, in bed and border, tree and shrub, are eager to drink life to the lees.

145

## OF GARDENS

Not only the poets and the gardeners are aware of this. Philosophers know it, too, for they are poets at heart. We have spoken of Bacon at St. Albans. His essay *Of Gardens* surely is poetry in prose and as true as when he penned it. Speaking of his seasons, he says: "God Almighty first planted a garden." It is unfortunate that we, in our day, so easily forget the verities in our search for truth. "And indeed," Bacon goes on, "it is the purest of human pleasures. It is the greatest refreshment to the spirits of man. . . ."

Month by month, he lists his favourites, blossom and bloom and scent. We could do worse than read him now and then by way of refreshing our own souls.

In England more than here there seems to be a flair for wildflowers as well as for scent, perhaps because as a people the Anglo-Saxons love and know the land as few others do. They cannot long keep out the flowers and the scents.

> "Here's lavender and love and sweet wild thyme,
> And dreams and bluebells that the fairies chime,
> Here's meadow-sweet and moonlight, bound in posies,
> With ragged-robin, traveller's-joy and roses,
> And here—just three leaves from a weeping willow;
> And here—that's best—deep poppies for your pillow."

Shadow-of-a-Leaf, in Sherwood, knew his woodland well.

## A TIME TO PLAN

In July, with luck, we have a chance to think a bit and plan. Half the year has gone by now. We planned in January for spring and summer. Now we can have a look at things and see what is needed for the next six months. Perennial borders may be perennial, but they are not presentable very long without care. Weak spots show up. When they do, our scale plan and our colour scheme must be considered in replacements. A seven-foot hollyhock does not go well in a foreground of a one-foot Cupid zinnia. A startling crimson naturally will not keep the peace with the cool pastels of some of its neighbours. Most perennials tend to spread—some more than others. July is a good month to note this. Plants need not be disturbed now, but notes should be made of what needs replanting, what colours must be checked or encouraged, what must come out altogether.

## THE GARDEN RECORD

Then there are the complete changes. Beer and skittles every day will pall in time. Without notes and a useable system of filing them in our record book, it would soon be impossible for us to remember from season to season just what changes we had in mind. In order to help in this, we use a month-by-month file, geared for next year's planting, with a tickler reference check that we have a look at regularly. For example, this July we noted that our east and south borders in the upper garden were short in white *Phlox suffruticosa,* the Miss Lingard variety. That fact has been entered in our work-to-do file. In the tickler file, we have another notation reminding us to order the phlox in September of this year for fall planting. When the planting moment arrives, the second check is there to see that we attend to it.

A simple calendar serves both purposes. Already there are things in it that must be seen to next June. To make this planning—and, what is more important—the execution of our plans—more easy still, we try to do our gardening equipped with a pencil stub and a small pad or notebook in our pocket.

## OUR FRIENDS' GARDEN

In other people's gardens we use our eyes and try to remember the cream, hoping that our good friends will not resent too much such filching of ideas. After all, it is a compliment. The poets have been at it for ages and some even admit it. Did not Kipling tell us:

"When 'Omer smote 'is blooming lyre,
He'd 'eard men sing by land and sea;
An' what 'e thought 'e might require,
'E went an' took—the same as me!"

Gardening is one of the rare, more cherished bonds, as hunting and climbing and all the field sports are. Rivalry is there, of course, and the natural spur of jealousy that stings so shrewdly but serves us a good turn when we grow torpid or settle on the lees. We could not do without the pain of seeing our best friends surpass us. One delight that any garden can give (but often does not) is that of reviving memories of happy days elsewhere. Few memories are keener than the scent or the sight of a flower or a shrub. Our garden here is purposely filled with such things. We have spoken already of some of them: stonecrop on the ha-ha wall, reminding us of the Blue Ridge, misty and cool against a June sunset years ago; wild thyme on the terrace—how that carries us back across the sea, and the years, to the slopes of a well-loved glen in the Highlands; the trumpet-creeper bringing to mind a Virginia lane with scarlet trumpets clustered on the fence post, an ordered line of cedars stretching up the hill; terns on the wall—how rich they are in memories of arctic fjords and ice-fields by the Circle; and the autumn crocuses, bringing back Baden in the fall and meadows by the Black Forest where oxen steam at the heavy wains. There are many more and we love them all, for in each we can re-live high moments, the white-stone days, as they used to call them. Our foxgloves and bluebells speak straight to the heart of Devon or Dorset lanes. Low yews carry us in memory to some wind-swept shoulder of the Rockies—Assiniboine snow-capped ahead, our pack train resting in the swale below.

Mountain laurel—and we have much of it—comes high in our rating, for always it brings to mind our happiest hours on the hills, brave days on rock and all the sweetness of the upland skies. Such a day is vivid now, a day of working downward through laurel-hells, well lost above the Little Pigeon—the slope almost sheer as we lowered ourselves, my friend and I, from laurel root to root, until we met the inevitable headwall, bare as a bald man's pate, below us. We had no rope, but made a flesh-and-blood one as my friend, holding firm to a laurel at the edge of the cliff, dangled his body over the lip while I went down him, as though he were a rope, until I was hanging in my turn at arm's length from his ankle. Scarcely accepted mountain technique, but it worked. Six inches below my toes was a tiny ledge—our halfway goal. To let go that clutched ankle was appalling, but no one could hang forever. So let go I did and dropped, landing with relief on the ledge, while my friend, in his turn, let go the laurel and came down with a bump on my shoulder, thence, *courte échelle,* over my back, just as I had come down over his.

My interest in that laurel bush and its holding potential must have struck deeply, for I rarely see one, even in the quiet of our garden, without feeling again that clutch at an ankle—that stretch of toes that would not reach the outcrop.

Rhododendrons remind us of the slabs above the Duck Hawk, knife-edged, sleek with rain, lying like gigantic shingles on a roof fantastically pitched, with every hold reversed and never a nick to take a finger. Our garden brings these memories back to us sweeter for the rough spots on the way, just as it brings again to us the kindliness of friends and well-remembered mirth and all the happy give and take of life that make the world so precious for our savouring.

## JULY CHECK LIST

Summer has struck its pace now. There is plenty of work in our gardens, but pressure is levelling off a bit. Also, July is a month to look ahead.

Cuttings should be made now for winter indoor plants—geraniums, fuchsias, begonias, and the like. Others may be seeded. Pinch back annuals as well as perennials to avoid leggy growth.

If July is dry, as it frequently is, keep up a regular and thorough watering, slow and deep. A good soaking once a week is far more valuable than a daily sprinkling that takes time but never gets below the surface. This holds good for the lawn as well as for the garden. Dahlias, chrysanthemums, and roses need constant watering.

Weeding never really ends till fall, but regular weeding now spells less work later. Mulching does more than anything else to keep down weeds. Remember a good mulch also conserves moisture where it is needed most.

July is a good month to divide madonna lilies and iris. It is also not too early to seed perennials for next year's blossoming: such things as foxgloves, delphiniums, columbines, English daisies, hearts-ease, and pansies. Mignonette, however, seeded now, will bloom by autumn.

Be sure to nip off the side-shoots of dahlias. This makes for finer flowers. Keep dahlias well watered always. This cannot be overemphasized.

Feed roses after each period of bloom. Remove faded blossoms as they pass their prime. This is true for all flowers.

By July, house plants that have blossomed during the winter should have been cut back, re-potted and dug in to the top of the pots in some cool and shady place.

Keep on with insecticide spraying or dusting. Japanese beetles add to our troubles in July. There seems to be little that we can do about them except pick and kill. Luckily the starlings help us a bit.

Be alert against mildew and fungus in July. Powdered sulphur or one of the commercial sprays or dusts will help enormously with phlox, roses, lilacs, and chrysanthemums. See that phlox especially is not smothered by being bundled to a stake too tightly. Circulation of air is essential to all plants.

Powdered sulphur also combats fungus and mildew in clematis.

Nicotine sulphate, rotenone, or pyrethrum serve against the usual hordes of enemies that vex us in midsummer—aphids, oyster-shell scale, red spider and the rest. Spray weekly now—roses, especially.

Shrubs need attention in midsummer. Look for borers in flowering almonds, flowering crabs, and the dogwoods.

Try miscible oil if scale shows up in the lilacs, magnolias, or other shrubs. For scale in euonymus use a miscible oil spray in July when the leaves are fully out, and again in August. Euonymus should also be sprayed in spring before the leaves are out, if scale is suspected.

Nicotine sulphate retards lace-bug damage in azaleas.

For fire-blight, wherever it occurs, cut off and burn all infected branches. This is a must.

For lace-bug injury to rhododendrons spray the leaves with a 50 per cent wettable DDT powder.

The sooner we spray in spring and early summer, the less injury will occur from pests, of course. And the less spraying required as the season progresses.

Lawns in July can be a problem. Crab grass and fall grass appear. Beetle damage shows up. Chinch bugs start working. Potassium cyanate, carefully used, will discourage crab grass. Nicotine sulphate spray, DDT powder, 1 per cent rotenone dust (25 pounds to 1,000 square feet)—all are useful against chinch bugs. 2-4D helps kill dandelions and plantain. Mercury compounds serve against brown-spot and pythium disease.

Be sure to let the lawn grass reach 1½ to 2 inches in the humid weather of July. This will help keep down fall grass and also offset disease by keeping the grass roots cool as they must be.

Watering, dusting, spraying, feeding, weeding, mulch renewals are July chores. So is the thinning out of zinnias and other seedlings that are crowding one another. Order fall-flowering bulbs now, such as colchicums and the fall crocuses. They can be a never-ending delight.

# CHAPTER VIII

# AUGUST

## *The Month of Thanksgiving*

The first of August, as many people are aware, has been known—ecclesiastically at least—from the earliest time as Lammas Day or Lammastide, but few of us are likely to remember the reason. It comes naturally enough, as so many of our older words have come to us, from the Anglo-Saxon. *Hlāfmaesse* in the old tongue meant *hlāf* or loaf plus *maesse* or Mass, that is, the loaf for the Mass. This, of course, does not refer to the Consecrated Element, The Bread of the Eucharist. The hlāfmaesse or loaf for the Mass—in English "Lammas"—means the loaves of bread baked from the first ripe wheat of the year, which were carried to the churches in every English village at Lammastide as a harvest festival, a thanksgiving for the season's bounty. What is known in the Bible as a feast of ingathering at the year's end. Lammas, really, is our older Thanksgiving Day, a custom known and faithfully observed by clergy and people for centuries before the Pilgrims, who had done away with the festivals of the church, felt the lack of them and had to think up a Thanksgiving of their own.

### LAMMASTIDE

Obviously, the fourth Thursday of November, as we celebrate it, is not so appropriate a day for harvest home as is the season of the year's first garnered wheat, but these things do not happen by chance. In Britain the seasons come earlier than with us. Midsummer falls in June, which we are likely to regard as the beginning of

152

summer. The harvest of the corn comes in late July and August. And we must keep in mind that the English word "corn" means grain and that it usually connotes wheat, never our Indian maize. In this country, however, our corn—the maize—is not cut until September. In the olden days it was always shocked. It still is in many places. Later, in October and November, when other chores on the farm have eased a bit, these shocks are overturned and husking begins, so that the actual harvesting of our grain crop (originally maize) was not finished until well into November, a month that would be regarded as winter on the other side.

## NAPKINS OF THE FAIRIES

Lammastide has been associated with heavy rains in Britain—the so-called Lammas floods. In Ireland, it stands for floods and the lifting of the new potatoes. Here, Lammas, indeed most of August, stands for the dog days—heat, humidity, holidays, and drought. But none of the four troublemakers should really worry us; they cannot last long now. We sense that. Nights are cooler—though we sometimes doubt it. Heavy dews show on the lawns at dawn. Grass picks up. Now and then a bejeweled cobweb in the garden reminds us of fall and September on their way. Thoreau calls the cobwebs "little napkins of the fairies spread on the grass." What an eye he had for seeing things. How great a heart for understanding what he saw.

August, really our midsummer more than June, carries us forward with many a hint of autumn in the air. August is never a resting, waiting month, as July can often be. Every moment reminds us of something to be done, that *must* be done, in bed and border. And all that we do is coloured in our minds by a longing for the cooler days ahead—a hunger and a yearning in our hearts for September and October and their resurgence of bloom, for the fresh greening of the grass, and for all the mellow glory of the turning leaves ahead. August can be every whit as exciting as April, so rich it is with promise. There is an end of midsummer resting.

## STIR OF LIFE

Life stirs again despite oppressive heat and burned-out lawns. All sorts of new blossoms begin to shape up. Chrysanthemums are almost ready now to fill our borders with their gold. The day-lilies have a happy trick of breaking once more into bloom. Fall asters, perhaps not fully blooming, are heavy nonetheless with opening buds. Strawflowers remind us that now is the time to watch their ripening so that we may cut them at the proper moment, just before their prime, and dry them for winter. Cornflowers, cosmos, calendulas, phlox, white vinca, fuchsias, begonias, gaillardias, houndstongue, petunias, all the dahlias, and all the zinnias are at their prime. Early marigolds bloom afresh while later ones are just beginning to flower. We may be sure they will keep at it until frost. Few months can *seem* to offer less in the garden than a dry August, yet give us more. Again it is anticipation that lends such zest—a feeling that the worst of the heat will soon be over, that the midsummer droughts must break, that the dulled green of our borders will soon be as fresh as ever spring could make them.

## FALL GLORY

Best of all, we know that colour is on the way: the scarlet challenge of the maples and dogwoods afire in the sun, the tawny russet of the oaks, the minted gold of the beeches, and all the pageantry of field and forest soon to match the splendours that will come to our jaded borders. Few can resist the glory of the fall—

> "When the maple turns to crimson
> And the sassafras to gold."

Though heat belies it, all sorts of fall and winter things are stirring. As early as the first week of August we have often watched the foxhounds at twilight put into covert, huntsman and whippers in on foot beside them, all eager to taste the scent of a cub once more and make the leafy woodland sweet with cry. We have thrilled to the sound of the hunting horn and the crack of a hunting-thong in air, warning new entry that fox is fox and they'd best know it. 'Ware wing! 'Ware hare! Or else!

At dawn, even in August, dew-soaked to the waist, we have followed the lively foot-beagles, entering this year's youngsters, like the foxhounds, except these are to hare. All this is winter work, of course, but the first high rapture of it comes in August twilights and in August dawns for those who can forerun the sun. Many an August morning in the old days we left kennel with the foxhounds a full hour before the faintest hint of light had touched the Tredyffrin hills, jogging through the misty by-ways so as to reach covertside as trees began to stir in the greying of the dawn. Aye, August is a living month and nowhere more so than in the garden.

## THE BULBS

One of the first things we try to do now is order and plant our fall-flowering bulbs. Usually, we have ordered them long ago, but by late August they should be in the ground—colchicums and autumn crocuses especially.

Speaking of bulbs, too many of us refer to everything that looks like an onion as a bulb. Actually, the onion *is* a bulb, but other things much like it may be corms or tubers or rhizomes or even tuberous roots. By way of definition, a bulb is an underground bud made up of overlapping scales that can be peeled off it. The bulb contains within itself its future stem, its flower bud, and its leaves. Further, the bulb serves as a storehouse for its own food. The lily, the colchicum (meadow saffron), the narcissus, and the daffodil are examples of bulbs. A corm, though like a bulb, is solid, lacking scales or a covering of concentric skins. The crocus is a corm. Tubers, like potatoes, are thick or roundish underground stems containing buds or eyes. Oxalis is a tuber. Strictly speaking, dahlias are not tubers, although we often refer to them as such. A dahlia grows from a tuberous root. A rhizome as found in iris, is actually a sort of

155

stolon, a trailing branch or runner that has rooted again at its tip and node. Strawberry plants send out true stolons. When a stolon goes underground or partially underground, as it does with iris, it is known as a rhizome. It is from bulbs, corms, tubers, tuberous roots, and rhizomes that our so-called bulb plants are reproduced and nourished.

## AUTUMN FLOWERING BULBS

There are many varieties of autumn bulbs, but the sternbergias, the colchicums, and the crocuses are our favourites. *Sternbergia lutea,* which we delight in, is an exceptionally beautiful flower, some two inches in size, pure gold in colour. We wish that we had hundreds of them clumped against the green of ferns or by the myrtle bank.

Sternbergia does not like too wet a footing; it can stand a certain amount of soil acidity. The leaves are a true green and delicately speared—a great addition to the flowers.

## COLCHICUMS

Colchicum should be planted in August. It flowers with us in September and October. There is a trick about the colchicums that fooled us in our salad days when we were green in judgment. When they blossom in the fall they have no leaves whatever. In spring, though lacking any hint of blossom, they do send up plenty of leaves. Several times in the old days we forgot that this foliage belonged to the fall-blooming colchicums so, when no blossoms appeared, we just pulled the bulbs up as a loss. Now, knowing their loveliness, we spare them in the spring and enjoy them in the fall.

Colchicums, as sternbergia, like rather dry soil and a touch of acidity. The old name "meadow saffron" is not used enough these days, as new colour and fresh varieties come in. The original meadow saffron, *Crocus sativus,* is usually purple, its stigma orange in colour. We plant both sternbergia and colchicum below our library window. As we get more of them, we shall try them among the myrtle and euonymus on the bank.

## AUTUMN CROCUS

Our autumn crocuses (*speciosus albus*) this year also have gone in by the library window. Others have grown for years at the foot of the garden walls. It is the autumn crocus that surprises us now and then by blooming in January. Usually we plant their corms in late August and they are in flower by early fall.

## LATE SEEDING

Next on our list of August chores comes the seeding of violas, pansies, and heartsease, ordered in July. We seed them in well-prepared soil, where they can get a start before frost and where they can be covered in midwinter with salt hay. August, as has been said, is the time to seed most of next year's biennials and perennials.

## TRANSPLANTING

The transplanting of flowers, some of it, can be done in August, but we try to keep our transplanting in summer to a minimum. Chrysanthemums, even in full bloom, are easily moved. The trick is to get the new site ready first, well fertilized and water-soaked; then lift the plant with as large a ball of earth about its roots as the spade will hold. Virginia bluebell can be moved in August, for it is completely dormant now, but unless the site of a clump has been marked in spring—June at the latest—it is hard to know just where its roots are. Mertensia leaves fade in late spring, then wither away. Often, by August, the last trace of them has disappeared. If located, however, the Virginia bluebells must be moved with plenty of earth and as undisturbed a root clump as possible. In transplanting any flowers in August, unless there has been plenty of rain, it is well to soak the plant thoroughly a day or two before you plan to move it. This will prevent the ball of earth from crumbling when lifted. Iris can be transplanted in August—in fact, that is the best month to do this with them.

## TOPPING PHLOX

One task, above all others, must be faithfully performed in August or the garden may be ruined next year; certainly any colour scheme is almost sure to be. Watch phlox, whatever its colour or variety, and cut off the flower heads before they go to seed. If this is not done, the phlox is likely to reseed itself and blossom next summer in colours you may not wish. Cool and frosty whites especially may revert to magenta. By care in topping phlox like this, we have managed to keep our white phlox for years—save for a few reseeded strays. With much phlox this cutting back of the flower heads also tends to produce bushiness and new bloom, so that we always count on some phlox blossoming from June until frost. What a godsend this is in our warm and dry midsummer weather.

## AUGUST CUTTINGS

Another August chore is the taking of cuttings from our begonias, geraniums, impatiens, plumbago, vinca, shrimp plant, and the rest. These are set out in sandy soil made more friable with peat-moss, to be potted later and, still later, brought indoors for our winter window. The re-potting of house plants follows hard upon our cuttings, but sometimes this is not done until September. In re-potting we take care to see that the pots are thoroughly clean. We try to use the richest soil we have, reinforced with fertilizer. Humus is essential. To obtain it we dig deep in our compost pile, where leaves have been rotting for at least two years.

## THE COMPOST PILES

Actually we have two compost heaps: one is made up of leaves that are not too acid, such as hackberry, apple, dogwood and maple;

158

the other is composed of oak leaves and pine and hemlock needles. This compost we keep for our azaleas, rose-bay rhododendrons, and the mountain laurel. By separating the strongly acid leaves and needles from the others, we get two useful and distinct types of humus. The acid sort must be avoided in potting or re-potting house plants.

## AUGUST ORDERS

August is an awakening month. Nearly every thing comes to life with a rush. Spring bulbs should be ordered now, that is, those to be planted in the fall so as to flower in spring: jonquils, daffodils, narcissus, hyacinth, tulips, snow crocuses, snowflakes, snowdrops, scillas, dogtooth violets, winter aconites, and chionodoxas—the lovely glory-of-the-snow. Also, oxalis and paper narcissus for the winter indoors. Freesias, *Tritonia crocata, Ardisia crispa, Tulbaghia violacea,* and *Jacobinia carnea* are ordered at this time for use indoors later.

Year by year, we make our budget for bulbs, then, weakening, exceed it. How many thousands have gone in here through the years it would be hard to compute, but in the end we have not begrudged them a penny of cost. Beauty can transcend price.

## DAY-BY-DAY

August work also includes the usual mixed bag of chores that must be attended to promptly. Among them is the noting of new bloom week by week.

1 August—watered upper lawn. Hand-picked crab grass there. Larkspur now in bloom in the south border.

2 August—zinnias and plumbago in fullest bloom.

3 August—dusted and fed roses. Tied up such phlox and dahlias as needed it. They had been staked long ago. Weed-killer on plantain and dandelions on rear lawn—a good dose this time *pour encourager les autres.*

159

4 August—clipped that maddening ivy on the lower windows and doors. There is no discharge in that war. Some late poppies suddenly in bloom. In the wild garden, alum root in blossom. Probably out for a good while, but not checked. Coreopsis in bloom.

6 August—weeded and cultivated east and south borders. Dahlias are really abundant there now and most lovely in colour. Bordeaux mixture on some of the roses. Tidied up the front bank. Staked the outline of the new south border which is to be moved some five feet forward this fall, out of the shade that now curtails growth at its back. Fall asters, a lovely blue, now out. We love them.

7 August—worked on the plantain and dandelions. Week by week we keep at it. Though patience be a tired mare, so we are told, yet she will plod.

8 August—watered upper lawn. Had work started today on transforming a root-cellar we have not used for years into a workable potting-shed, something we have long needed. It took a deal of doing to smash the reinforced concrete roof of the root-cellar, after a foot of earth had been shoveled off it. Blue lobelias and coreopsis blooming nicely.

9 August—more water on upper lawns. The drought has now been with us since May—with the exception of a shower or so in June. Broad-leaved evergreens suffer terribly in such weather, but we cannot water them all. Pruned the virgin's-bower from the branches of the pink dogwood outside the lower garden wall. Moved from above the terrace ha-ha to the terrace border 6 dianthus—3 Irene and 3 Silver Mine. Carnations need a good deal of sun.

10 August—planted ivy on west wall of the new potting-shed. We had saved it from the wall of the root-cellar. Not much is wasted here or thrown away. Watered lawn again. Watered terrace flowers and also such rhododendrons as showed the worst need for it. Day by day, the drought tells. In places the surface of the ground has cracked as we have never seen it do before. A man can put his fingers deep down where the parched soil has split.

13 August—ordered fall bulbs for spring flowering. An appalling number for us this year—892 bulbs, all told, but again we could not resist the promise of their loveliness in spring. Are gardeners sane?

15 August—new potting-shed finished today. It has a fine workshelf, high enough to be comfortable, under a wide window. There are storage

shelves on two sides for putting away pots and saucers and all the other gear. Pails are in place for sand and humus and peat-moss and good rich soil. An added luxury is a high bar-stool to use as a sort of shooting-stick or rest when working long at the bench. Cockscomb in blossom. Also penstemon and sundrops. Put in 10 European pennyroyal plants by the fountain. We love their aroma, so cool it is in high summer.

16 August—ordered 3 new climbing roses for fall planting. We have always put in our roses during early spring. This is a try at fall plant-ing. Watered ferns. Gathered first drop of our apples for sauce. Day-flowers and rose of Sharon blooming nicely.

17 August—put in four new chrysanthemums in the east border and transplanted 3 more to spots that needed something to succour their lack of colour.

18 August—edged borders, where the grass had encroached. Dug up an arborvitae under one of the west windows. Badly sited there. Cut back all white phlox that had gone to seed. Hand-weeded crab grass where it showed. Prepared a place by the trellis for the new climbing roses when they go in later this year. Found time, on the terrace at tea, to watch a hummingbird poise delicately in flight, as they do, while sipping nectar from every blossom of a shrimp plant. Usually they visit the fuchsias. The shrimp plant had over twenty-five flowers open.

19 August—slug-shot on all roses. Watered lower garden and the new planting of myrtle and ilex by the parking-place.

21 August—put out 7 more chrysanthemums.

22 August—pruned old canes from climbing roses. Looked into the possibilities of more herbs for next year's herb border. We now have the magic nine—plus two. Lavender, rosemary, sage, hellebore, comfrey, rue, vervain, verbena mint, wormwood, marjoram, and camomile. All are not easy to get, nor to grow.

23 August—virgin's-bower most lovely and most fragrant just in opening bloom.

24 August—weeded drive banks where swamp-maple saplings have a way of springing up all summer among the euonymus. Clipped back ivy runners at base of garden walls.

25 August—refastened climbing roses on the lych-gate. Transplanted an inkberry shrub from the terrace to a likely spot below the kitchen window. Clipped back the ivy on the upper summer-house, the little

gazabo that serves as a tool-house, as well, for the upper borders. Picked lots of dahlias and zinnias for vases indoors. By this date we had reached some 150 different varieties of bloom—by far our best year in spite of a most devastating drought.

26 August—put up two strips of small-meshed poultry wire on either side of the library window to help the silver-fleece vine and the climbing hydrangea take hold. Both are doing nicely there. Fed all roses. The floribundas really come to life in the early fall, when the beetles begin to ease off on their forays and cooler weather encourages bloom. Sprayed all roses. Asters are in lovely blossom. Beagled with the Treweryn this morning at dawn. A brace of hare put up in the stubble and chivvied about in the finest style. Called off as the dew lifted. Home for breakfast and work in the garden.

28 August—planted 20 autumn crocuses and 20 colchicums in lower garden border.

30 August—clipped and trained a few roses in lower garden beds. Staked one of the floribundas there, as it seemed to need a bit of bracing.

31 August—intensely hot and humid. Summer still can sting. We need rain most terribly. Dug out 6 peony clumps that have stopped blooming where they are. Separated the clumps and re-planted four of them under the dining room window, where the arborvitae has been dug up and removed. In the old days we used to grow hollyhocks here, tremendous fellows they were, reaching far over our heads. Perhaps the peonies may take on a new lease of life for the soil has been heavily fertilized and there is plenty of sun. Every so often peonies must be divided. They do not, however, like being moved.


## SUMMER DROUGHT

August can challenge us with heat and drought and sap the bravest of our good intents with humidity, but the real bite of summer has gone. Either that or our hopes are so high for the cooler days and richer colours of the fall that we do not mind the present weather. In our climate a prolonged, late-summer drought can be serious. If there be little rain in late spring and still less in summer, there is always the chance that the drought may hold until frost.

162

When this happens, we are indeed sore let and hindered for the ground may freeze before it is properly soaked. This means the springs will be low at the start of winter and brooks and streams even lower. Nothing could be worse because winter rains, if we have them, run off frozen ground instead of seeping in properly for storage. Should there be little snowfall (we have had none at all for the past three years) spring may come with the ground still dangerously parched and no reserves in the springs themselves. This starts another year off in a cycle of drought.

## EYES THAT SEE NOT

It is a commentary—and a saddening one—on our urban point of view to note how many people are wholly unaware of weather, especially of any lack of rain. It is disheartening to realize how little many of us know of the immediate world we live in—even of the most familiar things. How many of our friends, for instance, neighbours living in the country with us, can walk a mile down a country lane and name the wildflowers that make that wayside glorious? Yet we see these flowers every day, and surely, we enjoy their colour and beauty.

How many can tell the trees that cool these lanes with their shade or those that grow in the coppice on the hill? How many of us can read and adore the beauty so majestically spread above us in the starry cope of heaven? We know the Dipper? Well, we have at least made a start. How many—they will be few indeed—have the vaguest idea of the wildlife that lives so vividly and in such numbers all about us?

## THE EARTHS

There is joy past the telling in knowing, year by year, where the vixens have their earths and how cleverly they teach their cubs each summer to stalk and to hunt, lessons that go on evening after evening, perhaps in a neighbouring wood, quite unknown to us. It would surprise many people if they knew how close that fox's earth may be to their own doors.

Only a year ago, at midnight, a great dog fox, golden coated, drifted with the unmistakable glide, yet deceiving speed of his kind, across the beams of our headlights in Fairmount Park, with miles and miles of built-up city around him.

## UNDERCOVER FOLK

Hare, cottontails, woodchucks, coons and possums, muskrats, foxes (red and grey)—even the white-tailed deer of the mountain, are all about us, as are the bob-whites and the pheasants, the wild geese, ducks, and herons, though one must look for them. Not half a mile from our cottage door, right now, two brace of foxes, perhaps more, are thriving in a woodland covert—undreamed of by most of our neighbours. Only last evening a long-legged fox cub again crossed our headlights' beam scarcely a mile from home.

## THE OLDER WORLD

How can anyone living in the country or even in the suburbs be blind to the thrill of a tracking snow when all the story of the night is written there to read—a record of neighbours we may not have known we had? Naturally we do no snow-reading in August, but the life of the world is there, just the same. Busy and vivid in tree and shrub and flower, in the note of a bird or the high-pitched bark of a fox at midnight—shrill, skin-pricking, so strangely wild it is, coming to us from that older world we pretend we have forgotten, yet are always aware of. Or perhaps we find a hint of that world in the sudden plummet of a diving night-hawk, as the wind hums through the plunging feathers. Few sounds in nature are so tensed with the wilderness as that.

Actually all of us are closer to our forebears than we imagine—until something strikes a note that speaks to us through the patina of civilization; then we see how thin that patina can be. It is good for man to sense his old home about him now and then—the living world of glade and forest, pelt and wing, that he has known infinitely longer than any other.

## GOD'S HOUSE

We have not lived at all, actually, until we find the magic and the witchery of life for ourselves. The garden is as good a place as any to begin. And a country lane is not bad either. Juggling Jerry knew whereof he spoke:

> "Better than mortar, brick and putty
> Is God's house on a blowing day."

Indeed, it is.

Men have hunted far and wide for the elixir, the philosopher's stone, that would make them less unhappy and keep them young and give them all that their hearts are seeking, but it is unlikely they will find what they are after in a city's fester of grime and noise and strain that harries to the marrow of the bone.

It is not without meaning for us that Christ the Saviour, when He had the need to think, went always to a desert place apart and there found unity with God. August is the time to find something of this in our own world, something that may help us to be more at one with God ourselves in the harmony of the ordered world He has created, but which man so pitilessly destroys.

## DRYING FOR WINTER

August is, for one thing, the time to start gathering some of the midsummer wildflowers so as to dry them for winter use. Garden strawflowers are not the only blossoms we use for this. Some of the bonesets and thoroughworts, pearly everlasting, bittersweet, broomsedge, ironweed, joe-pie, or wild bergamot can easily be dried, for they are stout-stemmed and holding. Early goldenrod shows in

August, but we have never had any luck in making it retain colour. Also if not cut just at its prime, it will crumble too easily. Most delicate flowers such as jewel-weed, are obviously unsuited for drying, as the leaves and blossoms wither at a touch. It pays, however, to see what the dusty roadsides of August have to offer to supplement our garden's store. There will be much. If you draw blank and can find nothing that appeals, at least, near some neighbouring wood, the scent of pennyroyal may repay you for your trouble. Many a time we have plucked a handful of this tiny herb and rubbed its leaves and stems between our palms, then filled our pockets—the sharp, cool savour of it reminding us long afterwards of woodland coverts. Mint, of course, is always a mnemonic, bringing to mind the wayside spring.

## UPS AND DOWNS

Our interest in wildflowers led us in the end to making some use of our banks and levels, especially of the steep gully already described. Here, at the cottage, these different grades proved first a bane, but now a blessing. We have five levels and are the better for them all. Trying to work a car up our driveway in winter, after an ice storm or when damp snow has melted and then frozen as slick as a frog's hind leg, is disheartening, to put it mildly, until sand and chains have helped us snatch a foothold. On such days it would be difficult for anyone to see much advantage in our hill. During most of the year, however, these five levels have made easy all sorts of planting and planting effects, especially those of distance and depth that would have been unobtainable had our small place been all on the same plane.

## FIVE LEVELS

We count the first level—our datum-plane, as it were—that of the road. Here our trees, mostly oaks, begin. There is no sidewalk. Here, too, are our summer-sweet bushes, *Clethra alnifolia,* and back of them, a very steep bank planted with ferns, lilies-of-the-valley, mountain laurel and, nearer the top, just along the garden wall but outside of it, clumps of dogwood and hemlock and viburnum, so placed that we may have the evergreen boughs of the hemlocks as a backdrop for our wall in winter and the blossoms of the dogwoods and viburnums to brighten the top of the wall in spring as we see them from inside the garden.

The second level, coming up from the road, is that of the driveway by the door. Here there are two flanking shrubbery and myrtle beds with one border, below the library window—all of them approximately on the same level. Three steps lead up to the lych-gate and the third level of the cottage terrace inside it. Once within the walled garden, five steps lead down from the terrace to the fourth level—that which we have called the lower garden beds. The upper garden, across the drive from the house, constitutes our fifth level, for it is separated from the driveway by our myrtle bank and reached by seven steps of fieldstone.

## THE BANKS

It can be seen that these varying levels, while vexatious and troublesome before they were planted, have now added enormously to our planning for vistas, no matter how tiny these vistas may be. At the start, the slopes between levels were bare and grass would not thrive there. In the end, we carpeted our slopes with pachysandra and periwinkle and euonymus. The driveway, flanked by very steep banks, has euonymus on either side, filled in spring with daffodils and Virginia bluebells. The slope below the upper garden is covered with blue myrtle. Here it is that the squills are spreading. South of the upper garden steps, sweet honeysuckle covers the bank. We have kept that gadding vine in bounds for years by the simple expedient of ramming the lawnmower into it once a week all summer. The edge of the honeysuckle is persistent, but it has not encroached six inches onto the lawn since we put it there. Obviously, there is no particular daintiness of touch in our mower technique. One cannot hurt the feelings of honeysuckle.

Inside the garden wall, the slope below the terrace is covered by spurge—the pachysandra—and it gives the garden almost as green a setting in winter as in summer, especially when backed by English ivy on the walls and hollies, cherry laurel, and leucothoe in the beds. Daffodils are also in flower each spring, clumped here and there among the pachysandra and in the beds.

## PACHYSANDRA AND MYRTLE

One thing we found out early about myrtle and pachysandra as well as euonymus. The planting and the initial care pay off just as handsomely as they do with flowers. Before setting out the myrtle and the rest, we spaded the banks deeply and broke up the heavy clods. We then fertilized generously, using some cow manure, now hard to get and expensive. Bone-meal we did not spare. Nor did we spare a deep and thorough watering. Once the plants were in, we mulched up to four or five inches with peat-moss and watered regularly through the first year. As a matter of fact, we mulched and watered all banks for two or even three years in dry spells until they were completely covered by a rich deep growth and so could hold moisture by themselves. Even in this summer of appalling drought, hot dry winds, and high temperatures, our banks have kept as green as ever with no watering at all. They say that August has been the second driest August recorded here. We can readily believe it.

## OVER THE YEARS

Naturally, all this planting was not done at once. We could not possibly have afforded it. A bank at a time, the barest and those closest to the house were tackled first. The steep gully, to the east of our drive, was only attended to last year and the work on the wild garden above it has scarcely begun. The great thing is the mulching and the watering. Given a decent start, the most hopeless bank, arid and steep, can be transformed into as cool and lovely a part of the garden as any of the rest. Fall and spring bulbs bring colour aplenty. Best of all, a bank will remain green in the deepest of winter.

## THE LAWN AGAIN

We have spoken earlier of the care necessary if we hope to start a new lawn off right or to maintain an old one. Such care is needed in spring, of course, but early fall is the paramount season to do the real work, whether it be making a lawn or refurbishing an old one. It is most important to plan for this in August, because the actual work on the lawn, old or new, should begin as close to Labor Day as possible. In a real drought it is useless to attempt the seeding of grass. In a normal August, however, it is time to decide what should be done in September.

## THE WILDFLOWER CORNER

A start has been made on our wildflower corner, but August is one of the best months of the year to see which of the larger wildflowers we lack and just which sort would be suitable for the area in question. Small spring flowers, delicate and always beloved, are the first essentials for any wild garden, especially one limited in size. Midsummer and fall bloom, however, have at least some place and, if they be sited properly, will in no wise interfere with the less obtrusive flowers you may have already set out among the ferns and rocks.

## HINTS FROM THE NEAR-BY LANE

It pays to reconnoitre a near-by lane or shady glen to note what is in bloom, where it is growing, what kind of soil it seems to favour, how much or how little sun or shade it likes and how much or how little moisture it has at hand. Colour comes to our countryside especially in late August. You will find innumerable hints of what you may care to use in your own garden. The popularity of wild gardens, on a small scale, is growing every year, as attested by the number of nurserymen who are now specializing in wildflowers. The reason is obvious: few people nowadays can think of a formal garden of size. Gardens are smaller—they must be—and less formal in plan. This informality has led to the wildflower corner or slope or what you will.

## SHADE

The background of any wildflower area must include trees (size is of no particular moment, so long as they provide a good deal of shade), some weathered rock, and plenty of wood fern. Smaller plants, the spring sorts, naturally should be clumped near the path where we can see them. By "path" is meant the opening, the winding way between trees or rocks or laurel bushes. It may be only a few yards in length; that makes no difference. It must, however, look like a natural opening in the wood. The more leaves on it, the better, both for their loveliness of colour and for the essential moisture that they hold close to the ground where wildflowers need it.

## TOUCHES OF FALL

A little back from the path some open spots usually are found, on one or both sides of the way. These seem made for the planting of taller wildflowers: the midsummer goldenrods, boneset, joe-pie, wild phlox, ironweed, wild sunflowers, blue dayflowers, chicory, white wood asters, the lovely blue asters (glorious if massed), the cardinal-flower, and the blue lobelia. With luck, perhaps, you may have false foxglove, always difficult to move, and the snowdrops which are easily moved. The August countryside fairly glows with beauty, especially as hints of autumn weather appear. Wild lilies are gorgeous in bloom and should never be overlooked. There are several varieties—the wood lily, the Turk's cap, and the field-lily—all of them common in our neighbourhood. Lady's-slippers, of course, are something to boast of and worth any sort of trouble to have among

170

your ferns. They tend to bloom in June. Please do not dig them up in somebody else's wood and move them to your own garden without explicit permission to do so. No one should dig up any wildflower unless it is obviously abundant in the vicinity and well able to take care of itself. Even then, permission should be obtained from the owner of the property.

Ladies'-tresses and the rattlesnake-plantain; bouncing-bet; the campions; catch-fly, virgin's-bower, if you have a place for it to clamber over; monkshood; cinquefoil; the wild rose; wood-sorrel; milkwort; jewel-weed, if you have moisture enough for it; mallow; St. John's-wort; Queen-Anne's lace; wintergreen; the gentians; dogbane; heal-all; bee-balm; milkweed; butterfly-weed; blue vervain; nightshade; thorn-apple; moth-mullein—or even the taller Aaron's-rod; turtle-head; the harebell—if you are lucky enough to make it grow, few flowers are more lovely; black-eyed-Susan; cone-flower; feverfew; yarrow; tansy; hawk-weed—all these are treasures to be considered, most of them in August. The countryside is richer than we think.

It is interesting to remember that Kipling, when he made his crossing of the country from west to east en route from India, and recounted his impressions of it in his sarcastic *American Notes* wrote enthusiastically of the flowers he saw in Pennsylvania—the mulleins and the goldenrods striking his fancy especially.

Bedstraw; wild indigo; wild senna; alumroot; prince's-pine; Indian-pipe; tall meadow-rue; yellow star grass; sarsaparilla; black cohosh; the white snake-root; spider-lily—these and countless others can be seen and judged as we find them growing in their natural settings. It is easier then to decide which are suited to our particular needs and to the type of soil and sun or shade or moisture we can give them.

## FOREST BORN

Wildflowers are more choosy of locale than most cultivated plants. On the whole, they require less sun and more moisture. In the beginning, this being a forested country (at least the eastern part of it) most of our native wildflowers were woodland by nature. With the felling of the trees and the appearance of meadow and pasture-land and plough, some of these native flowers died out. Others clung to the cool banks of streams, in fuller sun than they had known, but doing well there. A few adapted themselves to the new conditions and throve as well as or better than before. We might be surprised, however, to know how many of our commonest wildflowers are really not natives here but immigrants from Europe.

There is pleasure in an August walk. Few of us, once we have set hand to making a wild garden, can resist casting forward to new venturing in it. The size of such a garden can be negligible and so can the cost, but its possibilities are endless.

How happily the Hermit of Walden speaks of his own, untouched wild garden at the door, and of his tramps about the countryside that he loved, taking time out *to live* while he was at it. It makes one envious in these harried days.

"A broad margin of leisure is as beautiful in a man's life as in a book— All things in this world must be seen with the morning dew on them, must be seen with youthful, early opened, hopeful eyes— morning brings back the heroic ages— I wanted to live deep and suck out the marrow of life."

We have come far from such an approach to the world, forgetting too often that the purpose of the world and the plan, as well as the beauty, flow from God. Man, however, has not finished his course. It is not without meaning that people have begun here and there to weigh a bit and ponder the price they have been paying and the pace they have been setting—for what?

Was it not the gentle lady of Wimpole Street who had the vision to remind us that—

> "Earth's crammed with heaven,
> And every common bush alive with God:
> But only he who sees, takes off his shoes.
> The rest sit round it and pluck blackberries."

And did not her husband, hungry for life and the rich joy of living it deeply, echo the same thought in lines that challenge still—

> "This world's no blot for us,
> Nor blank; it means intensely and means good.
> To find its meaning is my meat and drink."

A garden and work we do there, day by day, bring that meaning and that challenge home to us, for in the growing world we first sense, then come to know the sure and steadfast verities sprung from the eternal splendour of God, rooted by His will in the heart of men to flower there from seeds of beauty.

## AUGUST CHECK LIST

In August our thoughts are definitely turning toward fall and the wealth of colour soon to come. Yet there is much for us to do now. Be thankful, however, that the worst of the weeding is over.

Watch phlox to prevent it from going to seed. If you do not top the plants in time, colours cannot be maintained. The purest white will soon revert to magenta.

Early August is not too late to put in more fall-flowering bulbs: autumn crocuses, colchicums, and *Sternbergia lutea.*

Keep an eye on seedlings—the biennials designed for setting out in the fall. Thin them as needed, just as zinnias and other annuals were thinned in July.

Seed violas, pansies, and heartsease now for colour next spring. August, of course, is the month to seed most of next year's biennials and perennials.

Some plants can be transplanted safely in August, especially those whose clumps need to be divided: lilies-of-the-valley, iris, Virginia bluebells, and peonies, if you must, for they do not like moving.

Have a look at dahlia stakes. Their usefulness begins now. Keep all stakes as inconspicuous as possible on phlox, bergamot, lilies, delphiniums, foxgloves, wherever they may be.

Keep on watering and watering well, particularly the lawns and the flowers that have made their leaf growth and are getting ready to bloom in the fall—chrysanthemums, dahlias, and roses especially. Water the broad-leaved evergreens well. Rhododendrons, for example, suffer terribly from drought, even more than the moisture-loving ferns.

Cut strawflowers now for drying, just before they come to their prime.

Keep on taking cuttings from begonias, geraniums, impatiens, vinca, shrimp plant, and fuchsias, to be potted later and brought indoors for winter bloom.

August is not too early to plan for and order bulbs to be planted in the fall for spring flowering; jonquils, daffodils, narcissus, hyacinths, tulips, snow crocuses, snowflakes, snowdrops, scillas, dogtooth violets, winter aconite, chionodoxa. Also oxalis and paper narcissus, freesia, and such things as *Tritonia crocata, Ardisia crispa, Jacobinia carnea,* for winter colour indoors. Order roses now if you plan to set them out in the fall.

Have another go at crab grass and fall grass as they appear. Try a good weed-killer on dandelions and plantains.

Keep on dusting, spraying, and feeding roses. Old canes may be pruned now from climbing roses.

August is the time to re-make the old compost pile or start a new one, if you have not done so already. Compost is a *sine qua non* for every garden. Remember that the remains of the old compost pile, plus some well-rotted manure, and water are the best foundations for the new pile. Compost needs a lot of watering in midsummer.

Wildflowers can be picked and dried in August to delight us when most blossoms have gone. Boneset, thoroughwort, pearly everlasting, bittersweet, broom sedge, ironweed, joe-pie, wild bergamot —there is a wide choice.

Keep in mind the possibilities of a wildflower corner, if that be your pidgin, though August is not the time to plant one. It is, however, the very time to observe what nature can do in the lanes and woodlands about us. Have a good look at the goldenrods, boneset, wild phlox, ironweed, sunflowers, day-lilies, chicory, white wood asters, blue asters, cardinal flowers, blue lobelia—all of them begin to appear in mid- or late August. Wild wood lilies, the Turk's-cap and the field lilies, are now at their best. Bouncing-bet, virgin's-bower, wild roses, jewel-weed, the gentians, Queen Anne's lace, mallow, bee-balm, butterfly-weed, tall meadow-rue, the snakeroots, vervain, turtlehead, black-eyed Susan, yarrow, tansy, harkweed—these are but a few of the treasures that can add immeasurably to a wild garden in high summer.

# CHAPTER IX

# SEPTEMBER

## *The Month of Returning Gold*

Is September the last month of summer or the first of fall? We can answer that readily enough. It smacks of both. In heat, it can and often does match anything that July or the Dog Days can offer. This year it passed even the driest of Augusts in bitter and devastating drought. Gnats and moths and fireflies were as prevalent as in midsummer. The crickets and katydids did not noticeably slacken their evening charivaris.

All these are manifestations of summer, of course. The waysides were as dusty as ever July could make them, the hillside coverts as green. But—yonder a sumac flames in the hedgerow. Perhaps it is only a damaged branch, yet the fire of the fall is there. Higher on the slope is a flash of scarlet where Virginia-creeper has climbed a hickory stump. Sassafras at the coppice edge hints of its gold to come. A cloud of asters—blue, cool as the dew at dawn—seeps across the glade like drifting smoke where all was green before. Wood asters, too, are showing their feathery white as are the snakeroots in the lane.

### FRESH CHEER

Gold is everywhere—in garden and field we catch once more the glorious freshness of the colour that comes to us first in spring and now, toward summer's end, has come again to cheer us.

Chrysanthemums, marigolds, many of the dahlias, lantanas, some of the asters, coreopsis, sternbergia, some of the autumn crocuses,

176

clump after clump of yellow zinnias and the golden roses (Pinnoc-
chio, Rochester, Goldilocks, and the rest) all are blooming again.
Through the countryside the goldenrods, beggar's-ticks, cornflowers,
wild sunflowers, sundrops clothe the hills with purest gold. Tides of
loveliness that mock at heat and dust and fading flowers. This is not
summer's colour. We feel the very heart of autumn beating here,
and yet so early.

## VANGUARD OF THE FALL

Blossoms present and the promise of blossoms to come have
tipped the beam of the seasons in autumn's favour, summer yielding
to September as vanguard of the fall. Just as the gold of April
speaks to us in promise of the splendour of spring and as May brings
the sure fulfilling of that glory, so August is rich with promise that
September has redeemed in good measure—pressed down, shaken
together, and running over for our joy. In spring we are glad that
winter has passed. All the beauty, all the venturing of bed and
border lie ahead to stir the pulse within us. In fall, we rejoice in a
different way, yet joy is here to the full. Heat and dust will soon be
gone. New life has come—a rich and lavish beauty that speaks the
garnering of the year—not the sowing of the seed now, but the
harvest. The very knowledge that autumn has come and that winter
all too soon will gnaw at our cherished blossoms lends endearment
to that loveliness while we have it, a harvest of beauty that nature
is pouring all about us. In truth, we can enjoy now as at no other
time the precious things of the earth and the fulness thereof. Instinct
teaches the dullest of us to love that well which we must leave ere
long.

"The setting sun and music at the close,
As the last taste of sweets, is sweetest at the last."

## STILL THE APHIDS

Surprising throwbacks to summer still occur. Even late in September, if we look for them, we may be dismayed at the white swarms of aphids sucking the stems and the tender tips of plants. Once we thought June and July were their months. The remedy, of course, is the same as in summer—a nicotine sulphate or similar contact spray. This is essential, for aphids overlooked now mean a reenforced attack mounted by them next spring. Whatever spray or dust we use, we must be sure that it is a contact sort, for that is what it takes to kill them.

## TRANSPLANTING AND SEEDING

We have said that August is a good month for the dividing and transplanting of perennials such as day-lilies, peonies, and so forth. September is even better. Actually, peonies can be moved safely well into October. If we have such plants to move as arabis (rock cress) or bleeding heart, we try to do so in September. This year drought prevented that until the rain came in mid-October. September, however, is the better month when weather is kind.

## MARKING

In moving our plants in September, we must be sure that we mark where we have put them and also mark just what they are. If we do not do this, once frost has killed them back above ground we are almost sure to forget what is there or even that anything at all is there. October bulbs deserve a better bed than a newly divided peony root. And the peonies and day-lilies moved in September should not be sliced in half by a careless spade or trowel in October when we are planting bulbs.

## THE LAWN IN FALL

September is the month par excellence for restoring an old lawn or for making a new one. All lawns, old or new, have four essential requirements: (a) proper drainage; (b) proper enrichment of the soil by liming, by organic and chemical fertilizing and, if necessary, by the use of new topsoil; (c) adequate preparation of the soil by deep spading, when called for, and always by deep raking with a steel-pronged rake or by what is called pricking, that is, tamping with a nail-studded board so as to break up the hard spots. The board should be attached to a rake or broom handle for convenience in use; (d) proper selection of grass seed. This calls for a consideration of the sun and shade aspects of the area.

If there has been rain, the earlier in September we get our lawn work started the better. The greatest factor in successful seeding is that the grass should have a chance to make root and grow a bit before frost, hence the need for starting lawn work early. And also, the need for seeding in properly prepared ground. Every year we see good seed literally thrown away on thick crusted soil as hard as cement and as lacking in life. On such ground not even the best seed can take hold.

## DRAINAGE

In a walled garden, particular care must be given to drainage of the subsoil. Foundations of the walls go below the frost line in our climate. This can easily result in the retention of too much under-surface moisture, especially if the soil tends to be clayish. Provision must be made for adequate drainage *through* the foundations of the walls. We neglected this when our walls were first built, but have remedied it now. Any garden that does not drain properly, walls or not, must be seen to. A deep foundation of crushed stones or coal clinkers, at least 18 inches or 2 feet below the ground level often solves the problem of wet, clayish, and badly draining ground.

## FEEDING

The second essential is the feeding or enrichment of the ground upon which the lawn is growing—or is supposed to grow. Old lawns as well as new ones must be regularly and properly fed, especially

179

if an old lawn has been robbed of its very life year after year by close cutting and the raking up of every blade that is cut. If we insist on removing all cut grass, it is only fair that we repay what we have taken. September is an excellent month to do this. One thing we must never forget. In using any chemical fertilizer, we must follow instructions to the letter as to the quantity per square foot to be applied, regardless of the kind.

Pulverized phosphate rock and potash make fine fertilizers. They are easily obtained and widely used. Most good commercial compounds contain nitrogen, phosphate, and potash, water-solvent. Lime, obviously, is needed by all growing things. It is the magic that releases the wealth of the soil, a wealth that can be hidden and useless unless we have the wit to work with nature in order to profit by the treasures she has stored for us. Lime is the key, but it is best to hold over most of the liming until spring so that we may have its blessing when we are ready to use it. Other lawn feed should go in now. Organic fertilizer, some at least, is really processed sewage. Yet it makes excellent feed for old lawns and will help enrich the soil of a new lawn. Whatever it may be, organic fertilizer must be well worked in with the spade or rake. Mushroom mould does won- ders on grass. We put ours on about one inch thick and let it sink in of its own accord in rain. We must never forget that old lawns have baked hard in summer. They must be loosened. The founda- tion for a new lawn likewise must be able to breathe and receive seed properly.

There are, of course, other feeds and fertilizers than those we have mentioned. Peat-moss, rotted cow manure, humus from the compost pile, all have their place—quite as necessary a place as the chemical preparations. Indeed, it seems safe to say that we *must* have organic matter to feed any ground properly; we *may,* if we like, speed up our work by adding the phosphates and the rest. But the natural humus, decaying vegetation, manure—these no soil can do without and remain very long a useful soil.

## PREPARATION OF THE GROUND

The third requirement for a lawn is the preparation of its soil, apart from feeding and fertilizing, so that it may do a good job with the seed sown on it. A workable topsoil is basic for any lawn, old or new. Our first consideration must be an estimate of how much topsoil is needed. This can be a serious matter if we have to buy it. We can purchase everywhere what is sold as topsoil, but too often that is just what the bulldozer has scooped up somewhere—a modicum of topsoil and two or three feet of shale or clay, probably ripped from somebody's new cellar. We need *real* topsoil or none. Once the old lawn has been well raked and fed or the ground prepared and fed where a new lawn is to go, we should try, especially in the fall, to spread two inches of good, finely pulverized topsoil over it. This facilitates the seeding. In any case, do not try to seed unless the ground is ready for the seed, topsoil or not. By ready, we mean open and friable enough to give the new seed a chance. If topsoil is not obtainable or too expensive—as indeed it is for us— try to spread a little of it at least over the worn spots before seeding. Never seed too thickly. Some of the best Bent grass seed is very fine. If sown too thickly, it will spring up densely and the blades soon tend to smother themselves.

## CHOICE OF SEED

The fourth requirement is obvious. Buy the best grass seed you can possibly get and do not limit yourself to one kind. Try to see how much of your lawn tends to be shaded for the greater part of the day. And how much of it is in full sun. Shade grass is very expensive, but most lawns call for some of it.

## LIVE SOIL

No mention of lawns and their care would be complete without at least some consideration of the difference between live soil and that which is to all intent dead soil. A live soil, every foot of it, must contain a combination of organic matter: bacteria, nitrogen, and such minerals as phosphorus, calcium, and potassium. It must also contain moisture. It is the humus primarily that retains this moisture. And the moisture in turn allows the all-important mineral content of the soil to play its part in the cycle of sound growth. Lacking humus, hence moisture, hence life, what can a soil do with lawn grass or anything else?

The final work on a lawn, old or new, after it has been prepared, fed, fertilized, seeded and rolled, is to water it with the finest possible spray of the hose, unless nature vouchsafes to do this for us. The order of work on lawns is important. Rake deeply—even spade if you are starting fresh; feed thoroughly and see that most of the food is organic in nature; fertilize with chemical preparations in accord with their directions; apply topsoil lightly, if you can get it; seed with judgment as to sort and quantity; roll and water gently. And through it all pray heartily for rain. Nature's watering beats any amount of hose work.

## LAWN SOILS

In considering soils suitable for lawns (or for anything else for that matter) we should keep in mind that all soil falls roughly into three categories: clay, sand, and loam. A clay soil holds water and must be broken up, drained, and lightened with organic matter; otherwise it remains lumpish and is likely to sour. Coal ashes and clinkers, sand, even a basis of crushed stone as already suggested, are excellent for breaking up clay soils. Whatever is used, it must be well spaded in. Peat-moss and leaves are extremely useful in loosening clay soils.

Sandy soil tends to dry out too soon. It also lacks adequate humus —the very life of any soil. Sandy soil usually needs no breaking up, but it always does need fertilizing by organic matter—and plenty of it.

Loam soil—the best—while made up of clay and sandy soils, is by its very nature enriched with sufficient humus and organic matter, hence is never so dry as the sandy soil nor so wet and cloddish as the clay soil.

It is on loam soil that lawn and garden must be based—as deep and as rich a loam as the natural site or our own foresight and care can give it. Of course, it is nature that does the trick. We can but hope at best to work with her. One of the telling tests of whether or not nature is co-operating with us is the quantity of earthworms per square foot. Moisture and humus mean plenty of worms, and worms, in turn, mean a living, useful soil, with organic and mineral elements reacting one upon another in a beneficent cycle of growth. Where such reactions are lacking, gardening becomes a waste of time.

## HAVE A CARE

Once the old lawn has been re-seeded or the new one freshly made, two things are needed: rain or the regular weekly watering, and a determination to keep off the surface of the lawn until the new grass has had a chance to make sound sod. Short cuts to the flower beds are disastrous. A new lawn should not be walked over for several weeks. It takes a lot of time for several inches of loose topsoil to settle.

## DO NOT TAKE FOR GRANTED

The commonest error we are likely to fall into is of taking grass for granted. Or of supposing, in our innocence, that a lawn once made will stay made forever. So it will, but not without care. Was it not of an Oxford close, smooth as the surface of a putting green, free from any hint of weed, gloriously verdant in midsummer, that the American tourist received an unexpected answer when he asked the gardener what had been used as a foundation for such miraculous turf. "Three hundred and fifty years' hard work, sir," was the reply.

Few of us are likely to be dealing these days with that type of lawn, but there is truth in what the gardener said. All lawns call for yearly care and the longer that care is given to grass, the better it will show for it. By and large, the more we do in early September, the more progress will be made before frost and proportionately richer grass will reward us next year.

## SOUND ADVICE

"To everything there is a season," we are told, "and a time to every purpose under the heaven." Whenever it is possible, we should do our seeding, re-seeding, planting and transplanting either early in the day or, if that is not possible, toward evening. It is a mistake to seed in the heat of a September noon. Again we have the experience of the past to guide us. "In the morning sow thy seed and in the evening withhold not thy hand." Those of old knew whereof they spoke. They had not learned their gardening from a book.

## AWAKENING BORDERS

Next to its importance as a time to work on the lawn, September is the month to get the most from our borders. Perennials are already making a show of their own. We have expected that. Annuals, however, are usually suffering now from an overdose of summer drought or they are tired from a summer of blooming. It is surprising, though, what a little encouragement will do for them, especially early in September. Seed pods should have been cut off, of course, right along. If not, we must do this now and clip off all faded parts of the plant as well, nipping the tops and branches back a bit. Given rain, or a good soaking from the hose, many annuals will perk up amazingly, and break into the freshest bloom until frost.

## PERENNIALS IN FALL

Perennial borders are by all odds the easiest part of the garden to overlook when fertilizing is in order. As with lawns, we are prone to take borders for granted. Usually, however, we try to feed ours in spring with a dressing of cow manure, rotted leaves, and bone-meal. It is equally useful to rake in some bone-meal during the fall, but with us the beds and borders are too full of fall flowers for much of this to be done as early as September. We put it down at this time, however, in our tickler file, so that a top-dressing of bone-meal may be worked into the soil when the fall bulbs go in during October and the borders are being readied for winter. We cannot repeat too often that all gardens must have constant replenishment of humus and organic matter as well as all the essential minerals. One without the other is productive of little. If there must be a choice, the humus should come first. That is a bed-rock necessity for any soil.

## COLCHICUMS AND STERNBERGIA

Autumn-flowering bulbs, of course, have been in the ground since August. By early September, the colchicums and sternbergias are in full flower—the first, a lovely violet; the other, a bright gold. Both are a delight. Autumn crocuses, either purple, or white-and-gold like the *speciosus albus,* open for us toward the end of September or early in October.

## SPRING BULBS

The trouble with planting bulbs in September is twofold. Frequently the ground is too dry and hard for them to go in. And beds and borders where we wish the bulbs to show in the spring are too rich now with annuals still in flower for us to think of disturbing them. We leave that for the first real frost.

If you have space ready for the spring-flowering bulbs in September, some should go in by the end of the month, provided there has been sufficient rain to freshen the soil. Crocuses, chionodoxa, snow-drop, snowflake, scilla, jonquil, and most of the daffodils and narcissus are best got in early. Tulips can wait until October, if need be. And so can some of the daffodils.

## STRAWFLOWERS

So much must be done now, however, that it is hard to decide what should come first. We have already spoken of drying straw-flowers for the winter. Some of these blossoms have been cut in August and hung upside down in the potting-shed. More can be gathered in September. They must be hung in a thoroughly dry place or they will be ruined. Dampness makes them limp and useless. They do not need very much light either, while drying.

Too often we forget that some hardy annuals should be sown in the fall. Celandine and wild senna, although fall-sown, must wait for a frost. The cornflowers and snapdragons and calliopsis can go in before frost, in mid-September.

## SEEDLINGS AND CUTTINGS

September is the month for transplanting the tiny seedlings of delphiniums and foxgloves from where they have seeded themselves about the parent plants. It is also the time we pot our small cuttings from the fuchsias, impatiens, and all other plants that have been making roots since mid-August. In late September, we must watch out for an early frost. Plants potted for winter indoors can easily be nipped. We move ours by stages—border to pot to porch and finally, much later, into the house.

Many people pot chrysanthemums in September for winter colour indoors. This is easy to do and always they are lovely. We have never tried it, chiefly because our cottage lacks room for large pots and tall plants.

## MOVING SHRUBS

Above all, September is the month to start raking leaves and saving them. It is wasteful as well as stupid to burn a single leaf, so precious are they in making us the humus we need. While we are busy with the leaves, it pays to have a look at shrubs and foundation plantings so that we may decide if we ought to move or replace any.

September is a profitable month for this, especially where evergreens are concerned. In a dry September, it is best to wait for rain, even if we have to postpone all our transplanting until October. All moved or freshly planted shrubs must be well and deeply watered and mulched. It is impossible to stress too strongly or to repeat too often the need to mulch transplanted shrubs, whether they be moved in early or late fall or at any other time. Only recently have the real benefits of mulching begun to be properly appreciated.

## MULCHES

From spring till fall a good mulch, as we have said, pays its way in keeping down weeds, in conserving moisture, in preventing the topsoil from crusting or from washing away—in fact, a mulch does more for the near-surface feeding roots of plants and shrubs than anything else we could possibly do for them. Fall mulching is as useful as mulching at any season. It also prevents winter leaching so inevitable with open soil.

## MULCHING MATERIAL

Mulching material is not limited to leaves, salt hay, or peat-moss, though all three are commonly used. We have found that a mixture of sawdust and a little sand is splendid, especially when new plants are put in the ground and plenty of moisture is needed to help them root. Care must be taken to see that sawdust is not put on acid soil unless that soil has been given some lime before the sawdust mulch is applied. Should the soil be at all alkaline, the pulverized limestone is not needed. One great advantage of good mulches is that they can be worked into the ground as they rot away, thus providing the finest sort of humus and helping to break up clay soils and to maintain a sound texture in sandy soils which lack sufficient organic matter.

The straw found in manure and straw of such field crops as wheat, rye, and oats, grass clippings, corn stalks (if you have them), buckwheat hulls, peanut shells, the chaff from clover hay or alfalfa—all these make thoroughly useful mulches which add humus when decomposed and worked under.

We have not favoured scrap-mulches made of such odds and ends as wood-shavings, although they are sometimes used and will provide a reasonable amount of surface cover, especially in winter. Our stand-bys are peat-moss, partially rotted leaves, salt hay and the sawdust-sand mixture. Had we a supply of peanut shells or buckwheat hulls, we would gladly use them. In fact, we would use any of the organic mulches—the shredded stalk and stem and cob sort —were they available, as vegetable material of this sort is invaluable. Except on the broad-leaved evergreens, we do not use pine-needle mulches.

## START RAKING EARLY

The whole life of a garden depends, of course, upon humus balanced in the soil with the essentials of phosphate, nitrogen, potash, and lime, plus other minerals and trace elements in far lesser quantities. Humus is a September problem, for our supply usually must depend upon our own compost piles and they, in turn, depend upon a constant replenishing of leaves. With us, October is the chief month of falling leaves, but it is surrpising how many can be raked up and saved even by mid-September.

## THE COMPOST PIT

Compost is somewhat more than a pile of leaves, left to rot or blow away. Good compost should be started in a pit—not a pile. That helps keep the needed moisture there. Two feet is not too deep for it; sides can be carried up two or three feet more. Temporary sides are easily made of well-staked poultry-netting, but it pays in the end to have a permanent compost pit with sides of cinder blocks or good well-tarred boards. The blocks are cheaper in the end, for they will not rot. One end of the pit, regardless of its material, should be designed with a movable wooden entrance so that a wheelbarrow can be rolled in and out or its contents tilted into the pit sideways.

Once the pit has been dug (do not line the bottom with anything), and once the side walls are in place, start gathering your supply of leaves, flower stalks, corn husks, pea pods, grass cuttings, hedge clippings—in fact, any vegetable waste that you would otherwise throw away. Try to keep all sticks and very heavy stalks out of the compost, or chop the stalks up first. Sticks are just in the way and are troublesome as well as useless.

## LEAF TYPES

Even weeds can be used as compost material unless they have gone to seed. If they have, it is better to burn them. The best compost, naturally, is formed from leaves that are low in acid content or tannin and rosin. What we want are those high in calcium, such as the ash, the plane tree, the sugar maple, and the elm. We also use our hackberry, apple, pear, and dogwood leaves. In a properly managed compost pit, oak leaves and beech leaves do no harm and even pine needles are said to do none. We, however, try to save all pine and spruce and hemlock needles for compost intended to mulch the acid-loving shrubs—the rose-bays, mountain laurel, and azaleas. We usually put our oak leaves in this pile, too.

## COMPOST MAKING

The secret of good compost-making lies in building the compost pile right, that is, in layers. Four or five inches of leaves, well soaked; another layer of leaves, another soaking, and so on. If we are starting a new pile and cannot wait for nature to decompose the mass into well-rotted compost, we speed up the process by adding to each layer of leaves a good sprinkling of lime—say, 2 to 2½ pounds of it if the compost pit measures 4 by 6 feet, which is a handy size and not too obvious in the landscape. Commercial plant food, 3 to

3½ pounds of it for a pile of the size suggested, is sure to hasten the making of good compost if it is spread between the layers of the leaves. Manure used in this way is also extremely useful. Each layer must be well soaked with water and well tamped down. Obviously, one should use lime *or* plant food. Not both together.

We have also found that a little earth, the richer the better, is an asset if sprinkled between the layers of leaves. All compost must be kept damp. In drought, the pile or pit should be sprayed liberally with the hose from time to time.

## APPLES AND PEARS

One of the joys of September is that it brings to us the apples and the pears that have been ripening through the summer. Picking of apples is an October chore, but September gives us all that we can eat. Our apples begin with their first falls for sauce way back in July. Usually our late apples last on until Easter and after. In a good year we have eaten our own the twelve-month 'round. Seckel pears last us about two and a half months—September until early November. And extraordinarily good they are. The squirrels agree with us on that.

## FIRST FRUITS

No matter how small the place or how few the trees one may have, it is a joy to gather one's own first-fruits and to feel that our labours have been blessed in basket and in store, as they spoke of harvest in the old days. How vividly and how simply the seasons were portrayed, though quite unconsciously, when men depended upon the fruit of their own fields and upon the toil of their own hands to live. Fall meant more than the splendour of the turning leaf when they themselves "put the sickle to the corn." The very culmination of the year, the cycle of seedtime and harvest, are caught for us in the beauty of the phrase.

Just as we suppose our tasks are slacking off a bit, straightway new ones spring up to vex us—really, to delight us in the end, despite our grumbling.

"No field was ever so well cultivated that it contained no nettles, briars and thorns mingled with better plants," says Boccaccio in his *Decameron*. September, as a sort of second spring, can keep us busy with chores we love and others we hate. Or pretend to.

## DIARY JOTTINGS

1 September—clipped back the edge of the pachysandra where it was reaching out over the lawn.

2 September—cut back some honeysuckle and also some wisteria that had got out of hand since last attended to. Picked quantities of Seckel pears, our own particular favourite. Noted that morning-glories—intensely vivid blue ones—were more in flower than ever before.

3 September—re-tied a few dahlias where they needed it. How they do grow and blossom as fall comes on! Soaked them well. Some 25 different kinds of flowers now in bloom. A fortnight more and that number will increase.

4 September—asters in bloom everywhere. Virgin's-bower most lovely and more fragrant then ever. Camomile in tiny flower among the herbs. Also, pinks are re-blooming in the terrace border. Some of the English daisies are again in blossom. Dug out a wisteria vine by the west wall, so as to replace it later with virgin's-bower. We have enough wisteria already.

5 September—put in 2 blue aster clumps. Planted 10 colchicums, 10 *Sternbergia lutea*, and 10 autumn crocus in the library bed. Seeded Johnny-jump-up and mixed perennial pansies by the parking place. Trimmed some heavy branches from the viburnums in the lower garden where they were actually pressing the heavy wall out of plumb. It seems incredible, but such is the power of a growing tree. Lilies-of-the-valley at the foot of the drive are rich now with their crimson fruit. So are the yews, though with them the scarlet berries are scarcer.

6 September—lifted the potted plants that have been dozing all summer in the shade of the trees, well cut back, buried to their rims. We shall re-pot them now and give them to the sun again for winter blooming. Clipped ivy about the lower windows and doors. Thanked

191

God for a touch of rain in this maddening drought. In bloom today: petunias, verbenas, blue myrtle, white myrtle, virgin's-bower, ageratum, red impatiens, white impatiens, sweet alyssum, candytuft, camomile, floribunda roses, tree roses, climbing roses, tea roses, zinnias, dwarf French marigolds, begonias, fuchsias, plumbago, snapdragon, pink geraniums, white geraniums, shrimp plants, portulacas, lantanas, chrysanthemums, dahlias, cornflowers, hound's-tongue, rose of Sharon, white phlox, day-lilies, calendulas, cosmos, blue lobelias, cockscombs, butterfly-bush, honeysuckle, abelia, and hydrangea. The berries of the firethorn, lilies-of-the-valley, bittersweet, cotoneaster, and yew are lovely. Dogwood drupes are turning now. The sweet-bay fruit, always a surprise, shows scarlet among the polished leaves.

7 September—pruned a little from the shrubs in the east border, taking out dead wood and some branches not needed there. September is not really a pruning month. Put two additional mountain laurel in the east border, moving two inkberries to make room for them. Put the inkberries near the wildflower corner. Cut back some marigolds that were smothering the yellow Pinocchio roses in the lower garden beds.

8 September—weeded east border—not much to come out now. Picked some crab grass and mouse-eared plantain from the upper lawn. Night-blooming cereus now in its startling flower. Berries on the rock-cotoneaster are beautiful. Soon the scarlet of the barberry will join them. Here and there stray blossoms have opened in the viburnums, as they always do in early fall. The sour gum and the dogwood leaves are turning fast. Soon the squirrels and the birds will have a feast day with our dogwood berries. Dug up some Virginia creeper from outside the west wall where it was usurping too much space and threating our lovely clematis there. Had another crack at some poison ivy and stepped deep in a yellow-jacket nest unbeknownst. Paid heavily for that. How does a wasp know how to strike so viciously and so unerringly for his opponent's eyes? Stung three times there, in addition to the rest of the assorted stings. In spite of the defeat by the wall, managed to feed and spray all the roses. Set out some snare piles for the snails and slugs—still with us, drought or no.

12 September—watered all roses and the ferns in the wild garden as well. Ordered bulbs and pips for fall planting there: such things as stars-of-Bethlehem and wildflower. White wood-asters are now out among the ferns. They are the very spirit of fall.

13 September—got a little grass seed in after a shower. Still too dry

for real seeding. Slug-shot on the roses. Transplanted the bittersweet vine from the end of the fence to the garage wall. Watered the ferns again. Watered the new myrtle beds and the terrace border. Colchicums now in flower—Violet Queen.

14 September—watered again, hose going all day.

16 September—put a wild pasture-rose in east border. Also one virgin's-bower by the upper garden gazebo; two virgin's-bower on the west wall. Seckel pears most delicious this year and more of them than ever before. Squirrels are taking their quota of the best, but there are plenty for us all. Apples also are in great supply, partly as a result of regular spraying. It is fall now in spite of warm weather. "First the blade, then the ear, after that the full corn in the ear." Yet spring seems only yesterday. How swiftly the seasons press one upon another. Watered the ferns again. Never have we known such a drought. White snakeroot and goldenrod in blossom.

17 September—put in 7 new peonies—2 Duchess de Nemours, 3 Crystola, 2 Festiva Maxima. Cleaned out all the bird boxes. This should be done every year, but we too often forget it.

18 September—put 50 pounds of bone-meal on the road-bank ferns.

21 September—autumn crocuses out. Put in the wild garden gully 50 mixed ferns; 60 alumroot, 6 New England asters, 6 red baneberry, 6 white baneberry, 6 wild bergamot, 6 butterfly-weed, 6 wild pinks, 12 wild columbine, 6 cornflowers, 12 Jacob's-ladders, 6 jack-in-the-pulpits, 12 Virginia bluebells, 12 blue phlox, 4 white snakeroot, 12 spiderwort, 12 white trilliums, 6 blue lobelias, 6 cardinal-flowers. Gave the myrtle and other new plantings a thorough watering. Also watered the terrace and lower garden borders. Gave the compost heap a good soaking. The fall flowers, in spite of the drought, are magnificent this year.

22 September—pruned back the butterfly-bush. Slug-shot on the lilacs and on the climbing roses and also on the new virgin's-bower. Watered the south and east borders. Cut some more cornflowers for drying. Put 6 phlox (3 Fiancée and 3 Mary Louise) in lower garden beds. One Spitfire phlox in south border. Heeled in 10 hemerocallis for later planting in south border when we move the whole border forward into more sun: 4 Fulva, 3 Thunbergi, and 3 Margaret Perry. Monkshood now in blossom. Pinks are lovely. A busy day, but all the watering was done with the hose moved from time to time, so that was no chore.

23 September—put in 100 winter aconite in driveway bed. Clipped ivy.

24 September—heeled in 6 bearded German iris for the new south border (3 California Gold, 3 Gold Majesty). Also 6 Japanese iris (Gold Bound).

25 September—moved some of the potted plants to the porch and a few indoors. Re-potted some fuchsias.

28 September—sternbergia in golden bloom. Also, some very belated gaillardias.

29 September—began work today on the new lower garden lawn and a terrific chore it was! Five to six inches of topsoil dug up and taken off in a wheelbarrow. As many inches of new topsoil wheeled in. Fertilized this topsoil with bone-meal and lime. Worked peat-moss well into it. Then raked the whole surface free of the smallest lump. Still far too dry to risk seeding. That must wait. Also we started work moving the south border four or five feet forward. Many perennials, of course, had to be transplanted: day-lilies, peonies, chrysanthemums, German and Japanese iris, white phlox, foxgloves, and the rest. Our annuals we could not save, though they were lovely in color and freshness. Our English daisies in the lower garden beds are breaking into their usual fall bloom. Heartsease is still hard at it, blossoming bravely since the first of the year, nine months ago. In the wildflower corner goldenrod, Queen Anne's lace, and moth-mullein are in flower. Decided to help our espalier'd firethorns by taking down a cryptomeria overshadowing them. Topped it today. Quite a task single-handed, as the tree was a tall one. Last night it went to 38 degrees. First frost must be near. Indeed, there *was* a light frost in near-by low spots. Autumn crocuses love cold weather. They are coming up strongly.

30 September—gave the east border a final weeding. Cut down the rest of the cryptomeria tree. Moved the fleece-vine from the library wall to the west wall of the garden by the potting-shed. Cut and hung up more cornflowers. Potted for our winter window 2 *Tulbaghia violacea,* 1 *Jacobinia carnea,* and 1 *Ardisia crispa.*

How maddening is this drought! Yet in spite of it we know in our hearts that the fall rains will come just as they always have and all will go well again.

## SEPTEMBER

### THEY NEITHER KNOW NOR CARE

City dwellers doubtless are spared worry over the vagaries of weather for they know nothing of it and, apparently, care less. But they are also ignorant of the joy and the faith that so surely come to those more fortunate than they who have learned to know and love the world they live in. Actually how many of those caught in the trap of our mechanical civilization have the slightest concept of the effect of a day's rain or lack of it upon the food they eat? Indeed, few people bred to the town really believe that they have any connection with the soil at all. Such an attitude would be childish or just run-of-the-mill stupidity were it not so tragic, containing as it does the seeds of our civilization's destruction.

### NATURE'S GOOD AND GOD'S

How differently and how triumphantly Robert Browning champions a faith that gardeners know to be true.

> "I trust in Nature for the stable laws
> Of beauty and utility. Spring shall plant
> And autumn garner to the end of time.
> I trust in God—the right shall be the right
> And other than the wrong, while He endures.
> I trust in my own soul, that can perceive
> The outward and the inward,—Nature's good
> And God's."

It is fascinating to note the difference between those who really love the growing world because they see it and are enraptured by its wonder and those who merely see and record for us the sight without the vision.

### TOO FAIR TO BE BELIEVED

"Very few," says Thoreau, "write as if they had seen the thing they pretend to describe." What a sting lies in those words, yet how

195

true they are. Gardeners should not overlook Thoreau. He has the root of the matter in him. He sees so vividly and so surely the beauty we can easily miss, whether it be in our own familiar gardens or in the countryside that frames them.

Fall stirred him mightily as it stirs most of us. Of September, he writes:

"The increasing scarlet and yellow tints around the meadows and river remind me of the opening of a vast flower bud. They are the petals of its corolla which are of the width of the valleys. It is the flower of autumn, whose expanding bud just begins to blush. As yet, however, in the forest there are very few changes of foliage— some single red maples are splendid now. . . . It is too fair to be believed."

## SILENT WONDER

We can understand that. All of us at one time or another have felt the ecstasy of a garden, the sudden revelation of its almost unspeakable beauty. Or the overpowering loveliness of a hillside at twilight. Or the strange bond that knits our souls in kinship with the sweetness of a sun-kissed meadow. These things lie outside the beaten way, yet when they come they warm the hearts within us to silent and transcendent wonder. Such things are in truth too fair to be believed, yet there they are for our discerning and delight. It is then that those who have caught the vision begin, perhaps for the first time in their lives, to grasp what the poet meant when he spoke of a simple flower giving us by its beauty thoughts too deep for tears.

## OVERSEAS

In September, it is the earnest of what lies ahead, the first hints of coming splendour, that touch us so surely. Autumn is the season of colour. No other months of the year can approach the turning of the leaf in vividness. Overseas, few people have the faintest conception of what our fall can be. Their autumn is golden and lovely, not flame and fire as with us. To see the beeches on a Hampshire hill caught in the rays of a setting sun that makes each leaf a thing of life, is something no man can forget. The same golden colour flows down the slopes of the Black Forest in September. Many a mile we have tramped there in that magic light. Even in rain or under sodden skies, the colour of thin-spun gold burns in the beech-wood. But the scarlets and the crimson pageantries of our forest are lacking.

## THE ROWAN TREE

We felt this miracle keenly after serving for several years in Iceland during the war, for trees are few there and other vegetation is confined to a narrow band about the coast. Each autumn, as the long dark of winter drew on, we missed most terribly the familiar colours of our woodlands, the heartening glow of the maples, the warm and ruddy welcome of the oaks, the sharp fire of the dogwoods. Rowans there were there—a few, at least, of the mountain ash. So much did they mean to us close by the Arctic Circle that here near our wildflower garden we have planted a rowan tree—for old time's sake and the memory of those torn and stunted rowans that once stood us in good stead, reminding us of home.

## A FOREST FRAME

Not every garden can be framed in fall by the glory of forest trees in their splendour. Here, though not ours, the edge of a neighbouring grove serves as backdrop to the south. When fall touches this, as we see it beyond our garden wall, we know how fortunate we are. By the border of our garden to the east, there grows an ancient sweet birch, evidently part of the older forest. Morning light streaming through its leaves transforms the tree to fairest, transparent gold, adding immeasurably to the colour in our borders close by.

What colour there is! Azaleas bronze, the barberry grows richer

197

with its crimson fruit, and all the flowers share the pageant of the turning leaves above. September really is the month of gold.

## SEPTEMBER CHECK LIST

Although few weeds grow as late as September, almost all of them will seed at this time if given a chance. Be merciless in destroying them.

September is as good a time as any to build a cold-frame, if you have none. It is hard, indeed, to do without.

Perennials may be seeded now for next spring's bloom, but this is as late as we can risk it. Those seeded now, however, must not be transplanted until spring.

The first of the spring-flowering bulbs should be got in by mid-September: jonquils, grape hyacinth, scillas, winter aconite, crocuses, chionodoxa, snowdrops, snowflakes, and some of the daffodils.

Day lilies should be divided and replanted in September. So may peonies, if you have to thin them out. Never put peonies deeper than 2 inches or they will not bloom.

It is a good time now to plant German iris if you have to move any.

If September prove dry, postpone transplanting trees and shrubs, but if there is moisture in the ground or if you can water them well, now is the time to start moving some of them. A few, however, must wait until spring or they will be winter-killed. These include birch, beech, dogwood, silver-bell, magnolia, and redbud. As a rule, all thin-skinned trees should wait till spring.

Water shrubs, old or new, if the month is a dry one.

In September get your potted plants under way for next winter. Remember to start them right with re-potting, new soil, and a good feeding. The list can be surprisingly varied: sweet alyssum, verbenas, calendulas, marigolds, petunias, fuchsias, ageratum, shrimp plant, heliotrope, snapdragon. Soil must be rich, light, and well fertilized, as well as well watered. Do not forget that indoor plants need sun.

198

Arabis and bleeding heart may be moved safely in September, but they will need regular watering until the fall rains come.

In September transplant the seedlings of delphiniums and fox-gloves from where they are growing about the parent plants.

Annuals in the borders, some of them, still have six weeks or more of bloom ahead. Tend them. Clip off seed pods. Nip tops and branches back a bit. Soak them well, for they need it.

Be sure to mark whatever has been moved or seeded. Spring is a long way off and we can forget what is where readily enough.

Remember the early fall is the time to restore, re-make, or start a lawn. Pay heed to proper drainage, essential feeding and liming, adequate soil preparation, and good seed. Above all, do not neglect watering. New lawns or re-made lawns require a lot of water, as a rule, in September.

Watch for the colchicums and sternbergia planted in August. They should be in flower now. Fall crocuses come towards the end of the month.

Keep drying strawflowers as they come to their prime. They can be lovely indoors in winter.

Continue cuttings from the fuchsias, impatiens, begonias, geraniums, and the like for potting in a winter window.

Chrysanthemums may be potted now for indoor bloom later.

Begin to rake leaves as they fall and save them for mulching and compost. Winter mulching is a later chore, of course, but we shall need all the leaves we can get. Remember leaves may be high or low in acid content. For compost, save those low in acid, high in calcium —the ash, sugar-maple, plane tree, elm, apple, pear. Oak leaves and spruce, pine, and hemlock needles, on the other hand, are high in acid content. Save them for the azaleas, rose-bays, and laurels.

Re-tie dahlias if they need it.

Keep after crab grass and fall grass.

Continue to spray and dust roses. Their fall blooming can be lovely. Aphids usually stage a comeback in September. Use nicotine sulphate or some other contact spray wherever it is needed.

Water roses, chrysanthemums, and dahlias, especially, in dry spells right through the month.

Never forget that every garden depends upon humus and organic matter for its very life as well as upon bacteria, nitrogen, phosphorus, calcium, and potassium. Plan now to renew humus content as soon as frost has cleared the beds. Cow manure, sheep manure, rotted leaves, compost—these are the answers.

# CHAPTER X

# OCTOBER

## *The Month of the Leaf*

~~~~~~~~~~~~~~~~~~~~~~~~~~~~~~~~~~~~~~~~~~~~~~

There is so much colour in September and so much lingering warmth in October that the transition between them seems less marked in a way than that between any other two consecutive months. Yet in spite of that, the difference can be great at times. This comes home to us with a vengeance when October claims privilege and greets us some nippy morning with a frost that has blackened the dahlias.

## FIRST FROST

The sad part of this is that we may have no other killing frost until almost December. Through most years, however, October is kindly here, bringing a glory of colour and a loveliness of weather that no other season can match. We are in fall by October and no mistake. The neighbouring hillsides flame in splendour. The tint of corn in shock, the ripening pumpkins in the stubble, beech trees caught in a mellowing sun carry on for us a richer gold whose harbingers cheered us a month back.

## THE SENSES

Now, however, heat gone, drought broken, October's magic brings all the senses into play—not merely that of sight. We *feel* the challenge of the sharpening air, warm and drowsy though it be at noon. We *scent* the fragrance of the ripened fruit, the perfume of

grapes, unforgettable, spiced to incense by a sun that soon must go
We *hear* the lovely whispering of the trees, the breathing of farewell
as leaves grow crisp before they float to earth in a glory that is not
death, but beauty transmuted into newer life. Touch, too, has spe-
cialties in fall—the smooth, sleek feel of a horse chestnut in our
pocket, the rough, staining toughness of a walnut, the different feel
of pignut and hickory. And once (alas, now gone), the sharp pricking of a chestnut bur clubbed downward in the crisp autumn air.
We need not speak of taste. The garnering of the year lies rich
before us. Indeed, we taste its very bounty in the air we breathe.
October is the savoury month, the month we live with relish just
because we are alive—and know it.

## BREAKING DROUGHT

This year the breaking of the drought brought home more keenly
the benisons of fall, the glory of October weather and the healing of
October rain. How humbly, yet how nobly the old prayer of thanksgiving expresses man's gratitude for rain. Always the Elizabethans
left this heritage in their stately, singing prose which was (and is, of
course) the purest poetry.

"O God, our Heavenly Father, who by Thy gracious providence
dost cause the former and the latter rain to descend upon the earth,
that it may bring forth fruit for the use of man; We give Thee
humble thanks that it hath pleased Thee, in our great necessity, to
send at last a joyful rain upon Thine inheritance, and to refresh it
when it was dry, to the great comfort of us Thy unworthy servants,
and to the glory of Thy holy Name; through Thy mercies in Jesus
Christ our Lord."

What inimitable phrasing that is—"to send at last a joyful
rain." We know the joy.

## RAIN

"Till a silvery play in the maples,
And a quickening stir through the leaves,

Send a savour of hope to the beeches,
A content that the covert believes;
For the wind it has fetched us a blessing,
All the meadows are kindly again,
And the pents of the kennel are drumming
With the heart-easing murmur of rain!

O, the breath of wet thorn in the hedgerow!
And the sheen where the coulter has passed!
And the joy of turned headland and furrow,
And a green that's our birthright at last!
For the wastage of drought is behind us,
And the streams they are lusty again!
And our woodlands ring merry in chorus
There's a chime above chimes—after rain!"

## THE LEAVES

By October, it is now or never in the garden. Another month will see most beds put away for the winter or dormant. October, above all else, gives us a chance at the leaves. Just as they offer us so lavishly of their beauty—saffron and crimson and all the lovely tawny bronzes of the oaks—so they enrich us far more with the boon they bring to our mulches. Every leaf that falls should be raked with thankfulness of heart and put to the use for which it was intended—as ground cover first against the winter's cold, and then as a source of fruitfulness to the earth below. We should heed nature's plan, not fight it. Leaves do not die. They simply change their outward form and live again in the cycle of re-birth that admits no death.

In October, the compost pile should be re-made in layers, as has been said. Other leaves should be spread about the rhododendrons, the laurels, all the broad-leaved evergreens, and the azaleas. A bit of well-rotted cow manure helps the azaleas, but the soil must be kept reasonably acid as well.

## OCTOBER BLANKETS

October is also the month we pile leaves deeply above the gully where ferns and wildflowers are transforming it. Care must be taken that we do not blanket too deeply the places where we hope our spring flowers will emerge in March or April. Even under ground, under leaves or under snow, all plants need some air. We must not smother them with good intentions. It is strange how often we think of the early spring flowers as dainty, shrinking things that must be coddled. Actually, they are the toughest of the year or they would not be there at all, daring snow and ice and the biting winds that other flowers could not face for an instant.

## WASTE

It seems incomprehensible how leaves and their potential for good are wasted. Everybody recognizes the cogent need for humus in the soil. Everybody nowadays seems convinced that organic matter is essential as well as chemical boosters. Yet year after year, as fall comes round, not only the village streets, but the very verges of the gardens are bright with pyres of burning leaves. By spring many of these good fire-tenders will be buying peat-moss and all sorts of material to mulch and work into their soil. And all the while, the best compost material in the world, based upon decaying leaves, is wantonly destroyed.

Leaves attended to—and that chore goes on through November—we must begin to lift such plants and bulbs as cannot face a winter out of doors. So we finish the potting of begonias, fuchsias, geraniums, ageratum, shrimp plant, nephthytis and the rest, begun in September. Peruvian daffodils and montbretias are lifted now. So are gladiolus and cannas, to be stored where it is dry.

## THE DAHLIAS

We do not dig up our dahlias until a few days after the first killing frost has turned them black. As John Jorrocks puts it, "Hurrah!

blister my kidneys! It is a frost!—The dahlias are dead." And that, of course, was a token of joy to him, for it meant hounds and hunting again.

Dahlias may be hit by frost early in October or blossom on well through November. It is well to leave them in the ground, however, for a little while after they have been frost-nipped because it is then that the last of the nourishment in their stems retreats with the sap to the tuberous roots where it belongs. Once lifted, stems cut to six inches, these roots are left with some earth about them, and stored in a dry, cool place, not freezing, for the winter. Each root clump should be marked with its name and colour. Such things are too easily forgotten.

In spite of chores to be done before frost or soon thereafter, October is a restful month of mellow charm and deepening colour—a happy month that bids us taste each golden moment to the full. No other season of the year affords us this same feeling of repose, a sense of work relaxing, pressure eased. October does not fret. And we should not.

## DAFFODILS AND TULIP BULBS

After our raking and mulching and the lifting of plants and bulbs, the next essential is the planting of such spring-flowering bulbs as were not put in during September. This includes some of the later daffodils and many of the tulips. We try to make mid-October more or less the daffodil deadline. Late November will do for tulips. We have even put them in during December, but that is unwise.

As always, we try to plant our bulbs in clumps and drifts rather than rows. Even tulips, which are stately flowers that stand some ordering and arrangement, will show to better advantage if planted naturally. After all, nature has been a long time at it. It pays us to work in harmony with her. We never tire of marvelling how the wildflowers group themselves in perfect balance and proportion with each other and with their surroundings.

## THE LAWN

This year, held up by drought, we did not get our lawn work, planned for September, completed until mid-October. As a result, new grass was caught by frost before it had made much root. That is one of the chances gardeners must face. Perhaps, by spring, the freshly seeded lawn, helped by its new topsoil and well-fed foundation, may stage a recovery. We shall re-seed again in March or April anyway.

## BORDERS

As for the perennial borders, we remove at least some of the annuals by the end of October, though a good many hardy zinnias, asters, and so on are still in flower. The south border, in process of being moved forward into more sunlight, was deeply spaded this year in late October and two tons of steer manure, well rotted, dug in—not buried under, but dug *into*—the soil. While at it, we divided the perennials that had to be shifted to their new stands.

We have found that it is a great help to dig in as much organic mulch as possible (leaves and so on), when spading a bed or a border in the fall. This sort of compost is in its way as valuable as manure and costs us nothing at all. It seems to keep the soil warm and moist, yet friable, until real winter sets in, and thus helps newly transplanted peonies, iris, phlox, and other perennials to establish themselves.

## OCTOBER ROSES

Roses should be cared for in October. We try to heap some five or six inches of loose soil about their stems, taking care not to scoop this up from close by, for if we do so a hollow is left beside each plant. Such depressions soon fill with water. And inevitably the freeze and thaw of winter will play hob with the roots of the roses, causing serious lifting and heaving at times. As we hill the roses, we give them a final aphid spray—nicotine sulphate and soap—just to

206

start next spring aright. Later, in November, when real frost has come, we clip them back a bit—enough at least to keep them from lashing about in the wind and so loosening the soil round their roots. We also add manure to the hilled-up earth, but that comes later on.

Part of October's preparation for winter concerns our vines—not merely the climbing roses, but others. We try to see that each vine —clematis, trumpet-creeper, honeysuckle, virgin's-bower, even the English ivy—is made fast where it belongs and clipped back here and there where it needs it. We give our trumpet-creeper a regular crew-cut, so rampant is its growth each summer all the way to the eaves.

## WATERING AGAIN

One autumn task is easy to forget, that is, the watering of ever-greens. Well-established shrubs, as well as new ones, lose an immense and unsuspected amount of moisture by evaporation in the cold, dry winds of winter, especially late winter. We must guard against this now, in October, by seeing that such evergreens are deeply soaked. Rose-bays, laurel, leucothoe, cherry laurel, all the hollies, as well as the retinosporas and the yews are the better for a thorough watering in fall.

Through October, we also keep in mind the need for tidying and cleaning up. Raking leaves makes this easy. Weeds and rubbish that cannot be used for compost, we burn or cart away. Peony stems are best burned, thus lessening the risk of botrytis blight. A surprising amount of the so-called garden trash is usable, however, and will soon decompose into the finest compost if given a chance. We try not to waste anything here which we would have to buy later on as replacement.

## GOODBYE TO THE ANNUALS

The great thing in October is to budget our garden time against frost. Early or late, we cannot shut our eyes to that. The thing which hurts the most, especially in the mellowing golden weather, the very crowning of the year, is the need to start work on some bed or border, putting it to sleep for the winter before we can believe that winter is near. Yet start we must—somewhere, sometime. This means that some annuals, still in flower, must be sacrificed, some perennials cut back or divided. Mid-October is as late as we dare leave this chore if we hope to have all snug and tight by the end of November. So, a bed at a time, we say goodbye to our summer glories, saddened, of course as the colours go, yet heartened when we look towards spring as the bulbs of spring go in. No garden ends; the last flower to bloom in the fall is linked so surely to April's promise. And just to keep us in good heart the Johnny-jump-ups are everywhere to see that we are merry. In summer we do not notice them much. Now they make the day for us wherever we may find them.

## INDOOR BULBS

It is in October that we start the first of our indoor bulbs for winter blooming, among them hyacinths, Grand Maitre, paper narcissus, Grandiflora and Soleil d'Or; oxalis, Bermuda Buttercup; and lots of freesias. We grow these in series, starting them a fortnight apart so as to lengthen their period of bloom. Narcissus are set in pebbles or in soil. We lean to soil, as the flowers of bulbs so planted seem to last a little longer. Oxalis, hyacinths, and the freesias are in bowls of rich earth. Such winter bloom helps bridge the gap between October's splendours and far-off April's fairy gold.

Even more surely we bridge the seasons by bringing colour indoors. October rooms are gay with scarlet leaves and gayer still with dahlias and chrysanthemums and the last of the asters. Our potted friends from the terrace—faithful begonias, fuchsias and the rest— are full of cheer now in our winter window. Below the terrace, the lower garden is green and will be green beneath the snow, for we have planned it that way.

# OCTOBER

## PATRON OF GARDENS

The link between the library window-seat and the garden, quite properly, is Saint Fiachra, for that gentlest of saints stands vigil indoors, the garden in view below him, one hand resting on his spade, the other holding a book. What surer comfort, what more abiding joy has life to offer than a friendly spade and a friendly book?

Saint Fiachra, Abbot of Breuil, Patron of Gardens, has an appeal all his own. There is something that few can resist in the story of his having no tools with which to work in the little garden he loved. And of his being compelled to use what he had at hand in lieu of a spade—his crozier. And of a Bishop wise enough to reward—not blame—this unecclesiastical use of an abbot's staff. Indeed, the good Bishop presented Fiachra with a plough and a spade and a fork, with cart and horse thrown in for good measure.

It was Saint Fiachra, 1300 years ago and more, who told us we should enter the miracle of each new day on our knees in gratitude for the wonder and the beauty of it. Through the centuries legends have grown up about him and his miracles, and of the hospice he founded, the abbey he built and the oratory he raised to Our Lady. But of them all, men have remembered longest his love for flowers and the skill with which he made them grow. They have remembered, too, his knowledge of herbs and how wisely he used them in healing the sick.

We love to see so human and so lovable a saint leaning on his pointed spade as he keeps an eye on our own little herb bed and on the green garden below him. As gentle a friend, our Saint Francis of Assisi, stands in a nook of his own, but further off, where he is close to the birds at his feet just where he loved them to be. What a trio Fiachra and Francis and Thoreau of Walden would make. They'd set our muddled world to rights again!

In October, it is extraordinary to see how many flowers are still in bloom. Day by day, we note them, as the chores of autumn keep us on the go. Yet the pace has eased, as it should ease, to lend enchantment to the ripened year.

## DAY BY DAY

1 October—final weeding and stirring up of mulches on south border.

6 October—cut September's cryptomeria log into lengths for the hearth. We buy no firewood here and usually manage to give a two or even three years' seasoning to what we burn. Watered the rhododendrons and the newer myrtle. Watered the terrace borders and the lower garden beds. This, of course, was before the drought had broken. Clipped ivy from the lower windows. Almost the last time of this for the year. English daisies blooming in the lower beds. Autumn crocuses out at the base of the garden wall. Seckel pears by the basket—amazingly sweet and juicy.

8 October—moved a weigela bush to a new site near the cellar steps. Moved a butterfly bush from south border to a new place near the ox-heart cherry. Leaves are falling fast now. Gathered apples.

9 October—monkshood in flower. Raked leaves for the compost pile. Cut back peonies.

10 October—planted 12 Virginia bluebells in the east bank.

12 October—put in 100 more myrtle plants to thicken those already in by the parking place. Set out arabis—the rock cress—at the foot of the drive on either side.

13 October—nicotine sulphate on the roses for late aphids. Potted 4 nephthytis plants for wintering indoors. Potted all the impatiens, shrimp plants and fuchsias we had room for. Planted 50 dogwood violets, 30 *Muscari armeniacum,* 25 white *Muscari,* 35 stars-of-Bethlehem, 10 *Anemone blanda atrocaerulea,* 30 *Chionodoxa Luciliae,* 7 *Fritillaria recurva* and 3 shortia where the wildflower corner merges into the upper garden. The dogtooth violets went into the wild garden itself. The others serve to link it to the perennials. Put in 250 more old bulbs, mostly daffodils, also a link between the wild garden and the borders of the upper garden. Seeded the greater celandine, *Chelidonium majus,* and wild senna, *Cassia marilandica,* where they would have a chance to spread. Both need cold weather so we waited for frost for seeding. They call greater celandine the swallow flower. Put in half a dozen or so new ferns and more mint by the fountain. Planted a matrimony-vine by the library window. Sorted all new bulbs and marked them for planting soon. It saves time to know just where each sort is to go, and also how many there are for each place.

14 October—checked what October has in flower for us today. Thirty-seven different kinds of blossom and masses of them all. Gathered more apples.

19 October—spaded in a lot of well-rotted cow manure about the dogwood in the upper garden. Planted an andromeda in the myrtle below the kitchen window. Moved 2 azalea, *mollis,* from under the spreading pyracantha bush to place where they would get more light.

20 October—planted 94 snowflakes, *Leucojum aestivum,* on either side of the front door in the myrtle; a few in the terrace border. 38 jonquils in the east bank of the drive among the euonymus there; 24 scilla also in the euonymus; with 12 chionodoxa, the glory-of-the-snow; 12 Giant Trumpet daffodils (Convent Garden); and 30 snow crocuses. In the little bed below the library window 50 snowdrops, 40 Giant Flowered crocuses; 12 *Chionodoxa sardensis;* 100 winter aconite, *Eranthis hyemalis.* Once the aconite was known as New Year's Gifts. Wolfsbane is another name for it. Above the ha-ha steps, 10 Giant Flowered crocuses.

21 October—hosed and scrubbed all garden furniture and stored it for the winter. Turned off the water tap in the upper garden and drained the pipe. How easy it is to forget these outdoor taps. The foliage of the sweet birch rising above the rhododendrons is a miracle of color this year as the October sun turns each individual leaf to shimmering gold. Transplanted some *Phlox divaricata* to the foot of the garden walls and some, also, to the banks of the driveway. Moved the last of the chrysanthemums from the lower garden beds to the east border of the upper garden, where they have a better chance and are more needed for colour in the fall. Watered the recently manured dogwood and the transplanted azaleas all day—a slow, steady soaking from the hose. Pruned back a gigantic rose of Sharon by the garage.

22 October—planted 9 Dutch iris (White Emperor and Golden Harvest) in the east border.

23 October—Clipped back the large yew in upper garden. Gathered apples.

27 October—lifted all the annuals from the terrace and lower garden borders. Planted in terrace border 20 snow crocuses—mixed colours; 25 snow crocuses (*sieberi*); and 25 Single jonquils. Also seeded there were Double Flowered Pink, Yellow, and Salmon portulaca. Planted in east bed of the lower garden, after deep spading and feeding, 36 tulips and

37 daffodils. The same number in the west bed. The daffodils were Giant Trumpet King Midas and Special Mixture Poeticus and Poetaz. The tulips were Double Early Tea Rose and Peach Blossom, Cottage Tulips—Belle Jaune, and Giant Ideal Darwin Cum Laude.

28 October—wild pinks still in bloom. The witch hazel now is out. Spaded the east border deeply and fed it with bone-meal and pulverized cow manure, worked in. Put in there 100 old daffodils and tulips, lifted last spring and stored through the summer. Also planted 12 new Golden Harvest daffodils and 24 new Early Single Diana tulips. Put 100 old bulbs in new south border—daffodils and tulips, half-and-half, together with 60 new daffodils and tulips, half-and-half. The daffodils were King Alfred; the tulips were Single Early Rising Sun.

29 October—re-seeded back lawn. Planted more Dutch iris in the upper garden borders (Golden Emperor and others). Put in 5 new white peonies.

30 October—raked the terrace and the lower garden. Leaves are useful, but not on newly seeded grass. Gathered several baskets of apples for winter storage. Planted two loosestrife plants in the wild garden.

This year we put approximately 1500 bulbs—some 800 new, 500 old, and 200 smaller sort in or near the wildflower corner.

## WITCH HAZEL

As always in late October, the witch hazel shows its first gold. It is not at its best, however, until the leaves have turned and fallen in November. Then, indeed, it is a fairy shrub, its pale yellow blossoms shining like stars. We expect this in our garden by the great hackberry tree, but a witch hazel is at its height when come upon suddenly deep in the autumnal woodlands, perhaps high on the ridges by Diamond Rock. To see it there, its blossoms brightening every bough like so many golden jack-stones, the richer for the bareness of the forest about it, brings us a taste of fairyland that no other tree can give us. At times we have seen the witch hazel in flower almost as late as Christmas.

212

## VIRGIN'S-BOWER

Another flower we enjoy late in the year is the virgin's-bower. Gone is the scent that delighted us in September. Gone are the starry snow-white flowers. But in their place we have the grey mist of faded blossoms that have given clematis its other name of Old Man's Beard. That was the name we knew it by in childhood, when it seemed to cover so many stone walls and old rail fences hereabouts. In the south we have heard it called Traveller's Joy. Now in late October our garden wall is not made sad by the grey veiling it wears. The colour adds something to the green of the ivy. A little later we cut back our virgin's-bower a bit so that it will not gad too freely. Sir Walter Scott knew a variety of this in his native Borderland. He calls it—

> "—the favoured flower
> Which boasts the name of Virgin's-bower."

## OCTOBER FIELDS

If one grows downhearted as October blossoms leave us, a sure pick-me-up is a walk on the bright October hills through the bright October weather. That never lets one down. It is well to remember that the garden gate lets us *out* now and then as well as in.

Our hills may not be Sherwood or the Forest of Arden, but they do; they serve. Few city folk, who really need it most, have experienced the healing and the balm of being alone for a while. How worth the knowing this countryside of ours can be! Stephen Vincent Benét has caught the soul of it in *John Brown's Body.*

"Peaches grew in the orchards; it was a fertile country.
Full of red barns and fresh springs and dun, deep-uddered kine.
A farmer lived with a clear stream that ran through his very
  house-room.
They cooled the butter in it and the milk, in their wide, stone
  jars.

. . . .

213

Country of broad-backed horses, stone houses and long, green
   meadows.
—The market women sold scrapple when the first red maples
   turned;
When the buckeyes slipped from their sheaths, you could
   gather a pile of buckeyes.
Red-brown as old polished boots, good to touch and hold in
   the hand.
—The pigs were fat all year, you could stand a spoon in the
   cream.

. . . .

So I remember you, ripe country of broad-backed horses,
Valley of cold, sweet springs and dairies with lime-stone floors!"

In October, this mellowed harvest land is at its best. We should
know and love it as our own. Where else can man find one so fair?

## "LET'S LEAVE WAR OUT"

Once during the recent war, I learned in a new way how potent
the healing of the natural world can be. We had been living for
five months under bombs, day and night. There was nothing we
could do about it. Once the billet I had left was struck, full on, by a
V-I. When I came back to look at the wreckage, there was none—
just open sky and a pile of rubble where the house had crashed into
the cellar. Most of it was dust—not even rubble. Work went on.
Some lived. Some died.

Then, in Brussels for a day or so, held up by fog from flying to
our destination, we found ourselves with an afternoon to spare. The
British General with whom I was serving said that he, for one, was
going for a walk in the nearby Forêt de Soignes and would I care to
join him.

It was early October. The skies were grey, the soft rain of the
Low Countries seeping chilly through our bones. Surely, it was not
an afternoon of promise, yet rarely in my life have I enjoyed a walk

214

so much or profited by one so richly.

Until then, I had not the least hint that the General was inter-
ested in anything except the task at hand—a savage, brutal war that
had to be won. That was our particular assignment at the moment.
It was *not* ours for the next three hours.

The instant we had reached the woodland's edge, I found myself
walking with a stranger—or perhaps I should say with a new and
fascinating friend.

"Let's leave war out of this. Do you mind?" he said. "Even Water-
loo and Quatre Bras over there. There's more to my liking here."

I should say there was! Deep into that lovely beech wood we
trudged in the rain. I never knew so many birds existed, as the
General spotted them for me. I never knew a man could name so
many trees and shrubs and autumn flowers, as we paced the silent
allées in that strange soft light, all mist and golden leaves on the
path ahead, all mist and richer canopy of gold above.

We were in another world—enshrined by quietude and peace and
a beauty utterly remote from the horror and the wastage of war, a
beauty more fair with man and all his deviltries left out. How tragic
a realization that is. Much of the time not a word was said. Why
should there be?

Before we had left the wood, a calm had come to us such as we
had not known for years. Strain vanished. Life had meaning again.
That peace never left us, not entirely. Even in the darkest days of the
war, so soon to resume, something of that woodland quiet still re-
mained—a memory that held a certain steadiness and saneness in
our hearts when there was bitter need. We had found more than
beauty in those beech-tree aisles. I think we knew then, as never
before, that man, regardless of his fury and his madness, cannot destroy the divine soul of the world any more than he can set mete and
bound to the ultimate purposes of God. I shall remember that day
in the Forêt de Soignes.

Here, at home, a walk on our own familiar hills never fails to
bring that day to mind and with it the surety that not a single

October flower is lost to us in beauty or in memory though frost
may cut it down.

## A GAME OF TAG

October is never a month for dying. It could not be. For one
thing, the world about us is far too much alive. The very air tells us
that. Watch the squirrels as they play hide-and-seek up our hackberry. Not even in the heyday of spring itself do they romp so
merrily.

Once, years ago, at dawn, a rabbit joined in the fun—a rabbit and
two squirrels dodging and ducking and twisting and turning, all
about the upper garden lawn. When the game reached the point
where one squirrel and the rabbit took sides, apparently, against the
other squirrel, it really *was* a game worth the watching. In the end,
the squirrel to be tagged took to the tree, the second squirrel hot-
foot after him. And the rabbit, believe it or not, made a run for the
tree and tried himself (or herself, as the case may have been) to
climb it. Twice he (she) tackled the slippery trunk, once by leaping
up at it—to fall back, defeated. And once, from a standing start,
actually trying to crawl up. What frustration complex was that?

For the zest of life in October, watch dogs go merrily to work on
scent that is not there. Or watch some white-faced Herefords, sky-
kicking, as they romp from their shed or byre on a frosty morning
and feel the first nip of air that has October's tang in it. Or mark a
pheasant rise in splendour over stubble or glide more swiftly than
we think across new wheat. There is no repining over lost summer.
Nor need we mourn the faded colours, for our eyes feast on emerald
green and living gold of field and coppice and all the miracle of
beauty in the cock-bird's plumage. What livery he wears and how
proudly! Again remember the garden, be it ever so fair, must not
hedge us in too closely. Life is real in field and fallow.

## DAN RUSSEL THE FOX

On the green door of our lych gate there is another reminder to tie us to the countryside beyond—a beautifully modelled fox mask in bronze, the gift years ago from dear friends at Brookthorpe. How alive that mask can be! How clever its prototype, Dan Russel the Fox, as Chaucer called him long ago. Yet in all the legends we have heard of Reynard's craft and guile, none equalled what we ourselves saw one keen October day by Waynesborough Wood—that most delectable of coverts hard by Waynesborough House, where Mad Anthony was born and where he lived and hunted hounds before Stony Point and Paoli were heard of.

## WAYNESBOROUGH WOOD

I had come one morning late to a Leopard Meet and jogged on to find the Radnor pack as best I could, for they were already drawing covert somewhere. Soon I heard them chiming away in token of a find, just as I came to the slope southward from Waynesborough. The trees of the covert, still in autumn leaf, were below me to the left as I faced the ancient house where Waynes have lived for over two centuries.

Knowing, from the music, that they had found, I paused there. As I did so, out from the woodland below broke the hunted fox, floating along with that easy glide that seems not running at all. A full three hundred yards he moved fast, then stopped, turned on his tracks and glided back again, as quickly as before, rod for rod the line he had just travelled—straight towards the cry of the hounds still in covert. He seemed to be racing for certain death. Just as he reached the edge of the woodland where a stone wall led upward at right angles and climbed the slope across from where I waited, the fox gave a mighty leap to his right—a leap that landed him on the top of the wall. Up this he trotted briskly. When he was about as far up the slope on his side as I was on mine, he jumped down from the wall, to his right, and jogged a few yards from it out into the open field. Here, he sat down on his hunkers directly across from me, curled his white-tagged brush about his front pads and quite calmly watched the events transpiring below. Just as I was doing. We both were in the gallery, so to speak, the stage between us! To say I was fascinated would be putting it mildly.

There was no waiting for the show to start, for by the time the fox had made himself comfortable, hounds had burst from covert, glorious in cry. The instant they touched the line where it lay doubly strong, they put on more pace and fairly screamed across the meadow. Hard on their sterns came the field, perhaps three score riders, thundering forrard for dear life, scarlet coats gay in the sunlight, the huntsman doubling on his horn and cheering the pack.

I watched—mute, but bewitched. So did the fox. He was mute, too, but obviously delighted at what he saw. Why should he not be? He had planned it so. Not one inch did he stir.

As hounds reached the point where their quarry had turned, their zeal reached its peak. On they went like witches, where no scent lay, pealing like bells as though scent lay breast-high. Two hundred yards—five hundred—two fences and more—they flew, the galloping field behind them. And only then, they checked.

I did not move. Nor did the fox, save to shift his stance ever so slightly to get a better view.

The huntsman stopped his harking and hallooing; the field held hard. Horses' hooves poached and churned the line where once the fox had gone. Where he had not gone, the huntsman and the hounds made four beautifully executed casts, each in accord with the laws of venery. One forward, but no scent; one to the right; then one to the left, hounds fanning out magnificently as they tried for the line, but tried in vain, as well they might for no scent had ever been there. And then to cap it, a wide cast back—the classic round-the-hat maneuver which they might have tried at first with some chance of success. Enthusiasm had carried hounds far beyond where the line had stopped. And besides, the mass of riders, moving about, had neatly destroyed whatever vestige of scent there had been nearer the edge of Waynesborough Wood.

A perfect find in covert, a glorious burst across the meadow below, the making of a ten-mile point—and then, in half a mile, no scent, no fox, nothing at all. The horn sounded a wailing, doleful note as the pack moved off to try elsewhere.

Only then did the fox move. He stood up, stretched unconcernedly from the tip of his golden brush to tip of his outstretched toes, cocked his head for a moment towards the sound of the distant horn, front pad lifted—I can see him now—then daintily moved back to covert. He must have enjoyed his morning thoroughly. I know that I had. Needless to say, I saw no reason to give the show away.

We are wise and also happier if we can make such memories a part of our gardens. Life runs the sweeter for them. The fox on our lych-gate has earned his place.

## PRUNING TO COME

One pleasant chore that comes in October is the visit of our friend the tree man to give us an estimate and to see what our budget will stand in the matter of pruning through the winter. Actual trimming, of course, does not start until real winter when leaves are down, but we reckon the planning as part of October.

## OCTOBER HUM

There is a sense of satisfaction as the shorter days draw on and bit by bit the borders are made ready for the cold. One feels, even around this little cottage, the joy that comes when man has eared the ground and reaped the harvest. The place is far from neat now, for by late October the parking space itself is piled high with manure. Bales of peat-moss stand at the garage doors, below the spreading ox horns that adorn the front of the building up near the angle of the roof. Salt hay, baled and some of it cut free, fills the gazebo in the upper garden to overflowing, as it waits a good freeze before being spread on the borders. Baskets of apples are everywhere. The potting shed is crammed with house plants in various stages of transmigration from terrace border to window ledge indoors. All this is as it should be. Even the tiniest place and the smallest cottage should hum a bit in the fall. The squirrels are busy at their garnering. Why not we? Only we do wish they would not garner quite so many of our apples. Or eat so greedily of the pears. Or pilfer so of the bread crumbs and seeds we put out for the cardinals. Yet in the end, there seems to be enough for all.

Ground cover should never go on the beds in October—they are not ready for it until the ground is thoroughly frozen. We like to have it handy, however, and we like even more the touch of country it brings to our door. The manure (and we use a lot of it) is gradually spread on the borders, one at a time, and dug well in. That work we do begin in October.

And all the while, until the last annual has faded and the last perennial has been cut back, the glory of the garden holds through the ripe October weather—blue of sky above the ambered wood for our hearts' delighting. Small wonder we cherish these precious hours and lay them up in our hearts' own core.

## IN SPITE OF FROST

Still in flower through October were fuchsias, begonias, ageratum, petunias, autumn crocuses, sweet alyssum, tree roses, floribunda roses, geraniums, English daisies, colchicums, sternbergias, vincas, zinnias, marigolds, cockscombs, blue periwinkle, asters, dahlias, candytuft, heartsease, chrysanthemums, monkshood, lantanas, shrimp plants, snapdragons, impatiens, bleeding hearts, verbenas, white snakeroot, gaillardias, cosmos, goldenrod, white phlox, hydrangea, strawflowers, and abelia. Not so bad with frost already—luckily not a killer.

## NAMES WE HAVE LOVED

One joy that never fails in the country about us comes from the old names that cling so happily to the places we love. Many of these we learned as a boy from farmer friends who often were ploughing the same fields their kin had ploughed since Penn's day. That world has gone now; we are glad that we knew it. Other names we picked up from the hunters—men who loved the cry of hounds above all else the world could give them. Still other names, buried deep in the legends of the Welsh Tract, as the land hereabouts used to be called, came to us from the very old men, some of whom spoke of the Brandywine and Valley Forge as oddly personal and close. And indeed they *were* close, for their own grandfathers had fought and suffered there.

## WELSH MUSIC

A countryside long lived in, like ours, has a charm of its own; the more dearly men have loved it and cherished it, the deeper that charm can go. Names reflect this love for the land and the love for the homesteads that have grown so naturally from it. Welsh names are always beautiful, the lilt in them singing like Celtic music, which indeed it is. Tredyffryn—Town in the Valley; Nant yr Ewig—Glen of the Deer; Duffryn Mawr—The Great Valley; Bryn Clovis—Hill of Clovis (which is Lewis these days, for that is where the Lewises lived). And in the hill country is Nantmeal, once in the older Welsh, Nantmoel—the Glen in the Wild. We are the richer for these names.

Scarcely a copse or covert, no matter how small, but has a name of its own and a story to boot. There is Buzzards Glory, where they held camp meetings in the old days; and two hundred years and more before that, the Lenapes used to camp there. We have found their arrow points—knapped flint—many a time beside the waters above Crumdale. And once—a never-to-be-forgotten day it was— we found by Nawbeek Wood, below Buzzards Glory, a great stone club-head, delicately grooved to take a rawhide thong that once had lashed it to its staff. We forget sometimes that the Lenapes lived in our countryside a good deal longer than our people have. They never defaced it. Our record we face with shame.

And so the old names cling: The Admiral's Wood, that is newer than most; Fox Hill and Fairy Hill; Castle Rock where the highwayman hid and Sandy's Oak where the old men said he had buried his loot. How we longed in the old days to get at the roots of that gigantic oak and find trove for ourselves. Echo Valley; Willowdale and Blossomdale; Chestnut Sprouts and the Shellbarks; Sassafras Wood. What memories they bring! What devotion they tell of, what passion for the land to which such names were given. These are, as one can sense, friendly names, homely, natural names, rooted in the soil. Some of them have come to us almost from the days when all our hills were greenwood and our farms but clearings in the forest. Could anything be lovelier than the Glen of the Deer? Our heritage goes deep in these memories of the past. That is why we have cherished our names so dearly.

## COVERTS

"Such covert names are lovely as
The first sweet music of
A find. They live! They guard for us
Brave moments we have loved.
They hearten us again with cry
Of hounds on grass at dawn!
The strike of racing hoofs! The high
Leup-leuing of the horn!

Again and yet again we taste
Our breaks from Fairy Hill;
Or see again the Greenbank faced;
Or feel still fresh the thrill
Of wind across Bryn Clovis when
They race for Silver Spring!
And all our miles are true again,
Such witchery names bring.

We live—through them—the Shellbark views!
Or checks White Horse has known!

The points from Quaker Wood halleus
That marked them for our own.
So while the stars lend candle shine
And hounds draw Sumac Hill,
Let's draw from such spiced mem'ry's wine
Good Hunting and Good Will!


## ROCK WHENCE WE ARE HEWN

A garden should not be set apart from such things for they, too,
are life. A garden should reflect the soil from which it has sprung
and the people who are its neighbours. A garden should bring to us
some breath of the countryside that frames it—something that
should be a part of us to the very marrow of our bones. Are we not
told to look unto the rock whence we are hewn and to the hole of
the pit whence we are digged? It is no garden at all whose roots do
not hold to the land about us.


## TRUE GLORY

That is why we delight so in our wildflower corner. It brings the
things we love close in. And, just as important, it take us out. A
gardener, four-walled and unaware, is sad indeed. We need to see,
now and then, how nature is ordering her affairs. Wildflowers link
us to that, just as they link us to the sweeter freedom of the hills.

The stream of life runs deep in this keen October weather. Golden
hours wait for us, almost too beautiful to bear. In the garden or
beyond it, we should not grieve too much for summer gone. Sir
Francis Drake had caught the meaning and the challenge when he
prayed: "Grant us also to know that it is not the beginning, but the
continuing of the same until it be thoroughly finished, which yieldeth the true glory."

Life can be sweet in October. Day by day we find in it a glory
that abides.

223

## OCTOBER CHECK LIST

Chrysanthemums are October's prize. Do not forget that some can be potted and brought indoors.

Save leaves as they colour and fall. All will be needed for compost and mulching. Remember that real winter cover should not go on until the ground is well frozen. If leaves are used as a mulch this early, do not smother the plants underneath them. Whatever you do, do not burn leaves. Every one is needed.

As frost comes, but not before, dig up bulbs for winter storage: dahlias, gladiolus, tuberous begonias. Dry them well and store in peat-moss or papers or in sand. A dusting of sulphur or of 5% DDT helps. Bulbs need to be dry, cool, and not smothered.

Put in more daffodils, scillas, chionodoxas, and crocuses now. Mid-October to late October is about their deadline. Late November will do for the tulips. Plant bulbs in drifts—never in rows.

In October, remember the snowflakes and the snowdrops. Put in as many as you can afford.

October is as late as we dare risk house plants outdoors. By now they should have been re-potted, with fresh soil, well fertilized, nipped back to keep them bushy, and sprayed. Insect pests thrive indoors even better than out. Be on your guard early against them.

Potting over, clean up the potting shed, clean and oil garden tools you do not need, and try to keep the beds and borders in workmanlike order.

Beds should be full of colour now and hold it well on towards November with zinnias, asters, chrysanthemums, dahlias, marigolds, and the rest.

See to the lawn in October if drought has prevented work on it in September. Fall seeding is better by far than that done in the spring.

When a border is spaded in the fall, dig in as much organic mulch as possible (leaves and so on), as well as plenty of cow manure or sheep manure if you can get it. Bone-meal also helps.

Roses need care in October. Heap five or six inches of loose soil about their stems against the winter cold. Give them a final spray of nicotine sulphate and soap against the aphids. Do not clip them back until frost and then not too severely.

See that climbing roses and other vines have been made fast against winter winds.

October often is a dry month. Keep watering. Evergreens especially need to be well soaked before the ground freezes.

Save annuals as long as you can, but some must be sacrificed in October if we hope to get our borders ready for winter and spring. All beds and borders should be snug by the end of November. A start must be made in October.

Get the first of the indoor bulbs going in October: hyacinths, paper narcissus, freesias, and oxalis. They repay the time put on them a hundredfold.

As peony plants die back to the ground, cut off the stalks and burn them.

Virginia bluebells should be planted now for spring bloom. Myrtle set out in October does well. Also dogtooth violets, muscari, stars of Bethlehem, chionodoxas, fritillaria, and shortia.

Cow manure, well dug in, during October, helps flowering trees such as dogwood.

*Phlox divaricata* may be thinned a bit and transplanted in October.

Portulaca may be seeded. It likes cold.

Look for the witch hazel, the last of the shrubs or small trees to blossom. Virgin's-bower also adds to October's blossoms.

October bloom can include fuchsias, begonias, ageratum, petunias, autumn crocuses, sweet alyssum, tree roses, floribunda roses, asters, geraniums, English daisies, colchicums, sternbergias, vinca, zinnias, dahlias, candytuft, marigolds, cockscomb, heartsease, chrysanthemums, monkshood, lantanas, shrimp plant, snapdragons, impatiens, bleeding hearts, verbenas, snakeroot, hydrangea, strawflowers, cosmos, gaillardias, phlox, and abelia.

The garden year is by no means over.

# CHAPTER XI

# NOVEMBER

## *The Month of Blessings*

Much of the more obvious splendour of the fall has passed with October, yet in November new beauty is quick to take its place and can enchant us. True, the flaming tapestries of autumn, the glory of colour at its fairest, have gone from the hills. Only the oaks retain their foliage now, a stubborn bronze that will not yield till spring sap runs high again. But for all this, a different loveliness is here for those with eyes to see it. How sad it is so few will even try to see. W. H. Hudson knew this when he wrote in *Far Away and Long Ago:*

> "When I hear people say they have not found the world and life so agreeable or so interesting as to be in love with it . . . I am apt to think they have never been properly alive nor seen with clear vision the world they think so meanly of, or anything in it—not a blade of grass."

### NOVEMBER TREES

Trees in November give us a picture wholly new as they trace their patterns of trunk and branch, etched clean against the winter sky. This articulation we never see in summer; it can be lovely indeed. Too often we have not realized the grace and richness such traceries can bring.

### AUTUMN GREEN

There still is colour, of course, in the garden, but we must notice that, too, not close our eyes to it just because the more brilliant pigments of nature's palette are no longer there to bewitch us. Often in November, especially if frost holds off, our lawns are as deep a green as ever they will be in spring. We notice that green after a summer of drought.

English ivy on the garden walls and on the cottage adds a different green, more in evidence with no leaves of tree and shrub to hide it. Outside our lower garden, on the bank above the road, the hemlocks suddenly begin to assert themselves. During summer and earlier fall, with dogwoods and viburnums in leaf about them, we almost forget that the evergreens are there. This is true, of course, of all evergreens—holly, yew, spruce, pine, retinospora, arborvitae, as well as the broad-leaved shrubs—the rose-bay and laurel, leucothoe, andromeda, cherry laurel and the rest. We are more conscious of their presence and more grateful for their colour as we see them emerging from summer shade. Pachysandra and myrtle and the winter-creeper, too, bring us a fresh note in November that makes us thankful for their usefulness and beauty.

## COLOUR APLENTY

Green is but one colour. November is not sparing of others. As never before, we notice the fire in some of the azaleas, as the chill, sharp sunlight filters through the crimson leaves that will cling deep into winter. Barberry bushes and the cotoneaster come into their own now, scarlet berries transforming them both as frost brings miracles of colour to what may have seemed almost drab in summer. Leucothoe by November has changed its summer green for bronze. A treasure it can prove in these days when we begin to count our blessings more carefully. Euonymus also can be rich in the autumn.

Indeed, once we have accepted the fact that fall is passing and winter is at hand, we are amazed at the bright tints left us. And flowers, too, for that matter. Each year, while putting our borders to sleep for the winter, we leave at least one bed untouched as long as a single flower lives there, spared by frost.

## NOVEMBER BLOOM

This year in November we had in blossom floribunda roses, tree roses, geraniums, dahlias, chrysanthemums, bleeding hearts, blue myrtle, heartsease, sweet alyssum, candytuft, ageratum, Deptford pinks, lantanas, English daisies, abelia, gaillardia, white vinca, shrimp plant, impatiens, and witch hazel. Doubtless there were more not checked. This was after our first frosts and even after a light snow. By the end of the month, of course, real frost had scythed the annuals down and put a quietus to the perennials, but for half of November and longer we had blossoms aplenty to delight us in the garden and to bring colour indoors. Truly the lines have fallen unto us in pleasant places. Yea, we have a goodly heritage in the gifts that November can bring.

## READYING THE BORDERS

There is a great difference between readying a border for the winter and covering it for the winter. Readying it includes, among other things, putting in the last of the bulbs that are to go there, seeing that perennials are cut back neatly and tidied, spading in organic fertilizer and humus, earthing up the roses, and so on. Readying a border does not include, however, bedding it down with salt hay or other ground cover. That must wait until a good freeze has come, for the purpose of cover is primarily to prevent thawing and freezing and the subsequent lifting of roots and bulbs. Once the surface of the ground has been well frozen, two to three inches down, the cover should go on, but not before. If this be done, the ground will stay comfortably cold all winter and bulbs will not start up too early in the spring nor will they be heaved out of the ground in a thaw. Perennials also will stay dormant until it is time for them to grow.

We must not forget to count winter cold among our blessings.

228

Robert Frost knew this in his "Good Bye and Keep Cold," though he had a winter orchard in mind, not a garden:

"I don't want it stirred by the heat of the sun.
(We made it secure against being, I hope,
By setting it out on a northerly slope.)
No orchard's the worse for the wintriest storm;
But one thing about it, it mustn't get warm.
'How often already you've had to be told,
Keep cold, young orchard. Good-bye and keep cold.' "

## WINTER COVER

Cover has two uses as a matter of fact: to keep heat *out* of the ground in warm spells, but also to keep excessive cold out in sharp spells. This sounds contradictory, but it is not. Salt hay mulches and cover keep too severe frost from injuring or destroying rose bushes and other more or less tender plants. Our tree roses could not possibly survive a winter here unless they had been well bundled in salt hay, kept in place all about them and over their tops by staked burlap wrappings. That is an example of cover keeping *cold out*. The salt hay on the beds and borders, however, is designed to *keep in the cold* already there and to keep out the heat of winter thaws. We must bear this twofold purpose of cover in mind or damage will result.

## WORK IT WELL IN

At the risk of repetition, we must stress again that fall is the ideal time to work organic matter deep into the soil before the beds are covered. If we wait until spring to do this, the humus will not have quarter the chance to decompose and become an integral part of the soil itself. So each fall we try to work as much cow manure, rotted leaves, and compost into our soil as possible. It does little good to bury it far down in lumps. Rather it should be worked and edged in so that the manure—or whatever it may be—extends from the actual top of the ground downward for six or eight inches, every bit of it given a chance to touch and become a part of the soil it is intended to enrich. Buried in a lump half a foot under, it is largely wasted.

## NATURE'S COVER

The chores of late fall are obviously more related to winter work than to the tasks that have kept us busy since spring. When it comes to mulches and good cover—what to use and when to put it on— it is worth remembering that nature's winter mulch is the best of them all—snow. Here, for the past three years, we have had little or none of it. So each bed and border is made as tidy as possible, then covered when the time comes. As we have said, salt hay seems to serve our purpose best.

## PRUNING

November is not too early to start a bit of pruning. Both trees and shrubs can be trimmed now and a good deal more comfortably and carefully than in the bitter days of midwinter. Always we must guard against pruning shrubs that will bloom next spring on old wood. Dead wood is a different story. That must come out, be it on a tree or shrub. And so must all broken or diseased wood.

## CHRYSANTHEMUMS

In a mild winter our chrysanthemums, cut back to six inches, seem to survive very well out-of-doors. On the whole, however, it is safer to move them to a cold-frame. Mums have no objection to being moved at any time, even in full flower.

## LATE SEEDING

We are astonished year by year to remember how late in the fall seeds can go in. We have spoken of sowing the greater celandine and the wild senna in October. Even in mid-November it is not too late to sow cornflower and larkspur or plant the last of the spring-flowering bulbs—scillas and tulips especially.

## THE POTTING SHED

Before frost really comes, we take a pail or so of good earth to the potting shed for use in re-potting house plants during the winter. Indeed, by now our new potting shed has acquired the proper patina of use and is stocked, as it should be, with peat-moss, pulverized cow manure, sand, pebbles, and other essentials that we are sure to need later on.

## BEDDED DOWN

Much of our enjoyment of the fall and early winter stems from this sense of seeing everything in order, snug against the worst that winter can do. We love to know that our hearth wood has been cut to proper length and piled close at hand, under cover and dry for the burning. We like to feel that our apples are safely stowed. We like to see our roses warmly banked and the borders sleeping. This feeling is as old as the race; it is indeed, the instinct of garnering against the dark of the year. Like all verities, it goes deep. We are the happier if we heed it.

## WINTER RAIDERS

There is one hazard that every garden faces in November and through the winter—pillage by mice and squirrels, damage by rabbits. If a good cover, such as salt hay, has been put on the beds before the ground is thoroughly frozen, there is always the risk that field mice will regard it as the finest sort of new thatch set on to roof their winter quarters. Once they have moved in, under it, they will soon wreak havoc with the bulbs and plant roots waiting for them there in the soft, unfrozen ground beneath. Of course, if the ground has frozen properly prior to its being covered, these roots and bulbs are almost sure to go untouched. Once, at a neighbour's, field mice discovered a rich store of planted bulbs and ate them literally by the hundreds. The destruction was appalling—and costly.

## SQUIRRELS

Squirrels can be most troublesome. Our new lawn this year had not been in three weeks before it was pocked here and there where the gray squirrels had raided it to dig in the topsoil, probably after something buried there with the fertilizer. Certainly they were not after bulbs, because there were hundreds of these in the lower garden beds, fall-planted and handy to the new grass, yet they were not touched. No nuts are near the lower garden either, so it could not be that which they were after.

If only squirrels were more unattractive or less friendly, we might get around to destroying them. Like Hamlet, we never quite reach the point of saying in time—and with a loaded gun: "The interim is mine! The readiness is all!"

## RABBITS

Rabbits come and go. Some years the garden seems filled with them. Often they have nested in the deep pachysandra, yet they have done us no harm since the days of our vegetable garden where the south and east borders and the upper lawn now are. In those days, they were as vexing as could be, nibbling our choicest lettuce and parsley and vegetables just at the tenderest stage of each. Also, they occasionally showed a fondness for young fruit-tree bark in winter. A sapling can easily be girdled if left unprotected when rabbits or hare are about. We used to put wire guards around the bases of our young trees. That ended the trouble.

Actually, we do not worry much about rabbits and squirrels. They have a charm of their own. We should miss them were they gone.

Field mice and moles are of a different kidney. We wage war on both when that seems necessary.

## INDIAN SUMMER

The cream of November here is our Indian Summer—St. Martinmastide, as they used to call it. Truly, Indian Summer does come to us as summer again—delicious, doubly-blessed, sweet, easing days that make all out-of-doors a joy. It is so warm that we can sit on the terrace basking. Some years, flowers are with us. If they are not, the green of the grass and the ivy and the laurel, the sleek sheen of holly leaves, make up for gayer colours gone.

No season of the year leaves us more conscious than this of blessings given, for we realize that these warm lingering days are an epitome of all the beauty, all the loveliness and joy of bud and blossom, that have come to us since spring. We know, too, they cannot last. There will be no cloying now, no surfeiting on charms grown stale. It is perfection now. How eagerly we share in the rapture!

## THE STAG

As the shrubs lose their leaves in November, it is not only the evergreens that we notice anew. An old inn sign of handwrought iron emerges also. A golden stag that hangs flat against our garden wall in token of good cheer, close by the flagstoned corner where we like to have supper in summer with our friends. In summer, the stag is almost hidden by ivy and clematis and climbing roses about him, but now in November, he, like all warrantable stags, is more easily viewed, resplendent in his golden coat, his "rights" held proudly over brow, bay, tray.

## THE FARMLANDS

How vividly the signs and the names of our old inns hereabouts still tell us the story of our countryside—a story more true and far more interesting than that found in the history books. The farmland life of the old days lives, richly etched for us, in such names as The Plough, The Anvil, The Broad Axe, The Springhouse, The Bull, The Lamb, The Black Horse, The Sheaf of Wheat, The Ship (which once, though few remember it, was called The Sheep). The sign, long ago, showed a ship in full sail, but the older name grew from the land, not from the sea.

## THE ROAD

The story of the travelled roads and those who used them comes to us in The Drove, The Waggon, The Horse and Groom, The Coach and Four. Perhaps even in The Compass. The wild life of the earlier days, about the frontier farms, still is reflected in The Buck, The Eagle, The Swan and The Bird-in-Hand.

## HISTORY

Heraldry has its place in such signs as The Leopard, The Lion, and the Unicorn, saving for us, as they do, a hint of the British Crown and a reminder that our countryside from its settlement up to the present was a part of the British Crown for almost as long as it has been a part of the Republic. The Turk's Head traces, if we follow it back far enough across the seas, to the Crusades. The White Horse goes further still, its lineage harking back, through countless signs of the White Horse in England, to the great White Horses cut in the chalk of the downlands, and back of that to the battle flag of the Saxons—the White Horse Banner of Alfred himself. It is odd, how history clings to so little a thing as the sign by an old inn door.

We find history nearer to hand in The King of Prussia, The General Wayne and the Admiral Vernon (switched to its present name of The General Warren when Revolution brought new loyalties in). It was Admiral Vernon, we should remember, under whom young Lawrence Washington, George's half-brother, served at the

Siege of Cartagena and in whose honour he named his place in Virginia Mount Vernon. The Spread Eagle reminds us also of our country's birth, when the Eagle replaced the Lion and the Unicorn of Britain in popular favour.

Nature and a love for it and a love for colour, too, are back of such ancient signs as The Red Rose, The Rose Tree, The Rising Sun, The Green Tree, The Rainbow, The Blue Bell, The Sorrel Horse.

## OLD NAMES CLING

In nearly every case, these names antedate the Revolutionary War. Usually the name of the inn has passed to the hamlet that has grown up about it, so that we speak today of White Horse and the Leopard, just as they did two centuries ago, although the inns there have gone. This memory is as it should be. A countryside must have roots, just as a flower must, if it is to endure. Those who live there are the richer if they know the stories of the land that is their heritage. From this knowledge comes pride in and a caring for our own, whether we are dealing with far-flung acres or the tiny confines of a garden.

## THE LAND

Of course, the older generations tended to live longer in the same place. A few of our neighbours are still the happy owners of farms that their kinfolk have tilled for two hundred years. One good neighbour is the eighth in direct descent on the same farm. Not so long ago this was common here. We find this pride in a place, this devotion to it, reflected in the care many of our glorious old pastures have received, for much of the good farmlands hereabouts graze dairy cattle or fatten steers.

## JESSE RUSSELL

Again and again the passion for the chase (which is, of course, a part of the land, a heritage brought long ago from England and from Wales), shows in the names and the legends that are so surely a part of the countryside. Hunting Hill is known to all for it was here that Jesse Russell, farmer of Edgemont, who loved good tilth in summer and the cry of hounds in fall, was buried, at his own request, deep in the heart of that wooded hill where foxes still are found in the Rose Tree. His story has saved for us something of what land can mean to those who bear in their hearts a burning love for it.

## HUNTING HILL

"A churchyard lot? When I have gone to ground?
A stone that soon will tilt and moss, with whom to care?
What hint of horn, what wakening cry of hound,
What beat of hoofs on grass could ever reach me there?
You know I've always cheered them to the find!
So not the church. The grass is more my kind!

I've marked the place. They call it Hunting Hill.
Sound wood! I've jumped my foxes there past thirty years.
The sweetest find, I say, on Ridley still.
Rare scent for hounds to work at. Good spot, too, to hear
Them push him, once he leaves the white-oak side.
It's grass there—open, honest grass to ride!

I want to feel it near me when I'm gone,
That Ridley grass! I've scythed and ricked it since 'twas stump—
Lot pasture—poor starved barren stuff so long.
I'd like to hear the beech nuts falling in the clump,
The sound of chestnut clubbing in the fall.
But most—hounds' tongue on grass! That most of all!

It's in my bones! It's part of me, I say!
Some horn on Hunting Hill will sound the View again!
It must! Some challenge lift! Some ring-necks bay!
O God! To cheer! To hark them forrard in the lane!

You know I cannot leave it—not for good.
Not when my beauties wind him—no one could.

In spring there'll be the dogwood all about,
What spicebush gold and bloodroot, squirrel cup, cranesbill. Then
The blow of that wild cherry budding out,
So wide, just by the bare earth of the vixen's den.
I've watched her cubs there often try to chase
Our rabbits of an evening, brace for brace.

There'll be the cool of trees in summer, too,
The friendly stir of rain by Ridley Bend,
I used to rod for trout there. Many a do
Is good still, near the aspens and the Lower End,
Where poplar-cups lift candles in the sun.
I've always liked old trees—that oak's the one.

You'll find it easily—white-oak—near the top.
Fair open grass below. The lane must be cut back,
To make a decent hound-way. So just lop
The worst of it for me and trim the brushwood slack.
Not much. Leave there the white wood-asters all.
They'll make me think of hunting—and the fall!

What more to ask? I'll rest there year by year,
Content enough—till corn is in and harvest through.
Then maybe—some way—fall by fall, I'll hear
Once more the music of those sweet notes on the dew!
God's will I wake a while and feel the thrill
When hounds score true to cry on Hunting Hill!"

Such passion for the soil and for the life lived so richly and so
vividly upon it is important, especially in these rootless days when
many seem to live on wheels and never settle anywhere long enough

to count it home. We cannot but envy Farmer Russell.

Many a day I have galloped past his grave on Hunting Hill, as hounds spoke to a fox's line, fresh found, in the covert below. He has lain there for 130 years now, yet I suppose not a year has passed in all that time without the sound of the horn in the oaks about him.

One reason that gardens are so necessary for us these days is that they catch for us, on a smaller scale, yet with greater intensity, the love and the devotion of the wider days when men were closer to the land and could lavish their affection upon it naturally, as few of us today are privileged to do.

## A SMALL THING, BUT MINE OWN

The garden, however, no matter how small, still reaches deep to the heart-strings within us. When we cherish it, as so many do, we really are caring for all the countryside about us. Nor is this just a sentimental yearning for what we have not, nor a glorifying of the past till it glows in a romantic sort of aura as unobtainable as it is unreal. Actually, the smallest garden about the humblest cottage, made beautiful by care and the love spent on it, can bring to its neighbourhood gifts richer than we know. It takes so little to go so far with beauty—beauty that sometimes roots deeper than we give it credit for when first we meet it. That is another gift we should be grateful for.

## MEMORABILIA

A line of zinnias seeded year after year along an old stone wall— by whom we never knew. There was no garden there, not even a house very near, yet because of them and of somebody's care, a road has been made lovely. Often thousand of miles from home, across the seas, I have caught the memory of that wall and the cheer of the flowers there to share their boon with every passer-by. Was it not Charles Kingsley who wisely said: "Beauty is God's Handwriting."

A log cabin in a glen near the Great Valley had a climbing rose about its chimney end, as old, maybe, as the cottage itself. They used to tell us, when we were lads, that starving soldiers from Valley Forge had been fed there in what they called the Old War. That rose bush filled the whole glen with fragrant colour in the spring so that we would walk miles to view it. A more humble home could not be imagined; a more lovely garland I shall never see. I have carried the picture of those roses in my heart for a lifetime.

These things never come from money spent on them—not that alone. They root more deeply in the richer soil of love. Our garden can be more a part of us, really, than our house and every whit as cherished, for after all, it is not there for shelter or for use or for anything particularly practical, as our matter-of-fact friends are quick to point out. It has, however, a purpose more challenging than use. It speaks to the soul in a language of its own. That is still another blessing.

November, like October, is an easing-off month, it is true, but there still is much to be done—more always than we had counted on. That is part of the fun.

## WEEK BY WEEK

3 November—the long drought has broken at last. Some rain in October, but now Thursday, Friday, and Saturday, a soft and soaking rain that kept up night and day, seeping well in. The springs will be grateful for this. It is like the misty rains in Devon or on the Cornish coast—no angry floods to rush off in spate, scouring topsoil with it. Our wildings in the gully needed just such weather. Later in the day, the rain grew chilly, then turned for an hour to soft wet snow. No harm done. The floribunda roses were lovely showing through the white. A little later, of course, the snow had gone and all was fall again. Moved eleven wheelbarrows of firewood from the shed to the cover of the terrace porch.

4 November—first real frost last night. A killer this time. The dahlias told us that the moment we spied them in the morning.

10 November—scrubbed and put away all the garden pots. It pays to rub them clean now of stains and moss and mould. Next spring the

task would be much harder. Dug up the dahlias. Cut back all perennials in the south and east borders. Clipped back the long canes of the roses. Put one ton of cow manure on all roses in the lower garden—floribunda, climber, and tree—and on the peonies, virgin's-bower, new matrimony-vine, new beauty bush, and about the *Daphne cneorum,* the *Daphne mezereum,* and the climbing hydrangeas. Also manured the English hollies. Indoors, the *Jacobinia carnea* has come to lively bloom in the winter window. Unfortunately, so few of these cheery blossoms last long.

14 November—raked up the last of the leaves and stowed them above the gully, about the rhododendrons and on the compost pile. We planted in the wild-garden corner today 4 King ferns, 50 Lady ferns, 50 Christmas ferns, 25 white trilliums, 25 galax, 10 heartleafs, 12 foam-flowers, 12 hepaticas, 12 black snakeroots, 12 shooting stars. Then we added to last year's planting 6 red baneberries, 6 white baneberries, 6 wild berga-mot, 3 butterfly-weeds, 6 wild pinks, 6 coneflowers, 12 blue phlox, and 5 silvery spleenworts. And as valuable as anything in our plan, 6 great boulders, to hold moisture and to define the little path that winds be-tween them, were put in place above the gully not far from the new tree. Two years ago other great rocks were set in the gully itself, as has been said. All these boulders were sunk well into the ground, leaving their weathered surfaces exposed. In short, we put them in just as they had rested in their forest bed.

17 November—in spite of the frost, heartsease is still flowering here and there. Sprayed all rose canes with nicotine sulphate. Perhaps misci-ble oil spray would have been better. Gave the hollies some spray, too, playing safe against aphids in the spring. This is the last spray of the year. Manure on the new abelia and on the pyracantha by the east wall. Spread manure on the south and east borders and on the two beds in the lower garden. Potted the rosemary in the herb bed, above the ha-ha, and brought it indoors. How pungent-sweet it is—above all other herbs.

19 November—cut down a small maple above the gully where a little more light was needed. The sun at dawn today, shining through the leaves of an azalea near the sour-gum tree was incredibly beautiful, turning the foliage to a crimson, almost transparent, fire. Such miracles make the day for us. This has been a great fall for colour in berry and fruit. The Japanese holly berries seem a sleeker black than ever.

22 November—Thanksgiving Day—staked up a burlap screen filled with salt hay about the climbing hydrangeas on the terrace. Salt hay

cover about the hollies and on the terrace borders. Also on the Johnny-jump-ups and violas seeded by the parking lot and growing nicely there since August. Salt hay around the bases of the azaleas and the newer lilac bushes. Unusually cold for November—now in the low 20's. Christmas roses in bud, though not open, in the library bed by the drive. How eagerly we watch for them. It seems no time at all since we were watching for them last winter. *Tempus Imperator Rerum,* as the scroll on our old clock has it.

23 November—formerly on or about this date, we used to stake and cover with burlap the *Ilex crenata* by the lych-gate steps and the yews by the cottage door, so as to guard them against breakage by snow and ice falls from the roof. Now, however, they seem tough enough to fend for themselves. Perhaps, in a severe winter, we may regret this leaving them unprotected.

24 November—planted two little shad bushes above the gully. We look for their dainty flowers almost as early as any in the woodland when spring comes up our way. Staked burlap and salt hay around the kitchen trellis roses. Salt hay cover on the lower garden beds. Clipped ivy about the doors and windows—last time this year. Was it Adriana in the *Comedy of Errors* who called it a "usurping vine"? How right a term that is!

Years ago, when our English ivy was not so rampant in growth, we used to let it grow unclipped. Then it was that we came to know the greenish-yellow ivy flower, almost as late to bloom as the witch hazel. And we learned, too, how fond of the tiny blossoms were the bees.

## WONDROUS THINGS

One will note how the garden pace has lessened. A few hours each week end suffice now to keep things squared-away. Besides we cannot rush matters, even if we would, for frost in the ground and the depth of it control much of our work such as winter cover. A little at a time, however, we make our garden ready for what rigours may lie ahead. And while we are at it, we savour to the full the last sweet mysteries of fall—for mysteries they are, wonderful beyond our knowing. The storing of the sap deep below the bite of frost, the mulching of trees and shrub and flower by their own lost leaves, piled deep about them, the shield of frozen ground above the bulbs, the blanketing of the winter snows—

> O the depth of the riches both of the wisdom and
> knowledge of God! How unsearchable are His
> judgments and His ways past finding out!

## NOVEMBER MEMORIES

No Armistice Day comes to us in November without deep memories of the first Armistice in combat overseas so long ago. Of all Armistice memories, one most vivid has nothing whatever to do with war, thank God, but with a garden of roses, and sweet grass.

## STINSFORD ROSES

I had been stopping at Stinsford House in Dorset with an old friend of mine who has lived there for years. After breakfast in the library where a fire of logs kept the West Country chill at bay (such fires are almost unknown in England now where wood must be used sparingly) I walked about the great rose gardens below the house. In spite of the sharp November cold, roses were in bloom everywhere—literally acres of them! How I envied the lack of frost that keeps these English winters green. That garden was a heart's delight.

## THE WATER-MEADS

After lunch, I walked in the meadows below the terrace, and as I walked I thought of Thomas Hardy and of his affection for these very water-meads. And I knew again how deeply I was in debt to the Wessex Novels for they were warming my heart as I thought of them.

242

## THE HEATH FOX

Next morning, hounds met at Stafford Green near-by—our Armistice hunt. The field was small, for this was war time. The oldest was a hearty soul who informed me gaily that he was over eighty. The youngest, on a pony, claimed to be rising four! Both were going strong and proud of it!

We moved to covert promptly at 11:15, the first draw proving blank. The second saw hounds mark a fox to ground without his breaking covert. We found, on our third try, a dog fox sailing away at twelve. I had looked at my watch as I thrilled to the Gone Away! What a run that rascally chicken thief gave us! Rare pace, the bravest grass that man could dream of, no plough, a moment's check, a clever cast, left-handed, made by my old friend who has carried the horn for over sixty gallant years—and on with hounds still chiding, scent breast high—to a kill in the open, an even forty minutes from our find!

The mask of that fox hangs in our library now, but that is not what made the day. When I asked where we had run, my host told me many names that I knew, for I had tramped about these Wessex Hills before. The thrill came—and thrill it was—when he said we had crossed part of the upper moorland and killed by Egdon Heath! Had I ever heard of that? I could not believe it. Actually Hardy gave the moor this name in his *Return of the Native*. It has another. But the place is the same. Few writers have made a countryside so true to life.

## SHARED BEAUTY

Such memories are precious past telling, but cherished with the warmest of them are those November gardens, soft with rain, yet brave with roses still in flower. When the long drought broke with us this year and saved for us the sweetness of the fall, the sight of our own modest roses, responding to the benison of rain, brought back the picture of those stately terraced gardens overseas. How good it is that we can love another's flowers as well as our own and carry some share of their loveliness about us to keep the bonds of friendship green. We should be thankful for that, too. How these blessings mount, once we begin to think of them.

## A RE-CHECK

November chores, as can be seen, are light enough to give a gardener time to plan and look ahead. We have found that it is a handy season to check, revise, and list anew our winter work, all in its proper order, for often plans made earlier in the year have to be recast. If this reordering and rearranging be left too long, the rush of other things that must be done are sure to swamp us. It is good to feel, however, that we shall not have to hurry too much with our winter pruning, provided we know ahead of time just when we plan to begin it. This is true of all winter work. We cannot let it slide indefinitely—undone. So surely do the seasons tread upon each other's heels that winter spraying may well be upon us before we have finished our winter pruning. And once spraying starts, before we know it we have slipped into the busier chores of March. The secret is work plotted ahead of time—a little attended to, week by week. Many neglect this in winter.

## STUFF OF LIFE

How wise Ben Franklin was and how shrewdly he rated the value of time. Said he, "Dost thou love life? Then do not squander time, for that's the stuff life is made of. . . ."

## CHRISTMAS ROSES AGAIN

Already in November, as we have noted, the last flowers of this year or the first of next year are in the making, for by Thanksgiving the white buds of the Christmas roses are usually to be found, low hidden by the leaves above them, and almost, though not quite, ready to open! Such buds are exciting. They must be looked for, sought out on hands and knees. There can be no hurrying them on. When they themselves are ready and then only will they open, to offer us the richest guerdon of the year, because they come to us when most we need them.

## NO CODDLING

People, sometimes, set up frames and little hoods of glass to coax their Christmas roses forward. We do not do so, for it seems too close to smothering them in a greenhouse. Probably, in colder places, this coddling is necessary. There may be no other way to have them come to flower. Here, we'd rather risk the cold. In deepest snow, the Christmas roses come.

## THE VISION AND THE WONDER

November, is indeed, the month of blessings. There are so many miracles about us, who could list the vision and the wonder of them all? The stately pageant of the year, now drawing toward its close, so vivid and so varied in its bounty, the inestimable gifts of sun and shower, the healing of the rain, the tonic of the ice and snow, how humbly we should stand before them, yet how happily. How sad to know that things so wondrous we can take for granted, unbeholding. How smugly we hoodwink ourselves to the divine.

Even now, as winter closes in, there is no drabness here. Blind is he who will not see the glory or trust the coming of the spring at winter's end. November, like the poet's skyline, should be for us "a promise, not a bound."

## NOVEMBER CHECK LIST

Before deciding to use a winter mulch, you must keep two things in mind: its purpose and its hazards. A mulch is put on *after* the ground is hard frozen, to keep the cold in and thus prevent thawing and freezing. Field mice, however, are easily attracted to the shelter of a deep mulch and often will destroy every bulb under it, especially if the mulch has been put on too early, before the ground has had a chance to freeze.

In November, before mulching beds and borders, ready them for winter. Put in tulips now and scillas and the last of the other bulbs; cut back perennials. Spade fertilizer and humus well in and through the soil; do not just bury it where it can do no good.

Finish earthing up the roses. Do *not* put on winter cover yet.

Finish cleaning garden tools. Remove rust, then oil or grease them. Try to have everything left in the fall ready for use in the spring. Sharpen what needs to be sharpened now. There is more time than in spring.

Scrub flower pots clean, inside and out, before storing them for the winter.

Pruning may well start in November, but guard against pruning shrubs now that will blossom on old wood in the spring. Dead wood should be pruned from trees. Backward trees are helped by being given a balanced fertilizer in the fall.

Chrysanthemums should be moved now to the cold-frame.

Cornflower and larkspur may be seeded, even this late, as may sweet alyssum, candytuft, Shirley poppies, sweet peas and bachelor's buttons. They must not, of course, be moved now from where they are seeded.

Squirrels, rabbits, and field mice take their toll in November. There is not much that we can do about it. Young fruit trees, however, should be netted with close-mesh wire about their trunks to prevent rabbits from ringing their tender bark.

Do not forget that for indoor plants we can use a north window as well as a sunny one. African violets, ivy, philodendron, nephthytis, all the ferns, and fuchsias prefer the north.

Dig up the last of the dahlias one week after the first killing frost. This gives the last of the sap a chance to retreat to the roots for storage and nourishment.

Clip back the long canes on the roses.

Keep on raking leaves or they will soon blow away. The compost pile should be well filled by now.

In spite of frost, a final spray will help the roses, especially if none was given in late October before frost. Aphids seem indestructible.

Stake burlap screens around hollies, boxwood, and young yews or other evergreens that suffer from winter sun and winter winds.

Watch for the first of the Christmas roses.

Remember salt hay makes good winter cover for beds and borders as well as excellent protection around roses, if banked about them. Tree roses should be completely swathed in salt hay and burlap, well staked. Their bushy tops, of course, must be pruned well back. Leave breathing holes in the burlap.

Evergreens show their mettle in the fall—holly, yew, rose-bay, laurel, andromeda, cherry laurel, and the rest. No garden can afford to be without some of them. Barberry, cotoneaster, leucothoe, even euonymus, play their part with colour.

Late bloom can include floribunda roses, tree roses, geraniums, dahlias, chrysanthemums, bleeding hearts, blue myrtle, heartsease, sweet alyssum, candytuft, ageratum, Deptford pinks, lantanas, English daisies, abelia, shrimp plant, gaillardia, white vinca, impatiens, and witch hazel.

Of course it is a month for Thanksgiving.

# CHAPTER XII

# DECEMBER

## *The Month of Cheer*

December, oftentimes, seems to us more like the start of a new year than the end of an old one. It should not appear so, in a way, for certainly December is the darkest month and it can be a very cold one. Here, however, the cycle of the year certainly does come to end —and noticeably—in November.

Everything that could blossom since last January has blossomed, even the Christmas roses. Every bulb that we hope will bloom next spring is in the ground. Johnny-jump-ups and the violas have been seeded months ago. Portulaca, celandine, wild senna, and the other fall-seeders are long since in. Borders are snug against the cold. By Thanksgiving, we know for sure that the year has come full cycle.

### LOOKING AHEAD

In December, however, all sorts of chores come to mind that point to the new year and the new garden ahead. All that we do now is predicated on spring—never on the year that has passed.

The last of the old year's work was the covering of beds and borders with salt hay when frost had gone deep enough to warrant it. Usually, this occurs during the last week of November or in the first week of December, depending on weather. Once cover has been attended to, we can feel assured that the garden year has ended. There is nothing more we can do for this season. The rest of December's chores, however, are touched by the thrill of what lies ahead. Our look is forward now as at no other time.

# THE TURN OF THE YEAR

Actually, our tasks are not very numerous nor onerous, for December and January are slack months in anybody's gardens. Yet they are by no means dull. The stir of Christmas takes care of that. And the New Year. And the quickening pulse that comes to all who are in tune with the first faint gaining of the light and who understand what it means. Yet we must not race too far ahead; it is December, and dark December at that, which faces us now.

## FIRST PRUNING

One task is always waiting in these short days between the covering of the beds and the tightening of the cold. Usually, real cold and real snow do not trouble us until the turn of the year. For five or six weeks between Thanksgiving and New Year's the weather more often than not is delightful. This is the time we try to start our pruning, a little each year to keep expenses down, but always some share of it, so that we shall not have too ambitious a job all at once to swamp us.

It is amazing how clean trees can be kept and how fit, at little cost, if they are gone over now and then by a competent tree man. We try to cover a certain number each year until all have had their turn. Then we begin over again.

Our apple trees we do not prune in December or even in January, but leave them until mid-February. In very bitter weather we do not prune at all—it is too uncomfortable for one thing. And the branches tend to crack and split when the cut is being made in frozen wood.

## CHRISTMAS GREENS

There are, of course, other chores in December than pruning, so we always try to attend to them first and hold off the pruning of our hollies, yews, firethorns, cherry laurel, leucothoe, and other evergreens until as close to Christmas as possible so that we may have plenty of greens to work up into sprays and wreaths for indoors and out.

Every window and every vase should be merry now with Christmas colour and cheer. It is gratifying to see how much greenery is available if pruning has been postponed until we are ready to use what greens we have. Even the smallest snips are usable. We waste none of them. The shrubs are the better for their clipping, too, if it be done with judgment. As with all pruning, we try to take out the long, older canes close to their roots, never shearing the shrubs as though they were sheep.

## BRIGHT BERRY

Not only are greens in demand now for wreaths and sprays, but berries as well—and we need a lot of them. This is where our fall-fruiting shrubs come into the picture. It is a mistake to cut all the berries from one or two bushes, for winter colour out-of-doors in its natural setting is just as beautiful—and far more lasting—than it can be when cut and carried indoors to cheer us from Christmas till Twelfth Night. One should take a spray or two, sparingly, from each, leaving most of the berries or fruit where they grow.

It might surprise a non-gardener to mark how many varieties of berries there are in December. Everyone thinks first of the holly, but as a matter of fact hollies are not very plentiful in our neighbourhood. Their berries, when available, are usually saved for the one prize wreath or spray.

## OUR OWN

Far more abundant are the orange clusters of the firethorns. This year the birds have spared us many of them and incredibly lovely they are now against the snow. The low rock-cotoneaster gives us more colour with its bright, scarlet berries. In a spray, it is beautiful. Barberry, of course, is another source of colour. Bittersweet (not too popular these days, for it can get out of hand) was a favourite when all the land hereabouts was farm country and suburbia had not encroached on legitimate field and fallow.

## HOME WROUGHT

In those days we used to gather great masses of laurel and bittersweet in the wooded glens above Tredyffrin and make the whole house gay with them. There is something merrier and far more in the spirit of Christmas about one home-wrought green than there is in all the purchased wreaths that money can buy. The home-cut tree, though seldom feasible nowadays, has a place of its own in our hearts. There was a feel about it, a sensing of the Christmas pageant, a rite to be performed in the cutting of it, and the drawing of it home—aye, in the homemade trimming of it—that gave significance and meaning.

## THE MANGER

For one thing, the purpose of Christmas was not forgotten. Under our tree there was no glittering maze of track and engine. They could perform elsewhere. The Tree was sacred to the Manger that it sheltered. I can see the tiny straw-thatched byre now with the figures around the Crib—ox and ass and the gentle cattle kneeling, shepherds about the Holy Family, and the Three Wise Men bearing gifts. Most lovely figures these were, delicately carved in the Tirolean Alps, although as children we knew nothing of that and could not realize the beauty of their craftsmanship.

The Manger and the Stable meant much to us, however. I think the best part of it was their lack of motion. Nothing stirred there. Its passive loveliness was reassuring, changeless, year by year. Nothing had to be wound up. Nothing ran, then stopped or broke down. We knew very well that it was no toy. And we knew also that it was beautiful. Children remember such things longer than their elders suppose.

Even though the tree and the greens may have to be bought, the

251

sanctities of Christmas as well as its merriment and good cheer can be saved if at least some part of the sprays and the wreaths are homemade and if at least some part of our Christmas still tells the Christ Child's story.

## THE ORCHARD'S CHRISTMAS

In the old days, people liked to share so much at Christmas. Not even the orchard was neglected, for the apple trees were wassailed on Old Christmas Eve with song and fiddle and by a jack of hard cider poured over their roots! In these leaner days, I suppose we could not spare it. One thing has always seemed the purest magic to me—the scent of apple blossoms in the spring and the fruity scent of the apples in the fall; so different, yet both so lovely, so essential a part, each of its season. I like to think at Christmas of apple boughs in blossom.

## FIRST SPRAYING

Trees receive other attentions in December than pruning, for there is a chance now to give an early dormant spray to fruit trees and shrubs that are subject to attack by aphids. We have never sprayed quite this early ourselves, but it is a good time for it. When we do spray, a miscible oil is used as has been said. Lime sulphur is also excellent; we have used it often. We have not tried the dinitro spray (8 or 10 ounces to 100 gallons of water) but it has been found valuable by those who have tried it.

## DECEMBER PLANTING

This year we risked one hazard we have never attempted before. On the first of December which was pleasantly mild—even warm, we planted one Summer Snow climbing rose on our kitchen trellis, one climbing Pinocchio on our rail fence by the parking place, and one climbing Goldilocks at the base of our sundial in the upper garden—the old sundial that stood for so many years in the rose garden at Spring Bank when we were children.

We also planted 3 Wirral Supreme Shasta daisies in the south border; 8 Miss Lingard *Phlox suffruticosa* in the lower garden beds; and 6 Royal Robe violets and 6 Rossina violets in the terrace border. What luck we shall have with them remains to be seen. Never before have we tried winter planting of dormant roses. Or of anything else, for that matter.

## DIG THEM DEEP

In putting in the roses, we followed the same procedure as in spring. The holes were dug wide and deep. A generous supply of well-rotted manure and bone-meal with a handful or two of peat-moss were worked into the loose soil at the bottom of each pit. Then more soil, well crumbled, was sifted in about the roots of the plant and tamped down. As always, care was taken to spread the roots properly. No water was poured in this time, for the soil had been soaked by repeated rains. Loose soil was then raked up about the stems of the new roses for cover, and salt hay spread on top of that.

One thing we did in preparation for our late planting. The sites for all plants—roses, Shasta daisies, and violets—had been covered with salt hay since the first hint of frost had warned us. This meant that there was no frost at all in the ground where we planned to dig the holes. It is essential that this be so, for otherwise the ground would have been frozen and the lumpy soil could not have been sifted about the roots, as it must be. It will be interesting to see how these late plantings fare, especially in view of the very cold weather we have had since mid-December.

## COMPOST AGAIN

December is a good season to clean up whatever refuse has not already been turned into compost and put to work. It would be better to say it is a good time to put all useable refuse to work, as potential compost or humus, then clean up and burn what we know cannot possibly be used. We should not overlook the value of saw-dust, if there have been carpenters about. Sawdust makes a specially fine mulch for rhododendrons and laurels, for it is high in acid content. We use sawdust—when we have it—together with oak leaves and pine needles. All are helpful.

## KEEPING COVER IN PLACE

When this year's leaves are used as a mulch, many of them will blow away unless they are kept in place with a branch or so on top to weigh them down. Pine branches, needles still on, are excellent for this and permit proper ventilation as well. Even the branches of the discarded Christmas tree can be used, though by the time we take the tree down at Twelfth Night, it is fairly late for keeping down cover.

## OUR WINTER BIRDS

Late November and all of December bring our winter birds to mind, so we set out feeders for them at this time. Seeds, bread-crumbs, and suet must be replenished. One thing people are prone to forget: garden pots and bird-baths are usually turned upside down in winter to prevent them from filling with water and freezing. This is all very well for earthenware pots and garden jars, as ice will assuredly crack them, but at least one water holder, bird-bath, or what you will, should be kept in use, right side up and filled with water each day, not left as a solid chunk of ice, perhaps weeks on end, for daws to peck at! Available drinking water will attract birds in winter almost as surely as a feeding station. A squirrel-proof feeder assures the birds a reasonable share of their own dinners. Crumbs on the ground are soon devoured by squirrels, neighbour's dogs, and hosts of bickering sparrows. Bird feed should be kept somewhere off the ground where it can be of use to the birds.

Blue jays, nuthatches, the always welcome cardinals, chickadees (usually upside down), woodpeckers, juncos, tufted titmice—all are friends we delight to see about us. Blue heron and the broad-billed scaups are on the neighbouring mill dam.

## THEIR OWN TREE

A pretty custom, more frequent in the old days than now, was to set up a Christmas tree for the birds. It was trimmed with ears of corn from the crib and with suet and seeds, though we never quite worked out how to put seeds on the little tree. In the end, we stuck the seeds in the suet and the birds did the rest.

## TENT CATERPILLARS

Another December chore, now no longer necessary here, is the pinching of the egg masses of tent caterpillars from the wild cherry trees. They show up well once the leaves are down. In the end, we did away with the few wild cherries we had and so got the caterpillars under control. There have been none here for several years.

## STRAY LEAVES

Finally, until snow comes, we keep an eye on the lawn and rake up any stray leaves that may have settled there. A good flat oak or plane tree leaf, plastered to the grass all winter, means a bare spot in the spring. December winds see to most leaves, but a few always seem to stick. They should be removed. Those that pile against the foot of the garden walls we leave there, as they make a warm blanket for the roots of our ivy.

## NATURE THE GUIDE

Through every season of the year, we watch how nature does it and our wonder never ceases, for her lessons are the surest to follow. There can be no greater mistake than for a gardener to shut his eyes to her ways or try to oppose them. We strive out best to heed them. Nature really tells us all we have to know—when to mulch or put on cover, what to cover with, how deeply to pile it, until, in spring, she gives us notice to remove it just at the right time. In the same way, she tells us all the rest, if we will hark to her advice. It pays to look for these hints. Not always are they shouted from the housetops, but they are always there and they are always sound.

## THE END OF THE YEAR

Not all December chores are pointed toward Christmas, of course. By the end of the year we feel the magnet of spring at work within us—the miracles of returning life. How unbelievable it seems in the snow and cold of December to think that in two months on we shall be counting early bloom and plenty of it. But now—

1 December—planted the roses, Shasta daisies, and violets, as has been said.

2 December—the large holly tree above the drive is in berry for the first time although it has been growing there for many years. In flower today: periwinkle, some English daisies (blest be their hardy souls), and still the golden-starred witch hazel. Cut the last rose this morning, one of the floribundas, it was. The thermometer registered 20°, but the rose was still there, as chipper as in summer.

4 December—clipped ivy away from the eaves. Clipped back the trumpet-creeper. Had all the dead leaves scraped out of the gutters of the roof. We do all these chores at the same time, when we have a man with a long enough ladder to help us.

9 December—noted a great double wedge or arrow of Canada geese flying low overhead this morning. Some thirty in all. They could not have been more than one hundred feet up. We have never seen them so low; indeed, they were below the tops of the near-by trees, yet they were not coasting in for a landing on water. An incredible sight!

14 December—snow, five or six inches of it.

16 December—firethorn berries against the snow most beautiful.

Sunlight shining through the azalea leaves, against fresh snow, made the bush more lovely even than it had been in November. The leaves have a warmer glow of colour now. Our winter birds are much in evidence. They surely help to brighten up these dark midwinter days.

18 December—Christmas roses just opening after sleet and ice. Johnny-jump-ups and periwinkle still blooming.

22 December—put half a ton of rotted manure on the grass under the apple trees.

23 December—put 100 pounds of fertile peat on the myrtle. Raked some heavily matted leaves off the evergreens on either side of the drive. The snow had melted sufficiently to do this.

24 December—Christmas Eve, gave the apple trees their customary wassail gifts, even though fiddle and song were lacking.

## LATE FERTILIZING

By putting fertile peat on the myrtle so late in the year, we probably accomplish little. Usually, it is best to put on fertilizer of any kind when the plants are quick and can absorb it. Dormant plants do not feed much, as far as we know, if at all. In the case of the myrtle, however, its blossoming certainly bespoke life, so we risked the cost of the peat. Some of it may leach away before spring and do no good; part of it, however, may be retained in the soil and serve its purpose.

The manure about the apple trees was worth it, as it will gradually work its way down into the grass roots. Also it is sure to attract the earthworms needed there. It is hard to grow grass under fruit trees, for trees are heavy feeders themselves and the soil about them becomes impoverished before we realize it. Before it does, when we see the signs of weakening grass and hard-caked soil, then we must take steps to feed the trees themselves and so relieve the drain upon the earth about them. In addition to feeding the trees, we must also feed the topsoil. Our manure should do wonders under those apple trees by spring.

## EDELWEISS AND ALPENROSE

Winter flowers have fascination the more because they are so rare. We never see our Christmas roses buried in the snow or the hidden sapphire of the myrtle in winter without picturing the blossoms on some alpine slope—summer blossoms, it is true, but growing bravely on the verges of the lingering drifts. Indeed, we have found them many a time, under the snow, coy as our winter blossoms are here.

Once we climbed high on Grossgluckner in Austria, seeking edelweiss. It was August, but even then the snow on the approaches was ten or twelve feet deep. By afternoon, when the sun has a chance at it, such snow is dangerous. We could hear the roar and plunging hiss of the avalanches across the valley, as we kept to the shady side. Part way up, where snow and alp mingled, we found the lovely flower we were after. And lovely it is, though by no means so rare as legend would have it.

## ENZIAN AND MOHN BLUETE

Lower down, where snow gave place to upland corries and cattle grazed on pastures—steep-pitched, crisp, sweet-scented with springy mountain grass, the loveliest grass to walk on the world over, we found quantities of the beautiful *alpenrose,* as lovely as the *edelweiss* and easier to find, for it is red. And with it, these lower slopes were starred with *enzian,* low-growing, incredibly blue, its colour reminding us of the wild gentians we had seen high up on the Smokies at home. The *alpen-veilchen* was there as well, yellow and red, somewhat like the *alpenrose.* And the *mohn-bluete,* always lovely.

## THE POTTER

We picked a few of each. Back in the Tirolean village of Kufstein-am-Inn where we were stationed, we took the flowers to the potter who had promised to make us a tea set. In fact, we watched him throw the moist clay on his wheel and mould it magically with thumb and hand and fingers into shape—cup and saucer and plate, jug and teapot—amazingly swift and sure, in this most ancient of the crafts.

## SCHOEN TIROL

Plates and cups and the rest he then had baked. Now they were ready to be coloured, then rebaked and glazed. The potter's wife, as she had promised, took the little mountain flowers we had gathered and, as we watched her, re-produced swiftly and deftly, with her brush, three blossoms on each piece of the set. When she had finished, she said there would be no charge for this. She wanted us to remember Schoen Tirol. Perhaps, some hint of it might live in the pictures of these dainty mountain blooms. Nor did her husband, the potter, pick up the cost of the painting in selling us the finished set.

Not a day goes by without our using these cups and saucers when we take tea. Their makers would feel, I am sure, a warming of the heart if they but knew how well their handiwork has served us through the years and how often it has carried us back to their delectable country, where flowers have no fear of the snow. And where the people are as fond of the flowers as we are. Every Tirolean house has boxes gay with blossom and pendent green, set on the high balcony rails that run across the house front. Here, in summer we have followed their example and charming it can be.

## BALCONY BLOSSOMS

Each fall, as we have said, we take these balcony boxes of ours down, when frost has cut their blooming, and store them away for the spring. Yet there is no need to do this. Another year, when the colour has gone, we intend to remove the geraniums and the trailing vinca that have added so much charm in summer, but we shall leave the boxes filled with earth where they are.

## GREEN BOXES

Then, as greens are cut, at pruning time, we plan to set some of the smaller, fresh-cut branches in the boxes, pressing their stems deeply in the earth. By doing so, we hope to keep them green and fresh through most of the winter to provide a touch of green garden at the balcony level, above the green beds in the garden below.

It is astonishing how long cut evergreens will retain life and colour if kept out-of-doors in winter—the colder, the better. But their stems must be buried deep in the earth away from exposure to the air. If the boxes tend to dry out in a thaw, they must be watered, for it is the loss of moisture, chiefly by evaporation through the leaves, that causes evergreens to shed their leaves or needles and wilt. That is why a Christmas tree lasts so much longer and stays so much fresher if it has been based in a saucer containing two or three inches of water. We hope great things from our balcony boxes next winter. If the plan proves successful, we can thank our good friends in Tirol for it. *Nihil obstat,* as the clergy say. It is worth a try.

Was it not Plato who reminded us two thousand years ago and more that men are sustained by living amid things of beauty and by making of them a joy and a study?

## THE TREE

No Christmas can pass without at least some mention of the tree. The one that lives most surely in my heart was homemade, a tiny thing, yet brighter far than any I have known, so rich it was in the spirit of Christmas shared. For over thirty years I have cherished the memory of that tree with joy, yet with the knowledge that no price could possibly pay the debt I owe to it.

We were stationed that Christmas in France close to Reville, a small village near the Meuse. The war had ended on Armistice Day. Our billets were ruined huts built into the hillside. They had been captured by us a few weeks earlier.

The desolation of battle lay all about us, a horror of blasted fields, shattered farmsteads, and hamlets crushed into meaningless rubble by the shells. The reek of horses lying where these faithful creatures had fallen made hideous a countryside that once had been productive and beautiful. It would be difficult to imagine a scene so removed from the meaning of Christmas. Yet combat had ceased; some sort of peace, no one knew what, had come. And Christmas was Christmas still, had we the heart to make it so.

## CHRISTMAS EVE

On Christmas Eve, we sang the old carols together. Some of us had planned to ride over early on Christmas morning to service in a neighbouring church, where our Chaplain would be. So we had arranged for our horses to be saddled and ready. I was sleeping at the time on a rude bunk made of poultry wire nailed between two boards. Far better than the mud and the stench and the dripping hell of the dugouts.

I can remember after a lifetime how cruelly cold it was at dawn and how dark in that unheated shack, when I woke to be greeted with a Christmas gift that makes me humble even now as I think of it.

## AS NEVER WAS TREE BEFORE

Beside my bunk stood a Christmas tree—a real Christmas tree, perhaps two feet high and trimmed as never tree was before. How it got there, I shall never know, but there it was—carried in by someone on tiptoe, I suppose, while I lay sleeping.

What a tree! It stood on a memorable base, for beneath it was a board some three feet long by one foot wide and around the edges of this board ran a tiny post-and-rail fence, painstakingly carved and put together by the men of the Brigade who had planned it. They said the post-and-rails might remind me of the country at home. Need I say that it did? That fence brings unbelievable happiness even as I write of it now.

261

The board inside the fence was green with smoothest moss. In the middle was the actual support for the tree, a sort of base carved from wood taken from a cigar box, rubbed and polished until it shone like mahogany. Four 30-caliber cartridges adorned it, one jutting out from each corner. The detail of the work was amazing. How time had been found to do all this in our harried days, God only knows, but weeks had obviously been spent on it.

Rising from the middle of this little base or platform and held in place by cleverly whittled supports, was a one-pounder shell. And fixed firmly in the opening on top, where the fuse cap had screwed in, was the butt of the tree itself, knifed down to fit.

## GOOD WILL

No one could believe such a tree could exist. It sparkled and shone in the glow of my candle as though all the silver and all the gold in Christendom had gone to its trimming. As a matter of fact, its ornaments were bits of tinfoil, saved from chocolate bars, rolled into tiny balls and hung on the branches by wires, but I am sure that all the love and all the thought and care that ever made a Christmas merry went into that tree.

Here and there, fantastic coils of metal glittered in futuristic designs, past all comprehending. These were the insides of field telephones captured before the fighting had ceased along the Meuse. Everything that had a glitter to it seemed to have found its way to that amazing, that friendly, heart-warming tree, the kindliness back of it transforming what might have been pathetic into a glory undimmed by the years.

There are no scales to measure friendship by; no words to carry the affection and the pride that grow from honest kindness and good will. To this day, I draw fresh heart and joy unspeakable as I feel again the message of the tree, as bright and as dear in memory now as it was so many years ago that Christmas morning by Reville.

## CHRISTMAS HALLOWED

Each Christmastide it comes again to mind—how could it not— a gift renewed, enriched past understanding, to change a chill and sodden hutch on a battlefield into a shrine that Christ Our Lord had hallowed, for surely where men are kindly affectioned one to another some share of the Saviour's love, some knowledge of what Christmas can mean, must dwell in their hearts.

## PATHWAYS OF DELIGHT

And so, with the greens of Christmas about us and the joy of Christmas gladdening us, with the promised green of spring before us, the year we have followed, the Hobby we saddled a twelfth-month back, draw to a close, if we dare call it so, when every nook and corner tempt us to pry beneath the cover to mark what is happening there—below the leaves.

With the new year ahead, the growing year, to cheer us; with blossoms venturing (scarcely a month to wait for them now), how can we help but heed the carols in our hearts? The lovely sequence of the year, bud and blossom, scent sweet for our enchanting in the spring, high summer with its glory of the flower, autumn with ripened fruit and colour—surely we have trod the pathways of delight.

Nor has winter, lusty but kindly, failed to bring us gifts. Beneath the snow, in token of a goodly day tomorrow, the Christmas roses wake.

## DECEMBER CHECK LIST

December is the mulching month. As soon as frost has really hardened the ground, put on winter cover—leaves or salt hay, for instance—and thus keep the cold *in* the ground and the thawing-freezing-heaving out. Never smother beds and borders, however, with too many leaves that are likely to mat down heavily once they are wet.

Pruning starts in earnest during December, though fruit trees are usually left until January or February. In addition to pruning of trees, a start should be made in December at dormant spraying for scale. Use a miscible oil. Lime sulphur also is useful. Dinitro spray, 8-10 ounces to 100 gallons of water is good.

Make sure that broad-leaved evergreens have been well soaked before the ground freezes. Protect yews and other shrubs near the house from damage by ice falls from the roof. Screen tender shrubs with burlap if they are sensitive to winter sun and wind. This is really a November task.

Do not cut back evergreens, even if they need it, until you are ready to use the greens from them at Christmas: hollies, yews, cherry laurel, leucothoe, and so on.

Fall-fruiting shrubs come into the picture vividly—the firethorns, rock-cotoneaster, barberry, even bittersweet, all are lovely when sprays are brought indoors to add to the Christmas greens.

Indoor bulbs should be coming on toward bloom now. Do not bring them into sun or strong light all at once. Remember their root growth is made while they are more or less in the dark, before blossoming.

If frost has held off, dormant roses may be safely planted in December. Other December planting might include Shasta daisies, violets, and *Phlox suffruticosa.* Do not ram the plants into the ground; plant them even more carefully than in spring.

As the last of the windblown leaves collect in corners, gather them for the compost pile. Clean dead leaves out of gutters, before snow and ice arrive.

Keep winter cover in place with loose branches, especially pine branches with the needles still on.

Begin bird-feeding regularly in December with seeds, bread crumbs and suet. Drinking water, not frozen, attracts birds even as quickly as feeding.

Pinch off the egg masses of tent caterpillars if they show up in the bare branches of trees.

264

Rotted cow manure under fruit trees will pay dividends by spring. Most fertilizing, however, should wait until well after the New Year.

December bloom out of doors may well include periwinkle, English daisies, witch hazel, roses, Christmas roses, and Johnny-jump-ups, with a few autumn crocuses here and there to boot.

POTTING SHED

FRUIT TREES

THE HACKBERRY

SOUTH BORDER

GARDEN HOUSE

EAST BORDER

L.H. SELLERS - 1953